Liverpool

POCKET ANNUAL
1994-95

Edited by
Peter Fitzpatrick

Liverpool Pocket Annual 1994-95

Copyright © Peter Fitzpatrick – 1994

ISBN: 1-898351-10-4

Typeset by Bruce Smith Books Ltd

Cover Photograph: Teenage Robbie Fowler was the Anfield find of the 1993-94 season.
All Photographs supplied by Empics Ltd

Statistics supplied by Football Information Services.

The right of Peter Fitzpatrick to be identified as the Author of the Work has been asserted by him in accordance with the *Copyright, Designs and Patents Act 1988*.

This is not an approved nor an official publication of Liverpool Football Club.

First published in 1994 by
Words on Sport

Words on Sport Ltd
PO Box 382
St. Albans
Herts, AL2 3JD

Registration Number: 2917013

Registered Office:
Worplesdon Chase, Worplesdon, Guildford, Surrey, GU33LA

Printed and Bound in Great Britain by:
Ashford Colour Press Ltd, Gosport.

CONTENTS

Acknowledgements

Many thanks to all those people who, in one way or another, have contributed something to this first *Liverpool Pocket Annual*. In particular, I would like to thank Bruce Smith, Mark Webb and Martin Ritchie of *Words on Sport* for making it all possible, Tim Healy of Football Information Services for filling in some gaps and Liverpool FC for playing the football.

Disclaimer

In a book of this type it is inevitable that some errors will creep in. While every effort has been made to ensure that the details given in this annual are correct at the time of going to press, neither the editor nor the publishers can accept any responsibilities for errors within.

If you do notice any mistakes then please write in and we will try to rectify them for future issues. In addition, if there are other areas of information about Liverpool Football Club that you feel should be included in future editions then please let us know of your choices.

Introduction

Liverpool Football Club are the most successful English football team ever. They have won the league title a record 18 times, the European Cup four times, the UEFA Cup twice, the FA Cup five times and the League Cup a record four times. Along the way Liverpool have also established numerous other records which reflect the style with which they have achieved their success.

The greater part of these achievements have been made during the last thirty years since Liverpool were steered from the second division by Bill Shankly. Shankly engineered a club that was geared up to win – something it has done like no other.

There has been no real secret formula for Liverpool's success. It was built on the bedrock of getting the simple things right – *"never pass the ball to one red shirt if there are two in another direction"* – and evolved into a passing game that enabled Liverpool to dominate the European game for a decade.

Liverpool teams have always been more than the sum of their parts but that has not stopped many giants of the game donning the famous red strip. There have been many occasions when the Liverpool squad has overflowed with international caps.

This is the first edition of the Liverpool Pocket Annual and it has been designed to be the fan's guide to the club. All manner of facts and statistics about the club past and present have been included. The major historical records are here along with a complete run-down of all the Liverpool games in the season just passed.

For those travelling to away games in the Premiership there are details on how to get there and a street plan of the area around each ground.

The Season Reviewed

For Liverpool Football Club and its many followers the 1993-94 season was not a good one. What else can you say about a season in which the club records its lowest league position for over 30 years, gets nowhere in the League Cup, loses at home in the third round of the FA Cup to a team from the First Division and then sees a change of manager mid-season?

The final Premiership position of eighth place owed nothing to ill-fortune. In the league games against those clubs who finished above them Liverpool won two, drew four and lost eight. The team wasn't good enough. There were some positive signs it is true but for every ray of sunshine there was also a heavy black cloud.

And yet, despite all this – or was it because of this? – the crowds flocked to Anfield. Attendances rose yet again and there were many occasions when the ground was full to capacity. Maybe the novelty of not winning everything in sight had something to do with it or maybe the Liverpool supporters realised that following the club means a lot more than only turning up when times are good.

When the 93-94 season kicked off in bright August sunshine none of those woes were in sight. Liverpool had had a couple of bad seasons but they were behind them now. It was as if it were the dawning of a new era. The Reds made a clean sweep of their pre-season friendlies and stormed through their first three league games. The new signings of Clough and Ruddock looked like astute buys by manager Graeme Souness. Both blended in with the way the team played and Clough capped off his league debut by bagging a brace of goals. It wasn't just that Liverpool won those early games but the manner in which they did so that made one think that the glory days were making a welcome return. Sheffield Wednesday, Queens Park Rangers and Swindon Town were all brushed aside and Liverpool looked sharp and incisive starting off the season at a cracking pace. But, no sooner had Liverpool had a chance to savour the heady taste of success, riding high at the top of the first league tables of the season, than it began to fall apart. An unimpressive Tottenham Hotspur visited Anfield mid-week and went home with all three points. Another victory meant that August finished with Liverpool nicely poised in the league but then came September. Liverpool lost all their league games and didn't score a league goal. What had gone wrong? Souness responded quickly to the drop in form by swapping Marsh and Burrows for West Ham United's Julian Dicks but opinion is divided over whether that made a real improvement.

Souness began to swap players around to try and find the right blend and in doing so also brought some young blood into the team. Robbie Fowler became the find of the season. He scored on his debut against Fulham in the Coca-Cola Cup and then hit all five in the return leg.

That performance sparked a revival in Liverpool's performance and they began to climb their way back up the league ladder. But Autumn defeats by Newcastle United and Sheffield Wednesday were reminders that while Liverpool were still one of the top teams, they weren't championship material. What hurt most was Manchester United's runaway success at the top – doing a Liverpool. In the approach to Christmas Liverpool ran into Wimbledon in the Coca-Cola Cup. As on many occasions before, Liverpool found the south London team an immovable object. The fourth round match became a replay, became extra time and then became penalties which Liverpool lost.

Too many draws over Christmas when a strong run could have put the Reds back in with a title shout meant that the club's only realistic prospects of success lay with the FA Cup and the hunt for a place in Europe. The third round FA Cup tie against Bristol City turned into a protracted affair. The first match was abandoned after floodlight failure, the re-match was a draw and then the Bristol club was faced with a replay at Anfield. They came undaunted, played to win and were applauded from the field by the Kop when they did just that. But, while the Liverpool fans were generous in defeat to the Bristol players they were less generous to their own manager.

Graeme Souness had never been the most popular of Liverpool managers. He had upset fans with his abrasive style, his dealings with The Sun newspaper and by his wanting to redefine the Liverpool way of doing things. Most of all he had been unpopular because of his lack of success. One FA Cup triumph was insufficient reward from three years' effort and the fans called for his dismissal. The Liverpool board stuck by their promise to back him until the end of the season but Souness pre-empted any further speculation by tendering his own resignation.

His successor was announced quickly – the choice of Souness's assistant Roy Evans meaning a return to the days of promotion from within.

Roy Evans' task has not been an easy one. He inherited an unsettled squad with many older stars coming to the ends of their careers. Players like Barnes, Rush, Grobbelaar, Nicol and Whelan – cornerstones of earlier triumphs – are all in their thirties. Although players are continually extending their careers these days, they can't play forever. Souness's reign had also seen many expensive purchases with little to show for it and so, while money will be available to Evans, there may not be as much of it as he might have hoped.

Roy Evans was manager for the last third of the season. His record of played sixteen, won five, drawn two and lost nine is the stuff of relegation. More than anyone else he will be disappointed with that performance. It meant that Liverpool slipped back from fifth place – and the hope of a chance of earning a place in Europe – down to eighth. For any other club eighth place in the league would represent a respectable season but this is Liverpool we're talking about and eighth place quite simply won't do.

The end of the season saw the final game in front of a standing Kop. From the 1994-95 season onwards Liverpool will become an all-seater stadium. If the ground looks unfamiliar for the start of a new season then the team may look different as well.

The 93-94 season closed with speculation about any number of the Liverpool squad. Expect sweeping changes for the new season as the club seeks to establish a team to match the demands of the Anfield crowd. It's hard to know what to expect but that, as the saying goes, is what it's all about.

Liverpool Diary 1993-94

August

The season gets going in cracking style with Liverpool winning their first three games to take an early lead at the top of the Premiership. The first game in front of a full house at Anfield sees Sheffield Wednesday brushed aside 2-0 with new boy Nigel Clough grabbing both goals and fellow signing Neil Ruddock also impressing on his debut. This is followed by two away games where Liverpool's attacking style works wonders as they beat Queens Park Rangers (3-1) and Premiership newcomers Swindon Town (5-0).

   In their second home game Liverpool trip up against Tottenham Hotspur (1-2) but recover to beat the 91-92 league champions Leeds United 2-0.

September

After such a bright start in August, September is as bad a month as they come. Liverpool fail to score a league point or league goal all month and slump from 2nd to 13th position. The sequence of four consecutive league defeats is the club's worst form since the relegation days of the early 1950s. It is all that is needed to start the first rumblings of discontent about Graeme Souness's role as manager. For the record: Coventry City v Liverpool (1-0); Liverpool v Blackburn Rovers (0-1); Everton v Liverpool (2-0) and Chelsea v Liverpool (1-0). The only bright spot is victory in the Coca-Cola Cup over Second Division Fulham (3-1) featuring a debut goal from Robbie Fowler.

October

The rollercoaster continues as Liverpool don't lose a game all month. First up is a dull 0-0 draw at home to Arsenal to break the Reds' appalling sequence. That's followed by the second leg of their Coca-Cola Cup tie against Fulham. In just his 4th game for the club, 18-year-old Robbie Fowler scores all five goals as the Reds run riot (5-0). It's only the fourth time in Liverpool's history that a player has scored five times in a match and Fowler is instantly acclaimed as a prodigy, a genius, a saviour and the best thing since sliced bread. It's all true.

   Back in the Premiership Liverpool sneak two goals in the last two minutes to beat Oldham Athletic at Anfield (2-1) and perform a similar trick to share the points at Maine Road (Manchester City 1 Liverpool 1). The month ends with a couple of hat-tricks. Ian Rush bags three against Ipswich Town (3-2) helping Liverpool through to the fourth round of the Coca-Cola Cup. Robbie Fowler does likewise to make it 10 goals in 8 games as the Reds triumph against Southampton (4-2).

November

A quiet month as the fixture list is interrupted for international matches. Another newcomer, Dominic Matteo, comes close to scoring as Liverpool beat West Ham United 2-0 at Anfield to continue their climb back up the table. However, a trip to St James Park demonstrates how far Liverpool need to go to become title contenders. Kevin Keegan's men hold all the aces and look very good for their win with Andy Cole claiming all three Magpie goals (Newcastle United 3 Liverpool 0).

Back to Anfield and Aston Villa – last season's Premiership runners-up – fail to live up to their star billing. Liverpool win more comfortably than 2-1 might suggest.

December

A packed fixture list makes up for November's inactivity. Liverpool play eight games drawing six of them, three of which are against Wimbledon. In the first match against the Dons, in the Coca-Cola Cup fourth round, a late equaliser earns Wimbledon a replay (1-1). At Selhurst Park it's Liverpool's turn for a late equaliser (2-2). But after a goalless extra time the game goes to penalties and Liverpool lose 4-3.

Own goals feature strongly in Liverpool's trip to Sheffield Wednesday. The Reds score three goals but lose 3-1. There is more controversy three days later as QPR finish their match at Anfield with only nine men (3-2).

Bottom placed Swindon Town cast off their underdog status and give Liverpool a run for their money at Anfield (2-2). This sets the trend for a sequence of draws with which to finish the year: Tottenham 3 Liverpool 3, Sheffield United 0 Liverpool 0, Liverpool 1 Wimbledon 1.

January

A month that starts in drama ends even more spectacularly. Liverpool visit Ipswich Town to notch up their first Premiership away victory since August (2-1) before facing Manchester United at Anfield. United, the Premiership's runaway leaders and hot favourites for an unprecedented domestic treble, go 3-0 up in the space of 24 minutes. There then follows a remarkable comeback as Liverpool pile forward and lay seige to the United goal. In the end the Manchester club escape with a 3-3 draw.

Four days later Liverpool's FA Cup third round game at Bristol City is abandoned after 65 minutes when the floodlights pack in (1-1). In the league it's another away win as Oldham are dumbfounded by the passing game (3-0). Back to Ashton Gate for the FA Cup rematch and Liverpool struggle for their draw against Bristol City (1-1).

Manchester City visit Anfield and are undone (again) by a last minute goal (2-1). No such luck against Bristol City who come to Anfield for their FA Cup replay prepared to fight. They make a mockery of the form book winning 1-0. It's the second year in succession that Liverpool have fallen at the first hurdle in the FA Cup to a team from a lower division and it's more than the fans can bear. With Liverpool out of contention for any trophy this season Graeme Souness bows to the inevitable and resigns. His successor is promoted from within and is Bob Paisley's choice: Roy Evans.

February

The new manager endures a baptism by fire. The Reds look good for their 2-2 draw at Carrow Road against Norwich City but there then follows a visit to the Dell. England prospect Matthew Le Tissier runs amok grabbing a hattrick and Southampton go 4-0 up. Playing for pride Liverpool manage two goals to give the scoreline some respectability (2-4). There's no respite in a trip to Elland Road (0-2) and Leeds' victory makes Liverpool's prospects of European football next season seem very slim.

Roy Evans finally comes good in his first home game. It's against Phil Neal's Coventry and, although the Reds look like running away with the game, it's only Ian Rush's second minute strike which separates the teams (1-0).

March

Liverpool lose 2-0 to Kenny Dalglish's title-chasing Blackburn at Ewood Park for Roy Evans' third consecutive away defeat. Back at Anfield a week later things look rosier as Liverpool defeat Everton 2-1. Robbie Fowler returns after injury taking the place of Nigel Clough. A disappointed Clough is seen driving away from the ground before kick-off – Fowler scores the winning goal.

It's the last derby match in front of the Kop and after the game the club announce that supporters will be able to buy pieces of masonry when it is taken down at the end of the season with all proceeds going to local charities. Next season should see the completion of an all-seater Anfield.

Form team Chelsea visit Anfield and go two goals down inside 18 minutes. They get a goal back but can't stop Liverpool's ascendancy: 2-1.

April

Fortress Anfield cracks. The trouble starts as Liverpool let slip their one goal lead against relegation hopefuls Sheffield United and lose 2-1. Two days later Liverpool travel to form side Wimbledon and look like notching up their first victory over the Dons since flares went out of fashion. Almost. Elkins ruins the dream by grabbing a last minute equaliser to cancel out Redknapp's earlier effort, 1-1.

Grand National weekend means an early kick-off and both Liverpool and Ipswich look like they could do with a few more hours rest. Eventually Ipswich decide they are the worse team and concede a penalty which Dicks converts. It was the only way anyone was ever going to score. (1-0).

The following weekend and Kevin Keegan and Terry McDermott bring their Newcastle United team to Anfield. The high-flying Magpies play like Liverpool used to and easily win 2-0.

Despite conceding an early goal Liverpool win 2-1 at West Ham to give Roy Evans his first away win as manager. Unfortunately his team have now lost the knack of winning at home. They lose 1-0 in front of the Kop's last stand against Norwich City. It's an emotional moment which reminds all present exactly how good Liverpool used to be. Expect wholesale changes to the Liverpool side for next season; never mind the ground.

May

The last match of the season confirms Liverpool's eighth place – the club's lowest league position in over 30 years. It equals their finishing position in the 1962-63 season which was their first year in the top division since gaining promotion from the then Second Division in the 1961-62 season.

The game itself was a 2-1 defeat at Villa Park in front of the Premiership's highest ever gate of 45,347 with Robbie Fowler bagging the Reds' only goal. Talk starts in earnest about just who will be wearing Liverpool shirts in the 94-95 season.

Neil Ruddock made an impressive debut for Liverpool.

*John Barnes showing the sort of true grit that has made
him a favourite with the Kop.*

1993-94
Match by Match

Detailed analysis of every
Liverpool match – League and Cup

The Pre-season Friendlies

31st July, 1993, Prenton Park   Att: 10,101
Tranmere   3   Liverpool   4
Hooper (Grobbelaar 45), Jones, Bjornebye (Burrows 45), Nicol, Whelan (Redknapp 45), Ruddock, McMahon (Marsh 59), Molby, Rush (Walters 59), Barnes, Stewart

2nd August, 1993   Att: 3,121
Raufoss   2   Liverpool   7
Grobbelaar (Hooper 59), Jones, Bjornebye, Piechnik, Stewart, Ruddock, McManaman (Burrows 45), Redknapp, Rush (Molby 68), Barnes (Nicol 52), Walters

4th August, 1993, Nørwåy Cup   Att: 16,116
Rosenborg   0   Liverpool   1
Grobbelaar, Jones, Bjornebye, Nicol, Whelan, Rudock, Clough, Molby, Rush, Barnes (Walters 63), Piechnik

8th August, 1993, Burnden Park   Att: 13,242
Burnley   0   Liverpool   4
Grobbelaar, Jones, Bjornebye, Piechnik, Whelan (Redknapp 77), Burrows, Clough, Molby, Rush, Barnes (Walters 67), McManaman

Ronnie Whelan Testimonial, Anfield   Att: 21,757
Liverpool   1   Newcastle United 0
Grobbelaar (Hooper 47), Jones, Bjornebye, Nicol, Whelan, Ruddock (Piechnik 52), Clough, Redknapp, Rush, Wright, Walters

RESULTS SUMMARY

Date	Type	Opponents		Scores	Scorers	Att
14/08/93	FAPL	Sheffield Wed	(h)	2-0	Clough 39, 47	44,004
19/08/93	FAPL	QPR	(a)	1-3	Rush 18, Nicol 38, Clough 41	19,365
22/08/93	FAPL	Swindon Town	(a)	0-5	Ruddock 19, McManaman 36, 61, Whelan 70, Marsh 80	17,017
25/08/93	FAPL	Tottenham Hotspur	(h)	1-2	Clough 18	42,456
28/08/93	FAPL	Leeds United	(h)	2-0	Rush 24, Molby 40pen	44,068
01/09/93	FAPL	Coventry	(a)	1-0		16,740
12/09/93	FAPL	Blackburn Rovers	(h)	0-1		37,355
18/09/93	FAPL	Everton	(a)	2-0		38,157
23/09/93	CCC2R	Fulham	(a)	1-3	Rush 18, Clough 41, Fowler 83	13,599
25/09/93	FAPL	Chelsea	(a)	1-0		31,271
02/10/93	FAPL	Arsenal	(h)	0-0		42,750
06/10/93	CCC2R	Fulham	(h)	5-0	Fowler 13, 40, 47, 55, 70	12,541

Liverpool won 8-1 on aggregate

Date	Type	Opponents		Scores	Scorers	Att
17/10/93	FAPL	Oldham Athletic	(h)	2-1	Fowler 88, Barlow 90 og	32,661
23/10/93	FAPL	Manchester City	(a)	1-1	Rush 88	30,403
27/10/93	CCC3R	Ipswich Town	(h)	3-2	Rush 1, 16, 64	19,058
30/10/93	FAPL	Southampton	(h)	4-2	Fowler 14, 29, 85, Rush 63	32,818
6/11/93	FAPL	West Ham United	(h)	2-0	Clough 67, Martin 83og	42,254
20/11/93	FAPL	Newcastle United	(a)	3-0		36,374
28/11/93	FAPL	Aston Villa	(h)	2-1	Fowler 45, Redknapp 62	38,484
01/12/93	CCC4R	Wimbledon	(h)	1-1	Molby 15	19,290
04/12/93	FAPL	Sheffield Wed	(a)	3-1	Fowler 37	32,177
07/12/93	FAPL	QPR	(h)	3-2	Barnes 25, Rush 32, Molby 75 pen	24,561
12/12/93	FAPL	Swindon Town	(h)	2-2	Barnes 71, Wright 86	32,739
14/12/93	CCC4Rr	Wimbledon	(a)	2-2	Ruddock 38, Segers 90og	11,343

Wimbledon won 4-3 on penalties

Date	Type	Opponents		Scores	Scorers	Att
18/12/93	FAPL	Tottenham Hotspur	(a)	3-3	Fowler 48, 54 pen, Redknapp 51	31,394
26/12/93	FAPL	Sheffield United	(a)	0-0		22,932
28/12/93	FAPL	Wimbledon	(h)	1-1	Scales 27 og	32,232
02/01/94	FAPL	Ipswich Town	(a)	1-2	Ruddock 57, Rush 88	22,355
04/01/94	FAPL	Manchester United	(h)	3-3	Clough 25, 38, Ruddock 79	42,795

17

08/01/94	FAC3R	Bristol City	(a)	1-1	Rush 12	20,612
		(match abandoned after 65 minutes)				
15/01/94	FAPL	Oldham Athletic	(a)	0-3	Dicks 47, Fowler 54, Redknapp 81	14,573
19/01/94	FAC3Rr	Bristol City	(a)	1-1	Rush 62	21,718
22/01/94	FAPL	Manchester City	(h)	2-1	Rush 22, 90	41,872
25/01/94	FAC3Rr	Bristol City	(h)	0-1		36,720
05/02/94	FAPL	Norwich City	(a)	2-2	Culverhouse 53 og, Barnes 76	19,746
14/02/94	FAPL	Southampton	(a)	4-2	Dicks 68 pen, Rush 86	18,306
19/02/94	FAPL	Leeds United	(a)	2-0		40,053
26/02/94	FAPL	Coventry City	(h)	1-0	Rush 2	38,547
05/03/94	FAPL	Blackburn Rovers	(a)	2-0		20,831
13/03/94	FAPL	Everton	(h)	2-1	Rush 22, Fowler 43	44,281
19/03/94	FAPL	Chelsea	(h)	2-1	Rush 8, Burley 19 og	38,629
16/03/94	FAPL	Arsenal	(a)	1-0		35,556
29/03/94	FAPL	Manchester United	(a)	1-0		44,751
02/04/94	FAPL	Sheffield United	(h)	1-2	Rush 4	36,642
04/04/94	FAPL	Wimbledon	(a)	1-1	Redknapp 64	13,819
09/04/94	FAPL	Ipswich Town	(h)	1-0	Dicks 75 pen	30,485
16/04/94	FAPL	Newcastle United	(h)	0-2		44,601
23/04/94	FAPL	West Ham United	(a)	1-2	Fowler 14, Rush 87	26,096
30/04/94	FAPL	Norwich City	(h)	0-1		44,339
07/05/94	FAPL	Aston Villa	(a)	2-1	Fowler 17	45,347

CCC2R	Coca-Cola Cup 2nd Round
FAC3R	FA Cup 3rd Round
r	Replay or re-match

Liverpool
Sheffield Wednesday

(1) 2
(0) 0

Saturday, 14th August 1993, Anfield

Att.: 44,004

LIVERPOOL

1	Bruce	GROBBELAAR
2	Rob	JONES
5	Mark	WRIGHT
25	Neil	RUDDOCK
20	Stig	BJORNEBYE
4	Steve	NICOL
14	Jan	MOLBY (+73)
12	Ronnie	WHELAN
11	Mark	WALTERS
7	Nigel	CLOUGH
9	Ian	RUSH

Subs

15	Jamie	REDKNAPP (+73)
24	Mike	HOOPER (gk)
17	Steve	McMANAMAN

SHEFFIELD WEDNESDAY

1	Chris	WOODS
2	Roland	NILSSO
17	Des	WALKER
12	Andy	PEARCE
18	Phil	KING
14	Chris	BART-WILLIAMS (+57)
11	John	SHERIDAN
4	Carlton	PALMER – Sent Off
3	Nigel	WORTHINGTON
9	David	HIRST
7	Paul	WARHURST (*80)

6	Graham	HYDE (+57)
10	Mark	BRIGHT (* 80)
13	Kevin	PRESSMAN (gk)

Match Facts

- First Liverpool appearances in competitive games for Nigel Clough and Neil Ruddock.
- Liverpool have won their first game of the season 53 times in 91 starts, the best record.
- Carlton Palmer first Premiership player sent off in the new season (13 minutes).

Score Sheet

N. CLOUGH 39 min – 1-0

N. CLOUGH 47 min – 2-0

Referee:
Mr. G. Ashby (Worcester)

Result of this Season's Fixture

Sheffield Wed
Liverpool

A Flying Start

Liverpool made winning start to the season with the two expensive new signings, Nigel Clough and Neil 'Razor' Ruddock, looking impressive on their debuts. Anfield was packed to the rafters and even the sun was shining.

A mood of optimism was about, strangely at odds with the turmoil that had seen the preceding season's close. Graham Souness, at the heart of so much controversy only months before, had been building bridges. Talk of animosity between the manager and Ian Rush was dispelled by the appointment of the Welsh goalscoring ace as club captain, an honour which obviously thrilled him.

The new season kicked off with much at stake. Liverpool won no trophies in the 92-93 season and only finished sixth in the Premiership. It was the second year in succession that Liverpool had finished in such a comparatively lowly position making it three years without a championship – the worst sequence at the club since the end of the sixties.

The mood of determination was carried onto the pitch as Liverpool played with great conviction. The task of making a winning start to the season was made much easier by the sending off after just 13 minutes of Sheffield Wednesday's Carlton Palmer following a clumsy attack on Jan Molby.

By then Liverpool had already posted their intentions of taking charge and it was no surprise when the Reds took the lead just before half time. Clough gave himself time to take strike at a Steve Nicol pass which floated acrosss the Wednesday penalty area and left England keeper Chris Woods with no chance. Shortly after the break it was Clough who pounced on a chance after a powerful Neil Ruddock header had not been cleared.

Grobelaar had a relatively easy game and was only troubled by Wednesday's defender turned striker, Paul Warhurst. Warhurst volleyed wide on one occasion and forced a save with a header on another. For all their efforts, though, Wednesday were outclassed as well as outnumbered and Liverpool made a flying start.

League Records

	P	W	D	L	F	A	Pts	Pos
93-94 Premiership Record	1	1	0	0	2	0	3	–
92-93 Premier League Record	42	16	11	15	62	55	59	6th
All-time Premiership Record	43	17	11	15	64	55	62	–
All-time League Record	3567	1667	862	1038	6135	4582	5863	–

	Home	Away	Total
League Attendance	44,004		44,004

Queens Park Rangers   (1) 1
Liverpool   (3) 3

Wednesday, 19th August 1993, Loftus Road   Att.: 19,365

QUEENS PARK RANGERS

1	Tony	ROBERTS
18	Karl	READY – *Booked*
24	Seve	YATES
5	Darren	PEACOCK
3	Clive	WILSON
7	Andrew	IMPEY
4	Ray	WILKINS
14	Simon	BARKER – *Booked*
11	*Trevor*	*SINCLAIR (+73)*
9	Les	FERDINAND
12	Gary	PENRICE

Subs

19	*Devon*	*WHITE, (+73)*
13	Jan	STEJSKAL (gk)
15	Rufus	BREVETT

LIVERPOOL

1	Bruce	GROBELAAR
2	Rob	JONES
5	Mark	WRIGHT
25	Neil	RUDDOCK
20	Stig	BJORNEBYE – *B'ked*
4	Steve	NICOL
14	Jan	MOLBY
12	Ronnie	WHELAN
17	Steve	McMANAMAN
7	*Nigel*	*CLOUGH (+73)*
9	Ian	RUSH

15	*Jamie*	*REDKNAPP (+73)*
24	Mike	HOOPER (gk)
3	David	BURROWS

Match Facts

- Queens Park Rangers highest Premiership gate for a mid-week game.
- Steve Nicol's first goal for Liverpool since December '1991.

Score Sheet

I. RUSH 18 min – 0-1

R. WILKINS 24 min – 1-1

S. NICOL 38 min – 1-2

N. CLOUGH 41 min –1-3

Referee:
Mr. P Durkin (Portland)

**Result of this
Season's Fixture**

QPR

Liverpool

Turning on the Style

It wasn't so much that Liverpool won this game that pleased the fans so much, it was the manner in which they did it that counted. It was an emphatic win in which Liverpool played with great purpose and always looked in control. The will to win which had seemed absent for much of the last two years returned with a vengeance and for all QPR's skills and contributions to a richly entertaining game there was only ever one side in it.

The kick-off to the game was delayed by fifteen minutes as nearly twenty thousand struggled to get into the Loftus Road ground. The early play was largely QPR's as veteran Ray Wilkins orchestrated a series of attacks which called on all Bruce Grobelaar's expertise: first diving to stop a Les Ferdinand header then leaping acrobatically to parry a shot out for a corner.

After absorbing this early pressure Liverpool counter attacked and a Rob Jones pass split the Rangers defence leaving Ian Rush to do what he does best. But just when Liverpool threatened to take complete control they were rocked by a spectacular goal from old man Wilkins. Running onto a loose ball some thirty-five yards out he let go with a blistering shot into the top corner that left Grobelaar stranded and the fans stunned.

There was no denying Liverpool, though as they repeatedly pushed forward. Steve Nicol made it 2-1 latching onto a through ball from Nigel Clough. They reversed roles a few minutes later, the former Nottingham Forest number 9 scored the third Liverpool goal just minutes before the interval with a delightful back-heel flick from a Steve Nicol pass.

League Records

	P	W	D	L	F	A	Pts	Pos
93-94 Premiership Record	2	2	0	0	5	1	6	–
All-time Premiership Record	44	18	11	15	67	56	65	–
All-time League Record	3568	1668	862	1038	6138	4583	5866	–

	Home	Away	Total
League Attendances	44,004	19,365	63,369

Swindon Town (0) 0
Liverpoool (2) 5

Sunday, 22nd August 1993, County Ground   Att.: 17,017

SWINDON TOWN

1	Fraser	DIGBY
2	Nicky	SUMMERBEE – *B'ked*
14	Adrian	WHITBREAD
8	Ross	MACLAREN
6	Shaun	TAYLOR
16	Kevin	HORLOCK
7	John	*MONCUR (*47)*
5	Luc	NIJHOLT
10	Martin	*LING (+77)*
9	Jan-Aage	FJORTOFT
25	Andy	MUTCH

Subs

4	*Micky*	*HAZARD (*47)*
11	*Craig*	*Maskell (+77)*
23	Nicky	HAMMOND (gk)

LIVERPOOL

1	Bruce	GROBBELAAR
2	Rob	JONES – *Booked*
5	Mark	WRIGHT
25	*Neil*	*RUDDOCK (+76)*
20	*Stig*	*BJORNEBYE (*72)*
4	Steve	NICOL
14	Jan	MOLBY
12	Ronnie	WHELAN
17	Steve	McMANAMAN
	Nigel	CLOUGH
9	Ian	RUSH

21	*Mike*	*MARSH (+76)*
24	Mike	HOOPER (gk)
3	*David*	*BURROWS (*72)*

Match Facts

- The highest ever away win in the FA Premier League.
- First time that Liverpool have topped the FA Premier League.
- The first league meeting of the two clubs.
- Neil Ruddock's first goal for Liverpool.
- First goals for McManaman, Whelan and Marsh in 1993.

Score Sheet

N. RUDDOCK 19 min – 0-1

McMANAMAN 36min – 0-2

McMANAMAN 61min – 0-3

R. WHELAN 70min – 0-4

M. MARSH 80min – 0-5

Referee:
Mr. P. Don (Middlesex)

FA Carling Premiership League

Pos		P	W	D	L	F	A	Pts
1st	Liverpool	3	3	0	0	10	1	9
2nd	Everton	3	3	0	0	7	2	9
3rd	Ipswich Town	3	3	0	0	5	0	9
4th	Manchester Utd	3	2	1	0	6	1	7

Result of this Season's Fixture

No Fixture

Swindon's Greatest Loss

Swindon Town were the First Division play-offs qualifiers for the Premier League and the weakest of the three to gain promotion. Add to that the loss of player-manager Glenn Hoddle before the season started and it was no surprise that they were everyone's favourites for relegation before a ball had been kicked. Following a couple of defeats before this game and the club were in no position to be facing Liverpool.

Circumstances like those often serve to galvanise underdog teams to play above themselves but it was not the case with Swindon. To give them credit they tried to compete and play their own attractive brand of passing football but they were always on to a loser. It's not just style you need to compete at this level but style with steel. Once Liverpool had gone ahead it was just a question of "how many?"

The answer turned out to be "five" as Liverpool equalled their best ever win in the Premiership and set a new record for an away victory. More encouragement for those seeking signs of a return to old and winning Liverpool ways was in the goalscorers. Liverpool had four different goalscorers without contributions from either of the orthodox marksmen Clough or Rush.

The first goal came after 19 minutes when Summerbee fouled Steve McManaman just outside the area. Ruddock chested the ball down from Bjornebye's free-kick and fired past the strandede Digby. Summerbee was invovled in the second as well. He failed to stop McManaman who latched on to a Steve Nicol cross.

In the second half Swindon's defensive frailties were exposed when Nijholt was dispossessed by Ronnie Whelan. He put McManaman through for goal number three. Ten minutes later it was 4-0 when Whelan beat Nijholt to a partially cleared ball and sent in a low shot from 20 yards. Mike Mrash wrapped up the scoring after only three minutes on the pitch. He completed a neat one-two with McManaman by lobbing the Advancing Digby to complete a comprehensive victory.

League Records

	P	W	D	L	F	A	Pts	Pos
93-94 Premiership Record	3	3	0	0	10	1	9	1st
All-time Premiership Record	45	19	11	15	72	56	68	–
All-time League Record	3569	1669	862	1038	6143	4583	5869	

	Home	Away	Total
League Attendances	44,004	36,382	80,386

Liverpool (1) 1
Tottenham Hotspur (2) 2

Wednesday, 25th August 1993, Anfield   Att.: 42,456

LIVERPOOL

1	Bruce	GROBBELAAR
2	Rob	JONES
5	Mark	WRIGHT
25	Neil	RUDDOCK
3	*David*	*BURROWS (+57)*
4	Steve	NICOL
14	Jan	MOLBY
12	Ronnie	WHELAN
17	Steve	McMANAMAN
7	Nigel	CLOUGH
9	Ian	RUSH

Subs

11	*Mark*	*WALTERS (+57)*
24	Mike	HOOPER (gk)
21	Mike	MARSH

TOTTENHAM HOTSPUR

1	Erik	THORSTVEDT
2	Dean	AUSTIN
5	Colin	CALDERWOOD
6	Gary	MABBUTT
23	Sol	CAMPBELL
15	*David*	*HOWELLS (+82)*
12	Jason	DOZZELL
4	Vinny	SAMWAYS
14	Steve	SEDGLEY
8	Gordon	DURIE
10	Teddy	SHERINGHAM

20	*Darren*	*CASKEY (+82)*
9	Darren	ANDERTON
13	Ian	WALKER (gk)

Match Facts

- This was either Tottenham's third victory at Anfield in eight years, or their third in eighty – it all depends on how you want to look at it.
- The attendance of 42,456 is a new Premiership record for a mid-week game.

Score Sheet

N. CLOUGH 18 min –1-0
SHERINGHAM 30min Pen – 1-1
SHERINGHAM 42 min – 1-2

Referee:
Mr. D. Ellery (Harrow)

FA Carling Premiership League

Pos	Team	P	W	D	L	F	A	Pts
1st	Manchester Utd	4	3	1	0	8	2	10
2nd	**Liverpool**	**4**	**3**	**0**	**1**	**11**	**3**	**9**
3rd	Norwich City	4	3	0	1	10	4	9
4th	Everton	4	3	0	1	7	3	9
5th	Ipswich Town	4	3	0	1	5	1	9

Result of this Season's Fixture

Liverpool
Tottenham H

Spurs of Steel

In coming back from a goal behind at Anfield – the venue of so many of their defeats – Tottenham Hotspur displayed resilience, courage, application and a stomach for the fight. In short, all of those attributes that you don't normally associate with them.

Tottenham had been undergoing their own pre-season traumas with chairman Alan Sugar sacking Terry Venables in a much-publicised upheaval. However, the expected protests in favour of Venables never took off. One major factor in this was the arrival of Ossie Ardiles as manager and a subsequent resurgence in playing form. Tottenham brought with them a much more positive approach than had been in evidence in the previous season's final match when they had lost 6-2 at Anfield.

This time around Liverpool went ahead in the eighteenth minute when Steve Mcmanaman dribbled along the Spurs goal line before laying the ball back for Clough to fire in his fourth of the season. At that point Liverpool looked like taking charge but Tottenham were let back into the game when Burrows pointlessly pushed over Sheringham in a chase for the ball. Last season's Premiership top scorer needed no second bidding blasting the penalty past Grobbelaar to make it one apiece. Three minutes before half time a fluid Spurs move ended with Jason Dozzell firing in a low and hard shot. Grobbelaar got to the ball but could only parry it into the path of that man Sheringham who made no mistake.

Liverpool took the game to Spurs in the second half but lacked the final convincing touch. There was always an edge of desperation to their attacks when greater patience might have been more rewarding.

League Records

	P	W	D	L	F	A	Pts	Pos
93-94 Premiership Record	4	3	0	1	11	3	9	2nd
All-time Premiership Record	46	19	11	16	73	58	71	–
All-time League Record	3570	1669	862	1039	6144	4583	5869	–

	Home	Away	Total
League Attendances	86,460	36,382	122,842

Liverpool
Leeds United

(2) 2
(0) 0

Match Five

LIVERPOOL

1	Bruce	GROBBELAAR
2	Rob	JONES
5	Mark	WRIGHT
25	Neil	RUDDOCK
3	David	BURROWS – *Booked*
6	*Don*	*HUTCHISON (+64)*
14	Jan	MOLBY
12	Ronnie	WHELAN
17	Steve	McMANAMAN
7	Nigel	CLOUGH
9	Ian	RUSH

Subs

21	*Mike*	*MARSH (+64)*
24	Mike	HOOPER (gk)
11	Mark	WALTERS

LEEDS UNITED

1	John	LUKIC
3	Tony	DORIGO
22	Gary	KELLY
5	Chris	FAIRCLOUGH
16	Jon	NEWSOME
11	Gary	SPEED
10	Gary	McALLISTER
4	David	BATTY
7	Gordon	STRACHAN
9	Brian	DEANE
8	*Rod*	*WALLACE (+72)*

25	*Noel*	*WHELAN (+72) – B'ked*
23	Mark	TINKLER
13	Mark	BEENEY (gk)

Match Facts

- Ian Rush's 200th League goal for Liverpool.
- Leeds United have not won away since clinching their League title with a win at Sheffield United in May '92.
- Leeds have not won at Anfield since 1972.

Score Sheet

I. RUSH 24 min – 1-0

J. MOLBY 40 min Pen – 2-0

Referee:
Mr. R. Hart (Darlington)

FA Carling Premiership League

Pos	Team	P	W	D	L	F	A	Pts
1st	Manchester Utd	5	4	1	0	11	3	13
2nd	**Liverpool**	**5**	**4**	**0**	**1**	**13**	**3**	**12**
3rd	Arsenal	5	4	0	1	6	4	12
4th	Norwich City	5	3	1	1	9	4	10
5th	Ipswich Town	5	3	1	1	6	2	10

Result of this Season's Fixture

Liverpool

Leeds United

27

Rush's Double Century

Anfield is not the best place to bring a side with defensive uncertainties and a trace of desperation in their hunt for an elusive first away win since winning the championship back in 1992. For much of the game Leeds United competed on level terms and played with great conviction. When the ball was in their own penalty area, though, they lost all their composure and this led to both goals.

Leeds started out brightly enough and kept Liverpool pinned back into their own half. Early on Gary McAllister took the ball from Jan Molby, played a neat one-two with Brian Deane and shot low to Grobbelaar's left forcing a reflex save.

As ever, Liverpool gained their composure and started a series of flowing movements forward. A few chances went begging before Ronnie Whelan and Rob Jones engineered a delightful attack with Ian Rush running on the ball with only Lukic to beat. But the keper brought of a stunning instinctive save to deny him when a goal seemed inevitable. Rush wasn't to be denied a second time. Lukic and Fairclough were caught hesitating as he ran onto a Don Hutchison pass. It's the sort of half opportunity that Ian Rush seizes so well and the ball was in the back of the net before they could recover. It was his 200th League goal for Liverpool and in classic Ian Rush style, punishing the slightest defensive error.

At the other end Brian Deane was presented with what seemed to be a golden opportunity but the new signing from Sheffield United did little to justify his inflated price tag – at £2.7 million, he cost £500,000 more than Nigel Clough. A cross from the timeless Gordon Strachan opened the Liverpool defence but Deane's header was tame and wide of the mark.

Shortly before half-time a Molby through ball found Rob Jones springing the Leeds offside trap only to be brought down by Lukic on the edge of the penalty area.

Molby was composure personified as he sent Lukic the wrong way and wrap up the game. Leeds got the better of play during a disappointing second half without ever looking to score. For Liverpool there were encouraging signs in seeing them win comfortably without playing at their best – it's the sort of thing you need to do to win championships. The frustration is beginning to tell for Leeds. How many other managers can have felt under threat just 16 months after winning a club its first championship in 20 years?

League Records

	P	W	D	L	F	A	Pts	Pos
93-94 Premiership Record	5	4	0	1	13	3	12	2nd
All-time FA Premiership Record	47	20	11	16	75	58	71	–
All-time League Record	3571	1670	862	1039	6146	4583	5872	–

	Home	Away	Total
League Attendances	130,528	36,382	166,910

Coventry
Liverpool

(1) 1
(0) 0

Match Six

Wednesday, 1st September 1993, Highfield Road   Att.:16,740

COVENTRY CITY

23	Jonathan	GOULD
32	Lloyd	McGRATH
4	Peter	ATHERTON
20	Phil	BABB – *Booked*
3	Steve	MORGAN
16	Willie	BOLAND – *Booked*
17	Roy	WEGERLE
6	David	RENNIE
12	Peter	NDLOVU
7	*John*	*WILLIAMS (+87)*
10	*Mick*	*QUINN (*89)*

Subs

15	*Paul*	*WILLIAMS (+87)*
19	*Tony*	*SHERIDAN (*89)*
1	Steve	OGRIZOVIC (gk)

LIVERPOOL

1	Bruce	GROBBELAAR
2	Rob	JONES – *Sent Off*
5	Mark	WRIGHT
25	Neil	RUDDOCK – *Booked*
3	David	BURROWS (+68)
4	Steve	NICOL
14	Jan	MOLBY
12	Ronnie	WHELAN – *Booked*
17	Steve	McMANAMAN
7	Nigel	CLOUGH
9	Ian	RUSH

11	*Mark*	*WALTERS (+68)*
24	Mike	HOOPER (gk)
6	Don	HUTCHISON

Match Facts

● Rob Jones the first Liverpool player to be sent off this season.

Score Sheet

P. BABB 21 min – 1-0

Referee:
Mr. K. Burge (Tonypandy)

FA Carling Premiership League

Pos	Team	P	W	D	L	F	A	Pts
1st	Manchester Utd	6	5	1	0	14	3	16
2nd	Arsenal	6	4	1	1	7	5	13
3rd	**Liverpool**	**6**	**4**	**0**	**2**	**13**	**4**	**12**
4th	*Coventry City*	*6*	*3*	*3*	*0*	*11*	*6*	*12*
5th	Norwich City	6	3	2	1	11	7	11

Result of this Season's Fixture

Coventry

Liverpool

29

Not Good Enough

Coventry City won the FA cup in 1987, they finished last season's league campaign only seven points behind Liverpool and they've been in the top division longer than anyone except Liverpool, Everton and Arsenal.

Those may be the raw statistics but, in real life, you go to Highfield Road expecting to win – particularly if you are harbouring intentions of winning the championship. The previous December Liverpool got it wrong, horribly wrong, and a weakened team went down 5-1, one of the club's heaviest defeats in years.

This time around Liverpool played with much greater conviction and created several chances but none of them were converted. They started promisingly and fluid moves from midfield saw Jonathan Gould – the Coventry goalkeeper and manager's son – tested by a header from Mark Wright while Steve McManaman shot across the face of goal. But it was Coventry who scored in the 21st minute. John Williams forced a corner and from there Willie Boland chipped towards goal. Grobbelaar hesitated but Phil Babb didn't: 1-0. Liverpool's best chance of equalising came just before half-time when an exchange of passes between Nigel Clough and Steve Nicol found Nicol with a clear shot on goal but it wasn't to be his night and he put the ball wide.

After the break Liverpool kept pushing forwards but were never a match for the battling determination of the Coventry defence who were faster and more determined and kept upsetting the Reds' rhythm and putting their own forwards through on the break. Liverpool's frustration began to show and Whelan, Ruddock and Jones were booked for petulant fouls before Jones committed his second bookable foul on Roy Wegerle and was sent off.

League Records

	P	W	D	L	F	A	Pts	Pos
93-94 Premiership Record	6	4	0	2	13	4	12	3rd
All-time FA Premiership Record	48	20	11	17	75	59	71	–
All-time League Record	3572	1670	862	1040	6146	4584	5872	–

	Home	Away	Total
League Attendances	130,528	53,122	166,910

Liverpool
Blackburn Rovers

(0) 0
(0) 1

Sunday, 12th September 1993, Anfield   Att.: 37,355

LIVERPOOL

1	Bruce	GROBBELAAR
2	Rob	JONES – *Booked*
5	Mark	WRIGHT
25	Neil	RUDDOCK
20	*Stig*	*BJORNEBYE +60)*
17	Steve	McMANAMAN
12	Ronnie	WHELAN
14	Jan	MOLBY
4	Steve	NICOL
9	*Ian*	*RUSH (*79)*
7	Nigel	CLOUGH

Subs

18	*Ronnie*	*ROSENTHAL (+60)*
24	Mike	HOOPER (gk)
15	*Jamie*	*REDKNAPP (*79)*

BLACKBURN ROVERS

1	Bobby	MIMMS
20	Henning	BERG – *Booked*
2	*David*	*MAY (+72)*
21	Kevin	MORAN
6	Graeme	LE SAUX – *Booked*
7	Stuart	RIPLEY – *Booked*
24	Paul	WARHURST – *B'ked*
4	Tim	SHERWOOD
11	Jason	WILCOX
10	Mike	NEWELL
8	Kevin	GALLACHER

12	*Nicky*	*MARKER (+72)*
9	Alan	SHEARER
13	Frank	TALIA (gk)

Match Facts

- Liverpool's third defeat in four games.
- Blackburn Rovers undefeated away from home this season.
- Mike Newell's eighth goal against Liverpool.

Score Sheet

M. NEWELL 54 min – 0-1

Referee:
Mr. M. Reed (Birmingham)

FA Carling Premiership League

Pos	Team	P	W	D	L	F	A	Pts
3rd	*Blackburn Rovers*	7	4	2	1	10	6	14
4th	Coventry City	7	3	4	0	11	6	13
5th	**Liverpool**	**7**	**4**	**0**	**3**	**13**	**5**	**12**
6th	Aston Villa	7	3	3	1	9	5	12
7th	Wimbledon	7	3	3	1	9	6	12

Result of this Season's Fixture

Liverpool

Blackburn Rovers

Newell's Revenge

A disappointing game for Liverpool who created few chances but displayed great commitment. Too much commitment in fact, for the game was littered with crunching tackles that saw five players booked altogether. That four of those were Blackburn players didn't adequately reflect the levels of aggression and Dalglish was quick to complain after the game about what he saw as erratic refereeing by Birminham's Mike Reed. "I thought the referee's decisions were diabolical and contradictory" he said. Although he is far from the first visiting manager to Anfield to complain about partisan decision-taking, in Dalglish's case there is more credibilty than usual as his team won; so sour grapes don't come into it. Dalglish hardly set a shining example himself as he and Souness looked like they were going to square up to each other following a Jan Molby foul on Kevin Gallacher.

Blackburn won thanks to the only goal of the game from Anfield reject Mike Newell. Newell served his apprenticeship at Anfield before disappearing to Crewe Alexandra. Since then he has specialised in gaining revenge on his former employers and childhood heroes – he scored a hat-trick against Liverpool a few seasons back when playing for Luton Town. He has now scored eight goals altogether against Liverpool. His goal this time came after Tim Sherwood had forced Grobbelaar to tip the ball wide for a corner with a splendid rising drive. Jason Wilcox curled the corner in and found Mike Newell unmarked at the far post.

Ian Rush limped off ten minutes from the end with a groin injury and, with Blackburn's lead looking secure, Dalglish was under no pressure to experiment with bringing on recovering England hopeful Alan Shearer. If anything Blackburn had looked the more likely scorers with Newell testing Grobbelaar with a header from a rebound after Jason Wilcox had struck the bar.

After such a sparkling start to the season Liverpool have slipped back a little. But with Manchester United also losing there's no threat of anyone opening up a lead at the top of the table just yet.

League Records

	P	W	D	L	F	A	Pts	Pos
93-94 Premiership Record	7	4	0	3	13	5	12	5th
All-time FA Premiership Record	49	20	11	17	75	60	71	–
All-time League Record	3573	1670	862	1041	6146	4585	5872	–

	Home	Away	Total
League Attendances	167,883	53,122	221,005

Everton
Liverpool

(1) 2
(0) 0

Saturday, 18th September 1993, Goodison Park   Att.: 38,157

EVERTON			**LIVERPOOL**		
1	Neville	SOUTHALL	1	Bruce	GROBBELAAR
12	Paul	HOLMES	4	Steve	NICOL
2	Matthew	JACKSON	5	Mark	WRIGHT
6	Gary	ABLETT	25	Neil	RUDDOCK
3	Andy	HINCHCLIFFE	3	Julian	DICKS
7	Mark	WARD	17	Steve	McMANAMAN (†65)
10	Barry	HORNE	12	Ronnie	WHELAN – *Booked*
14	John	EBBREL – *Booked*	15	Jamie	REDKNAPP – *Booked*
11	*Peter*	BEAGRIE *(+81)*	11	*Mark*	WALTERS *(+52)*
15	Paul	RIDEOUT	7	Nigel	CLOUGH – *Booked*
9	Tony	COTTEE	9	Ian	RUSH

Subs

16		*PREKI (+81)*	18	*Ronnie*	*ROSENTHAL (+52)*
13	Jason	KEARTON (gk)	24	Mike	HOOPER (gk)
22	Brett	ANGELL	8	Paul	STEWART (†65)

Match Facts

- Everton's 50th victory in 149 league meetings between the two clubs.
- Liverpool's third consecutive league defeat.
- Bruce Grobbelaar's 34th Merseyside derby appearance – a record.

Score Sheet

M. WARD 27 min – 1-0

T. COTTEE 85 min – 2-0

Referee:
Mr. D. Elleray (Harrow)

FA Carling Premiership League

Pos	Team	P	W	D	L	F	A	Pts
7th	Blackburn Rovers	8	4	2	2	11	5	14
8th	Leeds Utd	8	4	1	3	8	10	13
9th	**Liverpool**	**8**	**4**	**0**	**4**	**13**	**7**	**12**
10th	Norwich City	8	3	3	2	13	10	12
11th	Wimbledon	7	3	3	1	9	6	12

Result of this Season's Fixture

Everton

Liverpool

The Wrong Sort of Battle

Out went David Burrows and Mike Marsh in a curious two-for-the-price-of-one swap for West Ham defender Julian Dicks. The straight swap meant that no money changed hands in an exchange estimated at £1.5 million.

Even more bizarre, though, was the sight of two Liverpool players squaring up to each other on the pitch in what Bruce Grobbelaar described as *"the worst of all derby matches"*. After the turmoil and indiscipline of last season seemed behind them as Liverpool began playing attractive and effective attacking football. A few defeats later and all the old uncertainties have surfaced once again. It was disheartening to see Bruce Grobbelaar and Steve McManaman letting tempers rise so far that their row became physical.

The immediate cause was Grobbelaar's irritation at a sloppy clearance leading to the opening goal for Mark Ward. After the game he explained that three goals from corners in the last three matches had been down to a defence not doing the simple things properly. A greater source of frustration though was the way in which Everton ran the show for much of the game forcing a succession of impressive saves from the Liverpool keeper. The first half in particular was all Everton's although they were pleased to score their second after a second half revival had threatened to see the scores levelled. Cottee clinched the game with a strike five minutes from time sidestepping challenges from Grobbelaar and Wright to steer the ball over the line.

After the match Souness was less concerned with the altercation between his two players than with the lack of fight the team had shown in capitulating to their Merseyside rivals. The overall display was best summed up by Neil Ruddock: *"It was a big day for the club and the fans, and we were crap."* Amen.

League Records

	P	W	D	L	F	A	Pts	Pos
93-94 Premiership Record	8	4	0	4	13	7	12	9th
All-time Premiership Record	50	20	11	19	75	62	71	–
All-time League Record	3574	1670	862	1042	6146	4587	5872	–

	Home	Away	Total
League Attendances	167,883	91,279	259,162

Fulham
Liverpool

(0) 1
(2) 3

Wednesday, 23rd September 1993, Craven Cottage   Att.:13,599

FULHAM

1	Jim	STANNARD
2	Duncan	JUPP
3	Simon	MORGAN
4	Glen	THOMAS
5	Martin	PIKE
6	Julian	HAILS
7	Udo	ONWERE
8	Martin	FERNEY
9	*Jeff*	*ECKHARDT (+60)*
10	Gary	BRAZIL
11	Peter	BAAH

Subs

12	Terry	ANGUS
13	Lee	HARRISON (gk)
14	*Sean*	*FARRELL (+60)*

LIVERPOOL

1	Bruce	GROBBELAAR
2	Rob	JONES
5	Mark	WRIGHT
25	Neil	RUDDOCK
3	Julian	DICKS
6	Don	HUTCHISON
8	Paul	STEWART
15	*Jamie*	*REDKNAPP (+67)*
7	Nigel	CLOUGH
9	Ian	RUSH
23	Robbie	FOWLER

17	*Steve*	*McMANAMAN (+67)*
19	Torben	PIECHNIK
13	David	JAMES (gk)

Match Facts

• Robbie Fowler's first team debut and first goal for Liverpool.

Score Sheet

I. RUSH 18min – 0-1

N. CLOUGH 41 min – 0-2

S. FARRELL 63 min – 1-2

R. FOWLER 83.min – 1-3

Referee:
Mr. P. Danson (Leicestershire)

Ringing the Changes

Souness promised changes from the squad that lost so miserably to Everton at the weekend and changes there were. Steve Nicol, Steve McManaman, Ronnie Whelan and Mark Walters were dropped and in came Rob Jones, Don Hutchison, Paul Stewart and Robbie Fowler.

Fulham are just the sort of team that a club like Liverpool need to face in harrowing times of late and Fulham dutifully played their part by losing 3-1 at home, effectively handing the tie to Liverpool. A team at the foot of Division Two should never have a realistic hope against one of the top sides in the country but cup ties are cup ties and the lesser sides have a disconcerting habit of playing several leagues above their normal ability when the occasion arises. Fulham didn't go quite that far but they did expose one or two defensive frailties that better opposition will be able to exploit to much greater effect.

Liverpool took the lead when a cross from Robbie Fowler was missed by Don Hutchison leaving Ian Rush with a simple tap in. Strange how he always manages to be in the right place at the right time. A second goal came just before the interval. This time Robbie Fowler's chip found both Martin Pike and Nigel Clough vying for the ball at the far post. One of them got the final touch and there was more than a whiff of suspicion that it may have been the Fulham defender. But it will be Nigel Clough's name that goes into the record books.

Liverpool eased up in the second half and were caught napping when an inspired substitution saw Sean Farrell get one back after just a minute on the pitch. He outpaced Neil Ruddock and lobbed the advancing Grobbelaar with a neat lob. After that Fulham took the game to Liverpool and left themselves exposed at the back. A Don Hutchison cross found Robbie Fowler who volleyed home to seal the game. It was an impressive debut for the England Under-19 international who was involved in all three goals.

League Cup Record

	P	W	D	L	F	A
Leagie Cup Record 93-94	1	1	0	0	3	1
All-time League Cup Record	141	76	40	25	272	119

	Home	Away	Total
League Cup Attendances	–	13,599	13,599

Chelsea (0) 1
Liverpool (0) 0

Match Ten

Saturday, 25th September 1993, Stamford Bridge   Att.: 31,271

CHELSEA

1	Dimitri	KHARIN
12	Steve	CLARKE
26	Andy	DOW
20	Glenn	HODDLE
35	Jakob	KJELDBJERG
6	Frank	SINCLAIR
18	Eddie	NEWTON
15	*Mal*	*DONAGHY (+58)*
19	Neil	SHIPPERLEY
9	Tony	CASCARINO
11	Dennis	WISE – *Booked*

Subs

14	*Gareth*	*HALL (+58)*
13	Kevin	HITCHCOCK
7	John	SPENCER

LIVERPOOL

1	Bruce	GROBBELAAR
2	Rob	JONES
3	Julian	DICKS
5	Mark	WRIGHT
25	Neil	RUDDOCK – *Booked*
6	Don	HUTCHISON (+66)
8	Paul	STEWART – *Booked*
7	Nigel	CLOUGH
9	Ian	RUSH
15	Jamie	REDKNAPP – *Booked*
23	Robbie	FOWLER

17	*Steve*	*McMANAMAN (+66)*
13	David	JAMES (gk)
4	Steve	NICOL

Match Facts

• Liverpool's fourth consecutive Premiership defeat.

• Liverpool collected no league points in September – their first time in 90 years.

• They didn't score any league goals either.

Score Sheet

N. SHIPPERLY 49 min – 1-0

Referee:
Mr. K. Hackett (Sheffield)

FA Carling Premiership League

Pos	Team	P	W	D	L	F	A	Pts
11th	Newcastle Utd	9	3	4	2	13	10	13
12th	*Chelsea*	9	3	4	2	9	7	13
13th	**Liverpool**	**9**	**4**	**0**	**5**	**13**	**8**	**12**
14th	Manchester City	9	3	2	4	9	8	11
15th	Ipswich Town	8	3	2	3	8	9	11

Result of this Season's Fixture

Liverpool
Chelsea

Just One of Those Days

Another disappointing result and the murmurings have started in the press about Graham Souness's suitability as manager. The Liverpool board have said they will stand by him for this season.

How very different things seem now from when the team had won their first three games and in a style that made them look like championship contenders. The team's fifth defeat in six league encounters will hardly have furthered Souness's cause but, in truth, it was a match in which Liverpool played well and, if not perhaps deserving victory, certainly merited more than defeat. Liverpool will play worse football than this and win games – I certainly hope so anyway.

They had two appeals for penalties turned down by referee Keith Hackett both following badly timed tackles by Glenn Hoddle. Jamie Redknapp and Nigel Clough were in turn brought down by the new Chelsea player-manager but on each occasion play was waved on. For all their endeavour a penalty looked like the only way Liverpool might score. Dmitri Kharin was impressive in the Chelsea goal making a series of good saves from Robbie Fowler, Julian Dicks and Steve McManaman.

The only goal of the game came shortly after the interval when an advance along the right flank for Dennis Wise and Steve Clarke provided a shooting opportunity. Grobbelaar dived acrobatically and juggled in vain with the ball which was adjudged to have crossed the line.

League Records

	P	W	D	L	F	A	Pts	Pos
93-94 Premiership Record	9	4	0	5	13	8	12	13th
All-time FA Premiership Record	51	20	11	20	75	63	71	–
All-time League Record	3575	1670	862	1043	6146	4588	5872	–

	Home	Away	Total
League Attendances	167,883	122,550	290,433

Liverpool
Arsenal

(0) 0
(0) 0

Saturday, 2nd October 1993, Anfield   Att.: 42,750

LIVERPOOL

1	Bruce	GROBBELAAR
2	Rob	JONES
3	Julian	DICKS
5	Mark	WRIGHT – *Booked*
6	Don	HUTCHISON
7	Nigel	CLOUGH
8	Paul	STEWART – *Booked*
9	Ian	RUSH
15	Jamie	REDKNAPP
23	Robbie	FOWLER
25	Neil	RUDDOCK

Subs

12	Ronnie	WHELAN
17	Steve	McMANAMAN
13	Mark	JAMES (gk)

ARSENAL

1	David	SEAMAN
2	Lee	DIXON
3	Nigel	WINTERBURN
4	Paul	DAVIS
5	Andy	LINIGHAN
6	Tony	ADAMS
7	Kevin	CAMPBELL
8	Ian	WRIGHT
10	Paul	MERSON
11	Eddie	McGOLDRICK
17	John	JENSEN

23	Ray	PARLOUR
9	Alan	SMITH
13	Alan	MILLER (gk)

Match Facts

- Robbie Fowler's home league debut.
- Liverpool's first draw of the season.
  A draw stopped Liverpool recording five
  consecutive defeats which would have been
  the first time since the side were relegated
  from the First Division in 1954.

Score Sheet

NO GOALS

Referee:
Mr. G. Ashby (Worcester)

FA Carling Premiership League

Pos	Team	P	W	D	L	F	A	Pts
11th	Coventry City	10	3	5	2	12	10	14
12th	QPR	10	4	2	4	16	17	14
13th	**Liverpool**	**10**	**4**	**1**	**5**	**13**	**8**	**13**
14th	Chelsea	10	3	4	3	9	8	13
15th	Ipswich Town	10	3	3	4	10	14	12

**Result of this
Season's Fixture**

Liverpool
Arsenal

Wake Me Up When It's Over

Arsenal have a reputation for being boring. It may be a little unkind to a team that have had so much success in recent years because you can't win trophies without playing some attacking football. Whatever the truth the reputation has stuck: Arsenal are boring. It's a reputation that was considerably enhanced here by a dour, dismal display of negative football.

Arsenal came to Anfield looking for a draw and after a goalless ninety minutes they achieved that ambition. Quite why they chose such tactics is open to debate as they were facing a team who had lost their last four league games without scoring a goal. A mid-week European match was blamed for the Londoners' lacklustre performance but this was on the same day that Norwich City and Manchester United added to their Wednesday wins. And is playing defensively really that much less demanding than attacking?

Many of the 42,750 crowd left well before the final whistle but the match may prove to have been just the respite Liverpool needed. There were solid performances from the Liverpool defenders and encouraging signs in Robbie Fowler's home league debut. He will have been disappointed not to score against the England keeper who made three good saves. Neil Ruddock shook off his reputation as a hard man and demonstrated his footballing skills instigating several moves from the back finishing one of them off with a rising shot from 35 yards out which was about as close as anyone got to breaking the deadlock.

For Liverpool the tide may be turning. After some poor performances the team are again beginning to play cohesively and they just need that extra something for the results to come their way. As Souness said after the game *"[The players] are buoyant – we've got to keep our heads up – sooner or later the results will come."*

League Records

	P	W	D	L	F	A	Pts	Pos
93-94 Premiership Record	10	4	1	5	13	8	13	13th
All-time FA Premiership Record	52	20	12	20	75	63	72	–
All-time League Record	3576	1670	863	1042	6146	4587	5873	–

	Home	Away	Total
League Attendances	210,633	122,550	333,183

Liverpool
Fulham

(2) 5
(0) 0

Wednesday, 6th October 1993, Anfield   Att.:12,541

LIVERPOOL			FULHAM		
1	Bruce	GROBBELAAR	1	Jim	STANNARD
2	Rob	JONES	2	Simon	MORGAN
3	Julian	DICKS	3	Martin	PIKE
5	Mark	WRIGHT	4	Martin	FERNEY
6	Don	HUTCHISON	5	Terry	AGNUS
7	Nigel	CLOUGH	6	Glen	THOMAS
8	Paul	STEWART	7	Jeff	ECKHARDT
9	Ian	RUSH	8	Udo	ONWERE
15	Jamie	REDKNAPP	9	Sean	FARRELL
23	Robbie	FOWLER	10	Gary	BRAZIL
25	Neil	RUDDOCK	11	Paul	KELLY (†68)

Subs

12	Ronnie	WHELAN	12	Duncan	JUPP (†68)
13	Mark	JAMES (gk)	13	Peter	BAAH
17	Steve	McMANAMAN	14	Lee	HARRISON (gk)

Match Facts

• Robbie Fowler scored five goals for Liverpool, a feat only achieved three times before: Andy McGuigan v Stoke City, Division One 4/1/02 (7-0h); John Evans v Bristol Rovers, Division Two 15/9/54 (5-3h); Ian Rush v Luton Town, Division One 29/10/83 (6-0h).

• Fewer people came to Anfield to see the second leg than turned up at Craven Cottage for the first.

Score Sheet

R. FOWLER 13 mins – 1-0
R. FOWLER 40 mins – 2-0
R. FOWLER 47 mins – 3-0
R. FOWLER 55 mins – 4-0
R. FOWLER 70 mins – 5-0

Referee:
Mr. A. Dawson (Jarrow)

'You Should Have Had Seven!'

Robbie Fowler scored five goals and was greeted from the field by Ronnie Moran's tongue in cheek reproach. It was an excellent way to bring the young tyro back down to earth after a goalscoring display which straight away placed him in the record books in only his fourth game for Liverpool.

Five goals in a game equals the all-time Liverpool record joining Andy McGuigan, John Evans and Ian Rush. It is the most goals scored by a Liverpool player in a cup tie and the most by any player in a League Cup game. The only worry for Graeme Souness is that he doesn't turn out to be one of those who don't live up to their early promise. Of Fowler's potential Souness has no doubt, saying that Fowler has the ability to be anything he wants to be.

It wasn't just getting five that made Fowler's performance special – it was the way he got them. He scored goals with left foot, right foot and head to put the finishing touches to an all-round display of striking excellence.

Robbie Fowler's first came after Rob Jones blasted in a fierce shot which Stannard could only parry. Fowler followed up and cooly slotted home with his left foot.

The second goal came when Clough sent Ruddock through. Ruddock squared and found Fowler at the far post for a simple stab home.

Goal number three came early in the second half. Hutchison put Jones through and Jones found Fowler ready to claim his hat-trick. The fourth was a spectatcular flying header from a Dicks cross and the fifth and final a right foot shot after Jamie Redknapp sent him through.

Could it have been seven? It was a possibility but Stannard in the Fulham goal managed a couple of excellent saves to prevent an easy victory turning into an absolute rout.

League Cup Record

	P	W	D	L	F	A
League Cup Record 93-94	2	2	0	0	8	1
All-time League Cup Record	142	77	40	25	277	119

	Home	Away	Total
League Cup Attendances	12,541	13,599	26,140

Liverpool (0) 2
Oldham Athletic (0) 1

Saturday, 17th October 1994, Anfield   Att.: 32,661

LIVERPOOL			OLDHAM ATHLETIC		
1	Bruce	GROBBELAAR	1	Paul	GERRARD
2	Rob	JONES	2	Craig	FLEMING – *Booked*
3	*Julian*	*DICKS (+61)*	4	Nick	HENRY
5	Mark	WRIGHT	6	Steve	REDMOND
6	Don	HUTCHISON – *B'ked (*45)*	7	Gunnar	HALLE – *Booked*
7	Nigel	CLOUGH	10	Mike	MILLIGAN
8	Paul	STEWART	11	Paul	BERNARD
9	Ian	RUSH	14	Graeme	SHARP
15	Jamie	REDKNAPP	15	Andy	BARLOW
23	Robbie	FOWLER	17	Darren	BECKFORD
25	Neil	RUDDOCK	25	Rick	HOLDEN

Subs

11	*Mark*	*WALTERS (+61)*	19	Roger	PALMER
13	Mark	JAMES (gk)	8	Andy	RITCHIE
4	*Steve*	*NICOL (*45)*	13	Lance	KEY (gk)

Match Facts

- Liverpool's first Premiership win since August 28th.
- Robbie Fowler's goal in the 88th minute was Liverpool's first Premiership goal in 588 minutes (or 9 hours 48 minutes).
- Oldham still without an away league win this season.

Score Sheet

D. BECKFORD 74 min – 0-1
R. FOWLER 88 min – 1-1
BARLOW 90 min (og) – 1-2

Referee:
A. Wilkie (Chester-le-Street)

FA Carling Premiership League

Pos	Team	P	W	D	L	F	A	Pts
8th	QPR	11	5	2	4	15	13	17
9th	Wimbledon	11	4	5	2	13	13	17
10th	**Liverpool**	**11**	**5**	**1**	**5**	**15**	**9**	**16**
11th	Newcastle Utd	11	4	4	3	16	12	16
12th	Everton	11	5	1	5	14	15	16

Result of this Season's Fixture

No Fixture

You Lucky, Lucky...

There used to be a time when Liverpool had the habit of scoring in the dying seconds of a game to salvage a draw or sneak a win but this one took the biscuit. With two minutes left to play Oldham were a goal up and looking to take three points home with them. Many of the crowd had started making their way home by then but when the final whistle blew the Latics left the pitch in a state of shock having had the game stolen from them.

In fact Oldham were unlucky throughout the match. Twice in the first half Grobbelaar was beaten but on each occasion Liverpool survived. The first came when Bernard rounded the keeper only to see Wright make a successful interception. Minutes later the same happened only for Beckford's shot to rebound from the post.

Liverpool probed away at the other end but without ever looking like puncturing a disciplined Oldham defence. Fowler was the only one to force a save from Gerrard in the first half.

Liverpool played more assertively in the second half with two shots from Stewart forcing impressive saves whilst Ruddock hit the bar, But it was Oldham who scored first. The Oldham goal came from a corner with Beckford forcing in Henry's cross in at the near post.

That looked like being the final result until, with just two minutes left to play, Fowler latched onto the end of a Neil Ruddock lob and bundled the ball past the keeper. Sensing that the game was theirs for the taking the Liverpool players charged forward. Clough knocked the ball wide to Ruddock who cracked a shot across goal. Oldham's Andy Barlow got the final touch helping the ball into his own net much to the astonishment and delight of the Kop.

It wasn't classic Liverpool but, after a couple of games where they had been unlucky to lose, being lucky to win made amends. As the saying goes: it's not over until the final whistle.

League Records

	Home				Away			
	P	W	D	L	F	A	Pts	Pos
93-94 Premiership Record	11	5	1	5	15	9	16	10th
All-time Premiership Record	53	21	12	20	77	64	75	–
All-time League Record	3577	1671	863	1042	6148	4588	5876	–

	Home	Away	Total
League Attendances	243,294	122,550	365,844

Manchester City   (0) 1
Liverpool   (0) 1

Saturday, 23rd October 1993, Maine Road   Att.: 30,403

LIVERPOOL

1	Bruce	GROBBELAAR
2	Rob	JONES
5	Mark	WRIGHT
25	Neil	RUDDOCK
20	Stig	BJORNEBYE
11	Mark	WALTERS – B'ked (*53)
4	Steve	NICOL
8	Paul	STEWART (+73)
21	Dominic	MATTEO
9	Ian	RUSH
23	Robbie	FOWLER

Subs

15	Jamie	REDKNAPP (*53)
13	David	JAMES (gk)
6	Don	HUTCHISON (+73)

MANCHESTER CITY

1	Tony	COTON
22	Richard	EDGHILL
15	Alan	KERNAGHAN
5	Keith	CURLY
7	Terry	PHELAN – Booked
7	David	WHITE
10	Gary	FLITCROFT – Booked
4	Steve	McMAHON
19	Fitzroy	SIMPSON (†53)
9	Niall	QUINN
8	Mike	SHERON

21	Steven	LOMAS (†53)
6	Michael	VONK
25	Andy	DIBBLE (gk)

Match Facts

- Liverpool debut for Dominic Matteo.

Score Sheet

D. WHITE 66 min – 0-1
I. RUSH 88min – 1-1

Referee:
Mr. M. Bodenham (Looe)

FA Carling Premiership League

Pos	Team	P	W	D	L	F	A	Pts
7th	Aston Villa	12	5	5	2	13	9	20
8th	Tottenham H	12	5	4	3	19	13	19
9th	**Liverpool**	**12**	**5**	**2**	**5**	**16**	**10**	**17**
10th	Wimbledon	11	4	5	2	13	13	17
11th	Newcastle Utd	11	4	4	3	16	12	16

Result of this Season's Fixture

Manchester City
Liverpool

The Late, Late Show

What's that saying about the game not being over until the final whistle? Cliche it may be but no-one's casting doubts on its veracity after Liverpool's second great escape in the space of a week.

Last Saturday Oldham came unstuck at Anfield when they lost a game they thought was wrapped up with only two minutes left to play. This time it was the turn of Manchester City to fall foul of Liverpool's late late show. Liverpool didn't win this time but they did force a draw that was hardly deserved.

With just two minutes of time remaining the City defence was caught dithering. They tried to pass their way out of danger, lost possession and watched helplessly as a Rob Jones cross found Ian Rush. The goal levelled the score and although City kept pushing forward through an extended injury time they had to settle for a 1-1 draw. That was the cue for more choruses of "Swales Out!"

The City fans had plenty to grumble about as their team played the better football and were able to disrupt Liverpool's passing game almost at will. They dominated the second half and might have scored more were it not for the customary excellence of Bruce Grobbelaar in goal – the Zimbabwean keeper playing as well now as he ever has done. His first save came from his own defender Mark Wright who went astray with his backheader. Bruce manged to scramble back and scoop the ball off the line. There was little he could do to stop the goal from White after a superb cross from Flitcroft breached the Reds' defence.

Minutes later Bruce was in action again this time stopping a Quinn shot with his legs after initially diving the wrong way. And at the end he saved the day for Liverpool with a diving stop to push a white volley wide just seconds before the final whistle.

League Records

	P	W	D	L	F	A	Pts	Pos
93-94 Premiership Record	12	5	2	5	16	10	17	9th
All-time Premiership Record	54	21	13	20	78	65	76	–
All-time League Record	3578	1671	864	1043	6149	4590	5877	–

	Home	Away	Total
League Attendances	243,294	152,953	396,247

Liverpool
Ipswich Town

(2) 3
(1) 2

Wednesday, 27th October 1993, Anfield   Att.: 19,058

LIVERPOOL

1	Bruce	GROBBELAAR
2	Rob	JONES
5	Mark	WRIGHT – *Booked*
25	Neil	RUDDOCK
3	Julian	DICKS
22	*Steve*	*HARKNESS (+71)*
4	Steve	NICOL
8	Paul	STEWART
21	Dominic	MATTEO
9	Ian	RUSH
23	Robbie	FOWLER

Subs

6	*Don*	*HUTCHISON (+71)*
13	Mark	JAMES (gk)
7	Nigel	CLOUGH

IPSWICH TOWN

1	Craig	FORREST
2	Mick	STOCKWELL
15	Phil	WHELAN
6	David	LINIGHAN
3	Neil	THOMPSON
4	Paul	MASON
5	John	WARK
7	*Geraint*	*WILLIAMS (*27)*
21	Stuart	SLATER
9	*Bontcho*	*GUENTCHEV (+65)*
10	Ian	MARSHALL

17	*Simon*	*MILTON (*27)*
14	*Steve*	*WHITTON (+65)*
13	Clive	BAKER (gk)

Match Facts

- Ian Rush hat-trick – his first since September '92.
- First game of the season for Steve Harkness.
- 22 different players have appeared for Liverpool so far this season.
- Ipswich have not won at Anfield in 32 visits.

Score Sheet

I. RUSH 1 min – 1-0
I. RUSH 16 min – 2-0
I. MARSHALL 22 min – 2-1
I. RUSH 64 min – 3-1
P. MASON 77 min Pen – 3-2

Referee:
Mr. J. Lloyd (Wrexham)

Ian Rush Hat-trick

Do scorelines ever truly reflect the story of a game? Liverpool have been going through a phase of winning games they should have lost and losing games they should have won. This time Liverpool were the better team by far and Ipswich's two goals were very much against the run of play.

After Robbie Fowler's five goal display against Fulham Ian Rush has obviously been a bit worried about being upstaged as the Reds' leading striker so he wasted no time in getting the scoring going in this game. It was still the first minute when he robbed the Ipswich goalkeeper, Craig Forrest, of the ball to score his first goal and the game was still only fifteen minutes old when he pounced on another defensive uncertainty this time stealing the ball from David Linighan – has anyone ever poached goals so effectively as Rushie?

2-0 and that should have been that but Ipswich managed to claw a goal back when Liverpool had their own defensive uncertainties. A backpass from Neil Ruddock flustered Grobbelaar and he hit his clearance straight to Marshall. The ball came back twice as fast and whistled past his ears into the net.

Liverpool threatened to increase their lead with almost every move and in the sixty-fourth minute Rush complete his hat-trick with a clean strike from a Fowler cross. A quarter of an hour later and Ipswich were back in the game. Mark Wright made an instinctive stop with his hand and the resultant penalty was a formality for Paul Mason.

League Cup Record

	P	W	D	L	F	A
League Cup Record 93-94	3	3	0	0	11	3
All-time League Cup Record	143	78	40	25	280	121

	Home	Away	Total
League Cup Attendances	31,599	13,599	45,198

Liverpool   (2) 4
Southampton (1) 2

Saturday, 30th October 1993, Anfield   Att.: 32,818

LIVERPOOL

1	Bruce	GROBBELAAR
2	Rob	JONES
4	Steve	NICOL
5	Mark	WRIGHT
25	Neil	RUDDOCK
8	Paul	STEWART
9	Ian	RUSH
20	Stig	BJORNEBYE (+45)
21	Dominic	MATTEO
22	Steve	HARKNESS
23	Robbie	FOWLER

Subs

18	Ronnie	ROSENTHAL (+45)
13	Mark	JAMES (gk)
7	Nigel	CLOUGH

SOUTHAMPTON

1	Tim	FLOWERS
2	Jeff	KENNA
3	Mick	ADAMS
6	Ken	MONKOU
28	Peter	REID
17	Kevin	MOORE
11	Francis	BENALI
9	Iain	DOWIE
7	Matthew	LE TISSIER
10	Neil	MADDISON
27	Paul	ALLEN

13	Ian	ANDREWS (gk)
8	Glenn	COCKERILL
24	Frank	BENNETT

Match Facts

• Robbie Fowler's hat-trick means he has scored 10 goals for Liverpool in just 8 appearances.

Score Sheet

R. FOWLER 14 min – 1-0
R. FOWLER 29 min – 2-0
M. LE TISSIER 40 min – 2-1
BJORNEBYE 63 min – 3-1
M. LE TISSIER 79 min – 3-2
R. FOWLER 85 min – 4-2

Referee:
Mr. D. Gallagher (Banbury)

FA Carling Premiership League

Pos	Team	P	W	D	L	F	A	Pts
5th	Aston Villa	13	6	5	2	15	10	23
6th	Leeds Utd	13	6	4	3	20	16	22
7th	**Liverpool**	**13**	**6**	**2**	**5**	**20**	**12**	**20**
8th	QPR	13	6	2	5	24	21	20
9th	Newcastle Utd	13	5	4	4	21	14	19

Result of this Season's Fixture

Liverpool
Southampton

49

Was it a Hat-trick?

Both goalkeepers have been in the headlines recently with Tim Flowers possibly on his way to Anfield and Bruce Grobbelaar maybe on his way out. Both played well in an enthralling match each making a series of reflex saves from close range and yet they still conceded six goals between them. How come? It was all down to the sheer quality of the strikers on display.

Robbie Fowler is making the sort of impact on the game that most players only ever dream about. Souness may be cautious in his praise for the player – scared perhaps of putting too much pressure on one so new to this level of the game – but you get the impression that he wants to sing his praises from the roof-tops.

The only question mark over Fowler's performance was whether he scored Liverpool's fourth goal or whether Rush got the tip of his boot to Fowler's curling free-kick that rounded the defensive wall. Something of a lucky strike perhaps, it didn't stop Fowler claiming the match ball. There was no such doubt over his first two goals. Number One was a subtle headed redirection of a Rob Jones cross. Number Two saw him chest down a Neil Ruddock cross and blast the ball home all in one fluid motion. With all the talk of Robbie Fowler it's worth remembering that the scorer of the other Liverpool goal was no mean striker himself – Ian Rush, back on form after a lean spell.

For Southampton Le Tissier has been sidelined recently but since his return has shown the sort of ability that makes defenders weep. Mark Wright was the man weeping on this occasion – Le Tissier left him stranded as he juggled the ball from left foot to right and back again before firing in his first goal.

For Tim Flowers it was something of a foretaste of what to expect from Anfield if he makes the move. The Kop was in voice chanting *"Flowers, Flowers, what's the score?"* as the goals mounted but it was he who stopped the game turning into a rout as he made fine saves from Matteo, Stewart and Rush to keep Southampton in touch.

League Records

	P	W	D	L	F	A	Pts	Pos
93-94 Premiership Record	13	6	2	5	20	12	20	7th
All-time Premiership Record	55	22	13	20	82	67	79	–
All-time League Record	3579	1672	864	1043	6153	4592	5880	–

	Home	Away	Total
League Attendances	276,112	152,953	429,065

Liverpool (0) 2
West Ham United (0) 0

Saturday, 6th November 1993, Anfield   Att.: 42,254

LIVERPOOL

1	Bruce	GROBBELAAR
2	*Rob*	*JONES (+18)*
4	*Steve*	*NICOL (*85)*
5	Mark	WRIGHT – *Booked*
25	Neil	RUDDOCK
22	Steve	HARKNESS
7	Nigel	CLOUGH
8	Paul	STEWART
9	Ian	RUSH – *Booked*
21	Dominic	MATTEO
23	Robbie	FOWLER

Subs

15	*Jamie*	*REDKNAPP (+18)*
13	David	JAMES (gk)
20	*Stig*	*BJORNEBYE (*85)*

WEST HAM UNITED

1	Ludek	MIKLOSKO
2	Tim	BREACKER
33	David	BURROWS
4	Steve	POTTS
18	Alvin	MARTIN
16	Matt	HOLMES
8	Peter	BUTLER
14	Ian	BISHOP
9	Trevor	MORLEY
25	Lee	CHAPMAN
34	Mike	MARSH

23	Keith	ROWLAND
28	Matthew	RUSH
13	Gerry	PEYTON

Match Facts

• Nigel Clough's first league goal since August.

Score Sheet

N. CLOUGH 67 min – 1-0

A. MARTIN 83 min og – 2-0

Referee:
Mr. K. Barrett (Coventry)

FA Carling Premiership League

Pos	Team	P	W	D	L	F	A	Pts
3rd	Aston Villa	14	7	5	2	17	11	26
4th	Leeds Utd	14	7	4	3	24	17	25
5th	**Liverpool**	**14**	**7**	**2**	**5**	**22**	**12**	**23**
6th	Arsenal	14	6	5	3	13	8	23
7th	QPR	14	7	2	6	25	21	23

Result of this Season's Fixture

Liverpool

West Ham Utd

The Road to Recovery?

What with all the recent fuss about Robbie Fowler's astounding entry into the Liverpool squad it has been easy to overlook another debutant who has also played exceptionally well. Dominic Matteo is, like Fowler, only 19 but plays with a maturity and composure that is only normally associated with one much older. Matteo certainly made his mark in this match and nearly rounded off his performance with his first goal for the club. His strike in the 83rd minute was eventually entered as an own goal by Alvin Martin.

Liverpool's revival continues apace – this game was their seventh without defeat. West Ham didn't prove to be the stiffest of opposition but they still managed to expose Liverpool's midfield weaknesses. Too many moves broke down before the ball reached any one of Rush, Fowler or Clough in a striking position and it was West Ham who came closest to scoring when Grobbelaar made one of those errors which only add to his reputation. He came storming out of his area to steal the ball from his own defender and slot a neat pass across to Morley. The Hammers' stunned forward waas to surprised to take full advantage of this gift and let Brucie and Liverpoool off the hook.

The second half saw a more resilient Liverpool but again they lacked true penetration and both goals had a little good fortune to them. Clough opened the scoring by volleying in a rebound past Miklosko in the 67th minute and Matteo's nearly goal was helped into the net by Alvin Martin.

Liverpool's recent sucesses have been helped by players making their way into the squad from the youth team – a system which Souness has said had broken down by the time he arrived at the club. The side is now packed with talent the equal of any club in the league. Souness has shown himself to be very capable at nurtuting young potential. Talent on its own is not enough and the next stage is in trying to get them to play effectively as a team. That could be the hardest part and one which hasn't been helped by injury problems. Rob Jones was the latest casualty being stretchered off in the 18th minute with knee trouble that is expected to keep him out for at least a month.

League Records

	P	W	D	L	F	A	Pts	Pos
93-94 Premiership Record	14	7	2	5	22	12	23	5th
All-time Premiership Record	56	23	13	20	84	67	82	–
All-time League Record	3580	1673	864	1043	6155	4592	5883	–

	Home	Away	Total
League Attendances	318,366	152,953	471,319

Newcastle United (3) 3
Liverpool (0) 0

Sunday, 21st November 1993, St James Park   Att.: 36,374

NEWCASTLE UNITED

30	Mike	HOOPER
19	Steve	WATSON
5	Kevin	SCOTT
2	Barry	VENISON
26	Robert	ELLIOT
10	Lee	CLARK
7	Robert	LEE
4	Paul	BRACEWELL
11	Scott	SELLARS
8	Peter	BEARDSLEY
9	Andy	COLE

Subs

1	Pavel	SRNICEK
21	Malcolm	ALLEN
14	Alec	MATHIE

LIVERPOOL

1	Bruce	GROBBELAAR
4	Steve	NICOL – *Booked*
19	*Torben*	*PIECHNIK (+45)*
25	Neil	RUDDOCK
22	Steve	HARKNESS
15	Jamie	REDKNAPP
8	Paul	STEWART
7	Nigel	CLOUGH
21	Dominic	MATTEO
9	Ian	RUSH
23	Robbie	FOWLER

15	*John*	*BARNES (+45)*
13	David	JAMES (gk)
11	Mark	WALTERS

Match Facts

- Liverpool's heaviest defeat of the season.
- Piechnik's first game since January.
- Newcastle's highest Premiership attendance.
- John Barnes' first game of the season.

Score Sheet

A. COLE 5 min – 1-0

A. COLE 16 min – 2-0

A. COLE 30 min – 3-0

Referee:
Mr. G. Ashby (Worcester)

FA Carling Premiership League

Pos	Team	P	W	D	L	F	A	Pts
7th	Blackburn Rovers	15	7	5	3	20	15	26
8th	*Newcastle Utd*	*15*	*7*	*4*	*4*	*27*	*15*	*25*
9th	**Liverpool**	**15**	**7**	**2**	**5**	**22**	**15**	**23**
10th	Tottenham H	15	5	5	5	20	16	20
11th	Coventry City	15	4	8	3	16	17	20

Result of this Season's Fixture

Newcastle Utd

Liverpool

Old boys Show the Way

For Liverpool's trip up to Newcastle there were some familiar names on display:
Kevin Keegan, Terry McDermott, Mike Hooper, Peter Beardsley and Barry
Venison and they were on Newcastle's side. In fact the Liverpool Old Boys did
rather better than their successors as Newcastle ran out comfortable 3-0 winners in
a rather one-sided affair. The goals came courtesy of the latest in a long line of
sharp-shooting Newcastle United centre-forwards, Andy Cole, who made his hat-
trick look easy.

Newcastle's forays down the left made the Liverpool defence appear leaden-
footed. Peter Beardsley has been on sparkling form of late and on several occasions
he orchestrated the destruction of Liverpool's last line. Sellars was also
instrumental in this and he made the crucial last pass for the second and third of
Andy Cole's goals. The third came after just thirty minutes and the game was over.

Souness can point to no less than 23 squad members ruled out of action for one
reason or another but that rather begs the question as to why Liverpool always have
so many injuries – is it all just misfortune? One injury-prone star made his return:
John Barnes coming on in the second half in an attempt to try and salvage some
pride after the mauling Liverpool received in the first forty-five minutes.

Liverpool's best chance fell to Jamie Redknapp who was put through after
Robbie Fowler latched on to a sloppy back pass. That forced the only save that a
revitalised and slimline Mike Hooper needed to make.

League Records

	P	W	D	L	F	A	Pts	Pos
93-94 Premiership Record	15	7	1	6	22	15	23	9th
All-time Premiership Record	57	23	13	21	84	70	82	–
All-time League Record	3581	1673	864	1044	6155	4595	5883	–

	Home	Away	Total
League Attendances	318,366	189,327	507,693

Liverpool
Aston Villa

(1) 2
(0) 1

Sunday, 28th November 1993, Anfield   Att.: 38,484

LIVERPOOL			ASTON VILLA		
1	Bruce	GROBBELAAR	13	Mark	BOSNICH
4	Steve	NICOL	17	Neil	COX
5	Mark	WRIGHT	5	Paul	McGRATH
25	Neil	RUDDOCK – *Booked*	2	Earl	BARRETT
22	Steve	HARKNESS	23	*Bryan*	*SMALL (*80)*
15	Jamie	REDKNAPP	7	Ray	HOUGHTON
14	*Jan*	*MOLBY (+80)*	8	Garry	PARKER
10	John	BARNES	6	Kevin	RICHARDSON
21	Dominic	MATTEO	14	Andy	TOWNSEND
9	Ian	RUSH	9	Dean	SAUNDERS
23	Robbie	FOWLER	10	Dalian	ATKINSON

Subs

11	*Mark*	*WALTERS (+80)*	22	*Guy*	*WHITTINGHAM (*80)*
13	David	JAMES (gk)	1	Nigel	SPINK (gk)
7	Nigel	CLOUGH	16	Ugo	EHIOGU

Match Facts

- Aston Villa's first away defeat of the season in all competitions.
- Liverpool's sixth consecutive victory at Anfield in all competitions.

Score Sheet

R. FOWLER min – 1-0

D. ATKINSON 53 min – 1-1

J. REDKNAPP 62 min – 2-1

Referee:
A. Wilkie (Chester-Le-Street)

FA Carling Premiership League

Pos	Team	P	W	D	L	F	A	Pts
7th	Norwich City	16	7	6	3	25	16	27
8th	QPR	17	8	3	6	29	23	27
9th	**Liverpool**	**16**	**8**	**2**	**6**	**24**	**16**	**26**
10th	Tottenham H	17	5	7	5	22	18	22
11th	Wimbledon	17	5	7	5	19	24	22

Result of this Season's Fixture

Liverpool

Aston Villa

Back Passes Go Astray

Liverpool's victory left them in ninth place in the Premiership table but only four points off second place and with a game in hand. The position of Premiership also-rans changes every week but at the top of the table Manchester United are running away with it. They have now opened up a 14 point lead over Leeds United in second place having dropped only seven points in 17 league matches. The bookmakers have stopped taking bets on United winning the title which, with over half the season left to play, doesn't appear very enterprising. At the end of 1981 Liverpool were 12th in the table before taking the division by storm and winning the championship.

There's a long way to go in the championship race and one of the clubs that might be expected to have a say in its outcome is Aston Villa. Last season they won both league encounters against Liverpool winning at Anfield after coming back from a goal down. They went a goal down in this encounter just before the interval thanks to a Robbie Fowler header. Dominic Matteo provided the cross and Fowler headed over the stranded goalkeeper. Villa equalised early in the second half, though, and started playing as though they expected to maintain their winning sequence.

Dalian Atkinson scored the Villa goal making the most of a weak back header by Steve Nicol that never reached Grobbelaar. Atkinson pounced showing a true striker's predatory instincts.

Villa's ascendancy didn't last for long as Liverpool's winning goal came in rather similar circumstances and again Atkinson was in the thick of the action. This time he was the one making the deficient backpass and it was Robbie Fowler's turn to steal in and demonstrate the striker's art. He picked up the loose ball and crossed it to Jamie Redknapp who fired in a terrific winner through Bosnich's legs.

League Records

	P	W	D	L	F	A	Pts	Pos
93-94 Premiership Record	16	8	2	6	24	16	26	9th
All-time Premiership Record	58	24	13	21	86	71	85	–
All-time League Record	3582	1674	864	1044	6157	4596	5886	–

	Home	Away	Total
League Attendances	356,850	189,327	546,177

Liverpool

Wimbledon

(1) 1
(0) 1

Wednesday, 1st December 1993, Anfield   Att.: 19,290

LIVERPOOL			**WIMBLEDON**		
1	Bruce	GROBBELAAR	1	Hans	SEGERS
2	Rob	JONES	17	Roger	JOSEPH
5	Mark	WRIGHT	15	John	SCALES
25	Neil	RUDDOCK	6	Scott	FITZGERALD
22	Steve	HARKNESS	3	Brian	McALLISTER
15	Jamie	REDKNAPP	2	Warren	BARTON
14	Jan	MOLBY	8	Robbie	EARLE
21	Dominic	MATTEO	4	Vinnie	JONES
10	*John*	*BARNES* (+76)	26	Neal	ARDLEY
23	Robbie	FOWLER	9	*John*	*FASHANU* (+47)
9	Ian	RUSH	10	Dean	HOLDSWORTH

Subs

11	*Mark*	*WALTERS* (+76)	7	*Andy*	*CLARKE* (+47)
13	David	JAMES (gk)	37	Perry	DIGWEED (gk)
7	Nigel	CLOUGH	18	Steve	TALBOYS

Match Facts

• Only the second time the two clubs have met in a cup competition: the previous being the FA Cup Final of 1988.

Score Sheet

J. MOLBY 15 min Pen – 1-0

R. EARLE 84 min 1-1

Referee:
A. Wilkie (Chester-Le-Street)

Dons Snatch It at the Last

Liverpool will need to play much better than this to stand a chance in the replay and Graeme Souness was unable to explain, after the game, why his players had performed so inadequately. Where they intimidated by the opposition, perhaps? The Dons have yet to lose to Liverpool under Joe Kinnear's managership and have a reputation for being the fly in the Anfield ointment. Wimbledon also have another reputation: for hard, some might even say brutal, football. Vinnie Jones and John "Fash the Bash" Fashanu are regular names in the press for overstepping the mark but there was little evidence of such a physical approach to the game at Anfield. Instead Wimbledon concentrated on trying to outplay Liverpool through good technique. In recent weeks Joe Kinnear has been urging critics of Wimbledon's long-ball approach to play to take notice of some of the subtler elements of their play. Some critics have responded by saying that they've been looking but they haven't had much to see. Brazilian it wasn't but here Wimbledon demonstrated that there's more to their approach than just hoofing the ball up the middle hoping to find a striker. When they left the pitch at the end of the game it was to some begrudging applause from the Anfield faithful who jeered their own team's departure.

After a fine display only three days earlier Liverpool failed to play as a team and once they had taken the lead through a Jan Molby penalty early in the first half they didn't have an accurate shot on goal. A one-two between Rush and Barnes saw Rush through into the Wimbledon penalty area only to find John Scales in combative form. Molby's spot-kick was low, hard and unreachable.

Wimbledon responded by taking the game to Liverpool and the only real surprise was that they left it so late before equalising. On two occasions the ball was scrambled from the Liverpool line before Robbie Earle headed home a McAllister cross to force a replay.

League Cup Record

	P	W	D	L	F	A
League Cup Record 93-94	4	3	1	0	12	4
All-time League Cup Record	144	78	41	25	281	122

	Home	Away	Total
League Cup Attendances	50,889	13,599	64,488

Sheffield Wednesday (1) 3
Liverpool (1) 1

Saturday, 4th December 1993, Hillsborough   Att.: 32,177

LIVERPOOL

1	Bruce	GROBBELAAR
2	Rob	JONES
22	Steve	HARKNESS
5	Mark	WRIGHT
25	Neil	RUDDOCK
4	*Steve*	*NICOL* (+79)
14	Jan	MOLBY Booked
21	*Dominic*	*MATTEO* (*69)
10	John	BARNES
23	Robbie	FOWLER
7	Nigel	CLOUGH

Subs

11	*Mark*	*WALTERS* (+79)
13	David	JAMES (gk)
9	*Ian*	*RUSH* (*69)

SHEFFIELD WEDNESDAY

13	Kevin	PRESSMAN
2	Roland	NILSSON
3	Nigel	WORTHINGTON
4	Carlton	PALMER – *Booked*
17	Des	WALKER
21	Ryan	JONES
14	*Chris*	*BART-WILLIAMS* (+71)
8	Chris	WADDLE
16	Graham	HYDE
19	*Nigel*	*JEMSON* (*79)
10	Mark	BRIGHT 80

23	Lance	KEY (gk)
28	Simon	*COLEMAN* (*79)
7	*Adam*	*PORIC* (+71)

Match Facts

• Ian Rush starting as substitute leaves Bruce Grobbelaar and Neil Ruddock as the only remaining 100% starters this season.

• Sheffield Wednesday unbeaten in 12 games.

Score Sheet

RUDDOCK 30 min (og) – 1-0

R. FOWLER 37 min – 1-1

M. WRIGHT 58min (og) –2-1

M. BRIGHT 80 min – 3-1

Referee:
Mr. J. Borrett (Harleston)

FA Carling Premiership League

Pos	Team	P	W	D	L	F	A	Pts
7th	Norwich City	17	7	7	3	27	18	28
8th	QPR	18	8	4	6	31	25	28
9th	**Liverpool**	**17**	**8**	**2**	**7**	**25**	**19**	**26**
10th	West Ham Utd	18	7	5	6	15	17	26
11th	Everton	18	7	3	8	20	23	24

Result of this Season's Fixture

Sheffield Wed

Liverpool

Putting the Ball in the Wrong Net

If there was a lesson to be learnt from this game it was a rather simple one – it's not just the scoring of goals that counts but that it's also important to put them in the right net. Liverpool scored three times to Wednesday's once but lost the game thanks to two strikes of defensive brilliance by Ruddock and Wright who managed to put the ball past their own keeper.

However, that isn't to suggest the result was fortunate for Wednesday becasue they demonstrated the greater organisation and cohesion and had, in Chris Waddle, an inspirational play maker. Their first goal came when Worthington drove across the goal-line and Ruddock managed to beat Jemson to the ball: 1-0. Rather against the run of play Liverpool grabbed an equaliser when a Rob Jones through ball presented Robbie Fowler with a half-chance. It's all he needs these days and quite how many goals he might get when Liverpool start dominating games again is anyone's guess. Just before half-time Liverpool nearly took the lead when John Barnes showed a fleeting glimpse of his true abilities with a chip from twenty yards out which hit the bar.

Wednesday regained the lead after the break with a Liverpool own goal similar in many respects to the first. This time it was a Chris Waddle cross which caused the mayhem. Mark Wright got to the ball ahead of Mark Bright and made an absolute hash of things stabbing the ball home when danger wasn't threatening. Bright got a goal of his own with ten minutes of the match remaining to seal the match. Waddle was again in the thick of the action chesting a ball down to Poric who provided the telling through ball. Grobbelaar's run from his area was ill-judged and let Bright round off a clear victory.

League Records

	P	W	D	L	F	A	Pts	Pos
93-94 Premiership Record	17	8	2	7	25	19	26	9th
All-time Premiership Record	59	24	13	22	87	74	85	–
All-time League Record	3583	1674	864	1045	6158	4599	5886	–

	Home	Away	Total
League Attendances	356,850	221,504	587,354

Liverpool (2) 3
Queens Park Rangers (1) 2

Wednesday, 7th December 1993, Anfield   Att.: 24,561

LIVERPOOL			QUEENS PARK RANGERS		
1	Bruce	GROBBELAAR	13	Jan	STEJSKAL
2	Rob	JONES	2	David	BARDSLEY
5	Mark	WRIGHT	5	Darren	PEACOCK – *Booked*
25	Neil	RUDDOCK – *Booked*	18	Karl	READY
22	Steve	HARKNESS	3	Clive	WILSON
17	Steve	McMANAMAN	7	Andrew	IMPEY – *Booked*
14	Jan	MOLBY	4	Ray	WILKINS
15	Jamie	REDKNAPP	22	*Mike*	*MEAKER (+86)*
10	*John*	*BARNES (+73)*	14	Simon	BARKER
9	Ian	RUSH	10	Bradley	ALLEN
23	Robbie	FOWLER	9	Les	FERDINAND

Subs

4	*Steve*	*NICOL (+73)*	12	*Gary*	*PENRICE (+86)*
13	David	JAMES (gk)	24	Steve	YATES
7	Nigel	CLOUGH	1	Tony	ROBERTS (gk)

Match Facts

- The crowd of just 24,561 was the lowest Premiership gate at Anfield and Liverpool's lowest league gate in over a decade.
- John Barnes' first goal of the season.

Score Sheet

L. FERDINAND 10 min – 0-1
J. BARNES 25 min – 1-1
I. RUSH 32 min – 2-1
S. BARKER 46 min – 2-2
J. MOLBY 75 min Pen – 3-2

Referee:
Mr. V. Callow (Southampton)

FA Carling Premiership League

Pos	Team	P	W	D	L	F	A	Pts
5th	Arsenal	19	8	7	4	18	13	31
6th	Aston Villa	19	8	7	4	23	19	31
7th	**Liverpool**	**18**	**9**	**2**	**7**	**28**	**21**	**29**
8th	Norwich City	17	7	5	5	27	18	28
9th	QPR	19	8	4	7	33	28	28

Result of this Season's Fixture

Liverpool
QPR

"Our Best Of The Season"

So said Graeme Souness after an exciting game where Liverpool were a better team than Queens Park Rangers over the ninety minutes. Both teams made light of atrocious conditions to reward the few who had braved the conditions on a cold December evening.

There is a saying that teams visiting Anfield are effectively a goal down before they start. Visiting fans often claim that this is because referees are so intimidated by the atmosphere that they automatically give decisions in Liverpool's favour. It's a good myth to have because, if visiting teams believe it, then they're not going to expect to win and if a team doesn't expect to win they haven't got a chance.

There was a penalty in this game and, yes, it was in Liverpool's favour. However, as it was given after a blatant and cynical challenge few would have disagreed with Mr Callow in awarding it. If he was in two minds about ordering the player to walk Simon Barker solved the problem for him by pushing Jamie Redknapp in the face, the player he had just sent crashing to the ground. Jan Molby's assured penalty sealed the game for Liverpool. Ten minutes later Rangers were down to ten men when Ferdinand was sent off for a second bookable offence – he frustratedly kicked the ball into the Kop after the whistle had gone for offside. Ferdinand claimed later not to heard the whistle in which case he should have been sent off for such an insult to the art of kicking a ball. If the judgment was a tad harsh, Ferdinand made no friends by marching so furiously towards Mr Callow that he had to be restrained by both Ray Wilkins and Jan Molby.

The whole affair was an ugly end to what had been such an entertaining game and meant that Rangers had lost both their goalscorers. Ferdinand's strike came in the tenth minute when Grobbelaar's "clearance" went straight to him. Barnes grabbed an equaliser a quarter of an hour later with a curling shot from the edge of the box and Liverpool went ahead shortly afterwards when a McManaman cross found Ian Rush waiting in the penalty area.

League Records

	P	W	D	L	F	A	Pts	Pos
93-94 Premiership Record	18	9	2	7	28	21	29	7th
All-time Premiership Record	60	25	13	22	90	76	88	–
All-time League Record	3584	1675	864	1045	6161	4601	5889	–

	Home	Away	Total
League Attendances	381,411	221,504	602,915

Liverpool
Swindon Town

(0) 2
(0) 2

Saturday, 11th December 1993, Anfield   Att.: 32,739

LIVERPOOL

1	Bruce	GROBBELAAR
2	Rob	JONES
5	Mark	WRIGHT
25	Neil	RUDDOCK
22	Steve	HARKNESS (†78)
17	Steve	McMANAMAN
14	Jan	MOLBY
15	Jamie	REDKNAPP
10	John	BARNES
9	Ian	RUSH
23	Robbie	FOWLER

Subs

4	Steve	NICOL (†78)
11	Mark	WALTERS
13	David	JAMES (gk)

SWINDON TOWN

1	Fraser	DIGBY
2	Nicky	SUMMERBEE (*67)
26	Terry	FENWICK
16	Kevin	HORLOCK
3	Paul	BODIN
6	Shaun	TAYLOR
7	John	MONCUR (+90)
10	Martin	LING – Booked
14	Adrian	WHITBREAD
25	Andy	MUTCH
27	Keith	SCOTT

9	Jan-Aage	FJORTOFT (+90)
11	Craig	Maskell (*67)
23	Nicky	HAMMOND (gk)

Match Facts

- Swindon still without a Premiership away win.

Score Sheet

J. MONCUR 60 min – 0-1

J. BARNES 71 min – 1-1

K. SCOTT 73 min – 1-2

M. WRIGHT 86 min – 2-2

Referee:
K. Morton (Bury St Edmonds)

FA Carling Premiership League

Pos	Team	P	W	D	L	F	A	Pts
6th	QPR	20	9	4	7	34	28	31
7th	Aston Villa	20	8	7	5	23	20	31
8th	**Liverpool**	**19**	**9**	**3**	**7**	**30**	**23**	**30**
9th	West Ham Utd	20	8	7	7	18	20	29
10th	Norwich City	17	7	7	3	27	18	28

Result of this Season's Fixture

No Fixture

Lack of Discipline

Three matches into the season Liverpool visited Swindon Town's County Ground and cruised to a 5-0 victory built on the bedrock of stylish passing and fluid understanding. There was much of the same on display at Anfield but it was split evenly between the teams who also shared a lack of discipline in defence. Swindon's league placing – bottom of the Premiership with just one win in twenty games – may fail to do justice to their ability to play attacking and attractive football but bottom of the heap they remain. If Liverpool can manage five goals away from home then a victory at Anfield doesn't seem to much to ask.

Liverpool's inability to play consistently well as a team is particularly frustrating considering the quality of players on the pitch and the club's own reputation. On this occasion the inconsistence was baffling as it was exactly the same team that had done so well against Queens Park Rangers. The corner count is particularly revealing as the score of 18 to 4 in Liverpool's favour shows that one or two opportunities either went begging or weren't created.

For their own part Swindon came to Anfield determined not to be overawed by the occasion and willing to attack as best as they could. The end result was a well-deserved draw and the generous applause of the Kop.

Swindon went ahead on the hour as Moncur passed wide to Summerbee and ran on the receive the return and stroke it past Grobbelaar. Barnes equalised shortly afterwards, meeting a Ruddock cross with a well-placed header, but Swindon went ahead again shortly afterwards. Grobbelaar could only parry a sharp header from Mutch and Scott was on hand for the rebound. Last season he was playing in the Vauxhall Conference, this year he's putting his team ahead at Anfield. Mark Wright spared Liverpool's blushes with a goal four minutes from time heading home from a well-flighted McManaman corner.

League Records

	P	W	D	L	F	A	Pts	Pos
93-94 Premiership Record	19	9	3	7	30	23	30	8th
All-time Premiership Record	61	25	14	22	92	78	89	–
All-time League Record	3585	1675	865	1045	6163	4603	5890	–

	Home	Away	Total
League Attendances	414,150	221,504	635,654

Wimbledon **(1) 2**
Liverpool **(1) 2**

Tuesday, 14th December 1993, Selhurst Park   Att.: 11,343

WIMBLEDON

1	Hans	SEGERS
2	Warren	BARTON
15	John	SCALES
6	Scott	FITZGERALD
3	Brian	McALLISTER
24	*Peter*	*FEAR (+102)*
8	Robbie	EARLE
4	Vinnie	ONES
26	Neal	ARDLEY
10	Dean	HOLDSWORTH
9	John	FASHANU

Subs

7	*Andy*	*CLARKE (+102)*
23	Neil	SULLIVAN (gk)
18	Steve	TALBOYS

LIVERPOOL

1	Bruce	GROBBELAAR
2	Rob	JONES
5	*Mark*	*WRIGHT (*26)*
25	Neil	RUDDOCK
4	Steve	NICOL
17	Steve	McMANAMAN
15	Jamie	REDKNAPP
14	*Jan*	*MOLBY (+ 34)*
10	John	BARNES
9	Ian	RUSH
23	Robbie	FOWLER

11	*Mark*	*WALTERS (+34)*
13	David	JAMES (gk)
22	*Steve*	*HARKNESS (*26)*

Match Facts

• Wimbledon have never lost to Liverpool in any cup competition.

Score Sheet

HOLDSWORTH 18 min – 1-0

N. RUDDOCK 38 min – 1-1

R. EARLE 70 min – 2-1

H. SEGERS 90 min (og) – 2-2

Referee:
Mr. H King (Merthyr Tydfil)

Liverpool Pay the Penalty

Out of the League Cup and with a Premiership title looking unlikely, the FA Cup is Liverpool's only hope of salvation for a season that started off promising much but which, so far, has failed to deliver. Should Liverpool fail then there is the awful prospect of another season at Anfield without European football.

Wimbledon have become the team that Liverpool fans love to hate. Actually Wimbledon have become the team that just about everybody loves to hate but it doesn't appear to have done them any harm; if anything they look like they are thriving on it. Their record against Liverpool is good and they have acquired a habit of saving important penalties. In the 1988 Cup final Beasant made a crucial save from an Aldridge penalty to prevent a Liverpool equaliser. In this game Hans Segers stopped a John Barnes penalty in extra time to hold the scores level and then made two important saves from Jamie Redknapp and Mark Walters during the penalty shoot out to hand the tie and a place in the quarter finals to Wimbledon.

During the first ninety minutes and the period of extra time both teams had plenty of opportunities to seal victory. Wimbledon went ahead early on when Vinnie Jones put Dean Holdsworth through but Liverpool equalised before half-time when John Barnes teed up Neil Ruddock from a free kick.

Half way through the second half Wimbledon went ahead again. Vinnie Jones again laying on the vital pass which put Fashanu through. Grobbelaar saved his effort but Earle pounced on the rebound. That appeared to have settled the matter but Liverpool scraped a fortuitous equaliser in the last minute of normal time when a Steve Nicol cross was floated into the Wimbledon penalty area. Robbie Fowler came to meet it but so did Hans Segers who was so keen to keep the ball from the young striker that he scooped it into his own net. But it was the last mistake that Segers made.

League Cup Record

	P	W	D	L	F	A
League Cup Record 93-94	5	3	2	0	14	6
All-time League Cup Record	145	78	41	25	283	124

	Home	Away	Total
League Cup Attendances	50,889	24,942	75,831

Tottenham Hotspur (1) 3
Liverpool (0) 3

Match 25

Saturday 18th December 1993, White Hart Lane, Att.: 31,394

TOTTENHAM HOTSPUR

1	Erik	THORSTVEDT
22	David	KERSLAKE
3	Justin	EDINBURGH
5	Colin	CALDERWOOD
14	Steve	SEDGLEY
16	Micky	HAZARD
4	Vinny	SAMWAYS
9	Darren	ANDERTON
20	Darren	CASKEY
12	Jason	DOZZELL
7	Nick	BARMBY

LIVERPOOL

1	Bruce	GROBBELAAR
2	Rob	JONES
22	Steve	HARKNESS – *Booked*
5	Mark	WRIGHT
4	Steve	NICOL
21	*Dominic*	*MATTEO (+82)*
10	*John*	*BARNES (*46)*
15	Jamie	REDKNAPP
17	Steve	McMANAMAN
9	Ian	RUSH
23	Robbie	FOWLER

Subs

13	Ian	WALKER (gk)
2	Dean	AUSTIN
23	Suizeer	CAMPBELL

13	David	JAMES (gk)
7	*Nigel*	*CLOUGH (*46)*
11	*Mark*	*WALTERS (+82)*

Match Facts

• Robbie Fowler has 14 goals from 17 matches.

Score Sheet

V. SAMWAYS 37 min – 1-0
R. FOWLER 48.min – 1-1
J. REDKNAPP 51 min – 1-2
R. FOWLER 54 min Pen – 1-3
HAZARD 68 min Pen – 2-3
D. CASKEY 77 min – 3-3

Referee:
Mr. R. Hart (Darlington)

FA Carling Premiership League

Pos	Team	P	W	D	L	F	A	Pts
5th	Arsenal	21	9	7	5	20	13	34
6th	Norwich City	19	8	7	4	30	21	31
7th	**Liverpool**	**20**	**9**	**4**	**7**	**33**	**26**	**31**
8th	QPR	20	9	4	7	34	28	31
9th	Aston Villa	20	8	7	5	23	20	31

Result of this Season's Fixture

Liverpool
Tottenham H

Young Guns do the Shooting

Two beleagured teams struggling to come to terms with their pedigree served up a game that was a joy to behold and full of the enterprising possession football and neat passing that has for so long been associated with both clubs. Tottenham took the lead towards the end of the first half and somewhat against the run of play. It was also somewhat against the style of play. Thorstvedt's long clearance led to a nod on from Dozzell to the waiting Samways. One crisp hard drive later and Tottenham's version of the long ball game had put them a goal in front.

Nigel Clough came on for an injured John Barnes after the interval and the swap made all the difference. He threaded a pass through to Robbie Fowler who made nonsense of the Spurs keeper's reputation putting the ball between his legs and into the net. Thorstvedt fared little better a few minutes later. Fowler's menacing of the Spurs defence led to Kerslake making a clumsy and frustrated challenge. Redknapp's free kick curled round the wall and then ricocheted off the post, off the hapless keeper and into the goal, 2-1.

Minutes later Liverpool were up again after Sedgley found Ian Rush in the penalty area and in possession. The Spurs defender dealt with the situation in the only way he could think of and Fowler scored from the resultant penalty. And that's the way it should have stayed but Liverpool's defence is not in the miserly form it once was and Tottenham were allowed to claw their way back into the game. Redknapp tripped Barmby inside the area when little danger was threatened and Micky Hazard scored from the spot. Ten minutes later Kerslake ran round Harkness and floated in a well judged cross for Caskey to glance home.

League Records

	P	W	D	L	F	A	Pts	Pos
93-94 Premiership Record	20	9	4	7	33	26	31	–
All-time Premiership Record	62	25	15	22	95	81	90	–
All-time League Record	3586	1675	866	1045	6166	4606	5891	–

	Home	Away	Total
League Attendances	414,150	252,898	667,048

Sheffield United (0) 0
Liverpool (0) 0

Sunday, 26th December 1993, Bramall Lane   Att.: 22,932

		SHEFFIELD UNITED			LIVERPOOL
1	Alan	KELLY	1	Bruce	GROBBELAAR
2	Kevin	GAGE	2	Rob	JONES
16	Paul	BEESLEY	5	Mark	WRIGHT
17	Carl	BRADSHAW	25	Neil	RUDDOCK
18	Dane	WHITEHOUSE	3	Julian	DICKS
10	Glyn	HODGES	4	Steve	NICOL
23	*Chris*	*KAMARA (+78)*	15	Jamie	REDKNAPP
11	*Mitch*	*WARD (*87)*	7	Nigel	CLOUGH
26	Jamie	HOYLAND – *Booked*	17	Steve	McMANAMAN
12	Jostein	FLO	9	*Ian*	*RUSH (+81)*
27	Bobby	DAVISON	23	Robbie	FOWLER

Subs

	Carl	MUGGLETON	13	David	JAMES (gk)
10	*Willie*	*FALCONER (+78)*	21	Dominic	MATTEO
22	*Andy*	*SCOTT (*87)*	11	*Mark*	*WALTERS (+81)*

Score Sheet

NO GOALS

Referee:
A. Wilkie (Chester-le-Street)

FA Carling Premiership League

Pos	Team	P	W	D	L	F	A	Pts
5th	Arsenal	21	9	7	5	20	13	34
6th	**Liverpool**	**21**	**9**	**5**	**7**	**33**	**26**	**32**
7th	Norwich City	19	8	7	4	30	21	31
8th	QPR	20	9	4	7	34	28	31
9th	Aston Villa	21	8	7	5	24	23	31

Result of this Season's Fixture

No Fixture

Blunt Blades Blow It

Sheffield United are the perennial strugglers. Since arriving in football's top division they have failed to set the world alight, preferring instead to scramble towards the safety of lower mid-table as the season comes to an end. The story goes that they only start playing properly come Christmas in which case they are a game or two late because there was little to celebrate about their play during this game. They have never rejoiced in the more elegant side of the game favouring "Route One", "Kick and Run", "The Long Ball Game" or whatever you want to call it.

For much of this game it proved an effective enough tactic and Liverpool struggled to come to terms with their opponents' approach. For their own part Liverpool failed to demonstrate the gulf that should exist between these two sides. Souness's millions looked cheap. Maybe the game was too soon after Christmas for Liverpool but where they should have given a team like Sheffield a stuffing, they served up a real turkey.

Dave Bassett was perhaps overdoing it when he said that his side had enough opportunities to win the game several times but they did have the majority of the goal-scoring opportunities. Grobbelaar made several fine saves and it was his efforts which gave Liverpool a point. He stopped Hodges and Flo in the first half and made a marvellous back-pedalling effort in the second half to tip over a Davison chip which looked to be a certain goal. But, for the most part he was assisted by the lack of belief that the Sheffiled players showed when confronted by the opposition goal. Happy Christmas, indeed.

League Records

	P	W	D	L	F	A	Pts	Pos
93-94 Premiership Record	21	9	5	7	33	26	32	6th
All-time Premiership Record	63	25	16	22	95	81	91	–
All-time League Record	3587	1675	867	1045	6166	4606	5892	–

	Home	Away	Total
League Attendances	414,150	275,830	689,980

Liverpool
Wimbledon

(1) 1
(1) 1

Saturday, 28th December 1993, Anfield   Att.: 32,232

LIVERPOOL

1	Bruce	GROBBELAAR
2	Rob	JONES
4	*Steve*	*NICOL (+79)*
5	Mark	WRIGHT
7	Nigel	CLOUGH
9	Ian	RUSH
15	Jamie	REDKNAPP
17	Steve	McMANAMAN
21	Dominic	MATTEO
23	Robbie	FOWLER
25	Neil	RUDDOCK

Subs

13	David	JAMES (gk)
22	Steve	HARKNESS
11	*Mark*	*WALTERS (+79)*

WIMBLEDON

1	Hans	SEGERS
2	Warren	BARTON
3	*Brian*	*McALLISTER – B'ked (+67)*
4	Vinny	JONES – *Booked*
6	Scott	FITZGERALD
8	Robbie	EARLE
9	John	FASHANU
10	*Dean*	*HOLDSWORTH – Booked*
15	John	SCALES
24	Peter	FEAR
26	Neal	ARDLEY

23	Neil	SULLIVAN
36	Gary	BLISSETT
7	*Andy*	*CLARKE (+67)*

Match Facts

• Liverpool have not beaten Wimbledon since September 1991.

• Liverpool's fifth consecutive draw.

Score Sheet

J. SCALES 27 min (og) – 1-0
J. FASHANU 40 min – 1-1

Referee:
Mr. K. Cooper (Pontypridd)

FA Carling Premiership League

Pos	Team	P	W	D	L	F	A	Pts
6th	Norwich City	20	9	7	4	33	22	34
7th	QPR	21	10	4	7	36	28	34
8th	**Liverpool**	**22**	**9**	**6**	**7**	**34**	**27**	**33**
9th	Aston Villa	21	8	7	6	24	23	31
10th	Sheffield Wed	22	7	9	6	39	29	30

Result of this Season's Fixture

Liverpool
Wimbledon

Oh No, Not Them Again

For all their endeavour Liverpool are still strugling to find their way past Wimbledon. There is nothing difficult or complex to the Dons' method of play for all Joe Kinnear's protestations that the critics are mising the subtleties. Wimbledon are doing well precisely because they employ a direct approach to the game. Bearing all this in mind you might expect Liverpool to have devised a counter policy to deal with it but we're still waiting.

This game saw Liverpool start by countering Wimbledon's approach by doing what they do best: playing football. Wimbledon were made to look a poor second best as Liverpool took possession, kept it and created a series of bright opportunities. A goal looked inevitable after a series of moves from Clough and Fowler put McManaman clear but he failed to capitalise. Eventually Rush broke away down the right hand side and sent in a sharp cross. Scales intercepted but failed to control the ball and instead sent the ball into the net off the underside of the bar.

A goal up but Liverpool failed to build and it was Wimbledon who took the initiative. John Fashanu broke clear and had two shots at goal after Grobbelaar cleared his first attempt, the second shot going in.

In the second half Liverpool strung together a series of attacking moves but each time Wimbledon's last line of defence held firm. Segers brought off a handful of athetic dives to deny the Liverpool forwards and keep the Londoners in the game. Although they created little of their own they were happy to soak up the pressure for the most part and return home with a point.

League Records

	P	W	D	L	F	A	Pts	Pos
93-94 Premiership Record	22	9	6	7	34	27	33	8th
All-time Premiership Record	64	25	17	22	96	82	92	–
All-time League Record	3588	1675	868	1045	6167	4607	5893	–

	Home	Away	Total
League Attendances	446,382	275,830	722,212

Ipswich Town (0) 1
Liverpool (0) 2

Sunday, 2nd January 1994, Portman Road   Att: 22,355

IPSWICH TOWN

1	Craig	FORREST
16	Eddie	YOUDS (+71)
5	John	WARK (*71)
6	David	LINIGHAN
15	Phil	WHELAN
2	Mick	STOCKWELL
7	Geraint	WILLIAMS
8	Gavin	JOHNSON
27	Gary	THOMPSON
10	Ian	MARSHALL
11	Chris	KIWOMYA

Subs

13	Clive	BAKER (gk)
19	Frank	YALLOP (+71)
9	Bontcho	GUENTCHEV (*71)

LIVERPOOL

1	Bruce	GROBBELAAR
2	Rob	JONES
25	Neil	RUDDOCK
5	Mark	WRIGHT
21	Dominic	MATTEO (*29)
22	Steve	HARKNESS
7	Nigel	CLOUGH
15	Jamie	REKNAPP
17	Steve	McMANMAN (+76)
9	Ian	RUSH
23	Robbie	FOWLER

13	David	JAMES (gk)
10	John	BARNES (+76)
20	Stig	BJORNEBYE (*29)

Match Facts

• Liverpool's first Premiership away win since August .

Score Sheet

N. RUDDOCK 57 min – 0-1
I. MARSHALL 75 min – 1-1
I. RUSH 88 min – 1-2

Referee:
Mr. A. Gunn (Burgess Hill)

FA Carling Premiership League

Pos	Team	P	W	D	L	F	A	Pts
5th	Newcastle Utd	23	11	6	6	40	21	39
6th	Norwich City	22	10	7	5	35	24	37
7th	**Liverpool**	**23**	**10**	**6**	**7**	**36**	**28**	**36**
8th	QPR	23	10	5	8	38	31	35
9th	Sheff Wed	24	8	10	6	44	33	34

Result of this Season's Fixture

Ipswich Town
Liverpool

New Year's Resolution

A game of two halves, as they say. One a rather soulless affair reminiscent of a New Year's hangover, the other with much more resolution.

Dominic Matteo limped off in the 28th minute and his replacement, Stig Bjornebye, looked keen to make a strong impression. Craig Forrest in the Ipswich goal was also doing his best to impress and saves from McManaman – still goalless since August – and Fowler kept the scores level till half-time.

Twelve minutes into the second it was a Bjornebye corner that found Ruddock waiting at the far post. His powerful header was beyond the goal-line attentions of the Ipswich defence and the Reds were a goal to the good. Minutes later Redknapp went on a surging run and fired in a shot from more than 20 yards out. Sadly what might have been a candidate for Goal of the Month crashed against the bar.

Liverpool were now in the ascendancy and so a goal for Ipswich seemed almost cheeky. Neil Thompson intercepted a Nigel Clough pass however and set up Bontcho Guentchev. He misfired but Ian Marshall followed through. Offside? Not according to Mr Gunn.

Normal sevice was resumed with the arrival of John Barnes. Short periods of play may be all that we get nowadays but he can still make all the difference. Shortly before time he did just that turning the Ipswich defence inside-out before crossing to Robbie Fowler. The young maestro's header hit the woodwork but if one of them doesn't get you the other will. Ian Rush followed up to nod the ball home: 2-1.

League Records

	Home								Away
	P	W	D	L	F	A	Pts	Pos	
93-94 Premiership Record	23	10	6	7	36	28	36	7th	
All-time Premiership Record	65	26	17	22	98	83	95	–	
All-time League Record	3589	1676	868	1045	6169	4608	5895	–	

	Home	Away	Total
League Attendances	446,382	298,185	744,567

Liverpool (2) 3
Manchester United (3) 3

Tuesday, 4th January 1994, Anfield   Att.: 42,795

LIVERPOOL			MANCHESTER UNITED		
1	Bruce	GROBBELAAR	1	Peter	SCHMEICHEL
2	Rob	JONES	2	Paul	PARKER
5	Mark	WRIGHT	4	Steve	BRUCE
25	Neil	RUDDOCK	6	Gary	PALLISTER
3	Julian	DICKS	3	Denis	IRWIN
17	Steve	McMANAMAN	14	Andrei	KANCHELSKIS
7	Nigel	CLOUGH – *Booked*	16	Roy	KEANE – *Booked*
15	Jamie	REDKNAPP	8	Paul	INCE – *Booked*
10	John	BARNES	9	Brian	McCLAIR
9	Ian	RUSH	7	Eric	CANTONA
23	Robbie	FOWLER	11	Ryan	GIGGS

Subs

13	David	JAMES (gk)	13	Les	SEALEY
4	Steve	NICOL	12	Bryan	ROBSON
20	Stig	BJORNEBYE	18	Darren	FERGUSON

Match Facts

- Manchester United are only the second team to score three goals at Anfield in the Premiership.

- Clough's second goal was Liverpool's 100th Premiership goal.

Score Sheet

S. BRUCE 9 min – 0-1
R. GIGGS 20 min – 0-2
D. IRWIN 24 min – 0-3
N. CLOUGH 25 min – 1-3
N. CLOUGH 38 min – 2-3
N. RUDDOCK 79 min – 3-3

Referee:
Mr. P. Don (Middlesex)

FA Carling Premiership League

Pos	Team	P	W	D	L	F	A	Pts
6th	Sheffield Wed	25	9	10	6	38	26	37
7th	Norwich City	23	10	7	6	36	26	37
8th	**Liverpool**	**24**	**10**	**7**	**7**	**39**	**31**	**37**
9th	QPR	24	10	6	8	38	31	36
10th	Aston Villa	23	9	7	7	26	25	34

Result of this Season's Fixture

Liverpool
Manchester Utd

Back from the Dead

Pride, they say, comes before a fall. Liverpool are a club with more to be proud about than any other and, sure enough, they fell. 3-0 down to Manchester United after only 24 minutes and worst of all – it was at home. There's more to pride than just plain vanity and it was this that gave Liverpool the edge in the rest of the match. It was the Liverpool pride that saw the players fight to the very death and level the game; 3-3. Manchester United may be sweeping all before them this season but they're not going to do it at Anfield.

It has been a season when the quality of football on display has had crowds flooding back to the Premiership clubs and yet nothing has matched this. The match of the season? There was more than one newspaper report that said so.

After withstanding a barrage of Liverpool attacks in the first few minutes it was United who scored first – Steve Bruce heading home a Cantona cross after a United corner. Worse still, the mercurial Ryan Giggs put the visitors further ahead ten minutes later taking advantage of a weak back pass to lob the advancing Grobbelaar. Liverpool hadn't had time to settle after that when United struck again. Denis Irwin struck home the sweetest of free kicks from some 25 yards. 3-0 and Liverpool looked dead and buried. How much worse could thing get?

Liverpool responded with what Alex Ferguson called *"kamikaze tactics"*. This translates as outplaying and outfighting United in all departments . Nigel Clough scored a minute after United's third goal with a hard, low drive from outside the area. Shortly before the interval he struck again – it was the same manoeuvre only on the other side of the pitch. The teams went in at half-time with Liverpool having reduced the arrears to a single goal. Everything to play for.

United showed considerable resolve in the second half soaking up attack after attack as Liverpool kept pushing forward looking for the equaliser. In the 79th minute the inevitable occurred and Neil Ruddock jumped to meet a cross from Bjornebye and levelled the game. By the end United must have felt relieved to escape the game with a point.

League Records

	P	W	D	L	F	A	Pts	Pos
93-94 Premiership Record	24	10	7	7	39	31	37	8th
All-time Premiership Record	66	26	18	22	101	86	96	–
All-time League Record	3590	1676	869	1045	6172	4611	5896	–

	Home	Away	Total
League Attendances	498,613	298,185	796,798

Bristol City (1) 1
Liverpool (1) 1

Match 30

Saturday, 8th January 1994, Ashton Gate   Att.: 20,612

BRISTOL CITY

1	Keith	WELCH
2	Stuart	MUNRO
3	Martin	SCOTT
4	Mark	SHAIL
5	Matthew	BRYANT
6	Brian	TINNION
7	Dave	MARTIN
8	Ian	BROWN
9	Liam	ROBINSON
10	Wayne	ALLISON
11	Rob	EDWARDS – *Booked*

Subs

12	Glenn	PENNYFATHER
13	Andy	LEANING (gk)
14	Leroy	ROSENIOR

LIVERPOOL

1	Bruce	GROBBELAAR
2	Rob	JONES
3	Julian	DICKS
4	Steve	NICOL
25	Neil	RUDDOCK
20	*Stig*	*BJORNEBYE* (+51)
7	Nigel	CLOUGH
23	Robbie	FOWLER
9	Ian	RUSH
10	John	BARNES
15	Jamie	REDKNAPP

Subs

13	David	JAMES (gk)
6	Don	HUTCHISON
17	*Steve*	*McMANAMAN* (+51)

Match Facts

- First FA Cup meeting between the clubs since 1974 (when Liverpool won 1-0).
- Before this game the teams had met five times in the FA Cup, Liverpool winning four.

Score Sheet

I. RUSH 12 min – 0-1
W. ALLISON 38 min – 1-1

Referee:
Mr. M. Bodenham (Looe)

Liverpool in the Dark

Bruce Grobbelaar's suggestion was that the rematch of this game should be played at Anfield. His theory was that Liverpool had done enough to merit playing the rematch at home and that it was unfair to expect the Reds to make the trip twice. The match was abandoned after 65 minutes when one of the floodlights packed in. If that wasn't bad enough the problem was compounded by the attempts to get it going again. For nearly an hour it looked hopeful that the match could be restarted but finally the organisers had to admit defeat and send a cold and disappointed crowd home.

The locals had rather more to be pleased about as Bristol City, who are struggling in the Endsleigh League First Division, had managed to earn themselves an equaliser somewhat against the run of play. Liverpool started off full of purpose and set about demonstrating the division-plus gulf between the two sides. The first goal came early on after Barnes lost his marker and sent in a cross to Ian Rush. Had the match been completed then it would have been Rush's 36th goal in the competition – just one short of Denis Law's record.

To their credit Bristol City refused to accept that they were being outclassed and started putting together some meaningful moves of their own. Shortly before half-time Scott completed a midfield venture by directing a cross towards the head of Allison. He kept his composure and glanced the ball home past Grobbelaar.

It was City's last conclusive move as Liverpool took charge in the second half. Bjornebye was replaced by McManaman and this redressed the midfield balance in Liverpool's favour. But if you can't see what you're doing you can't play football and when the lights failed all the efforts of both teams counted for nothing.

FA Cup Record

	P	W	D	L	F	A
FA Cup Record 93-94	–	–	–	–	–	–
All-time FA Cup Record	347	180	81	86	554	330

	Home	Away	Total
93-94 Cup Attendances	–	–	–

Oldham Athletic   (0) 0
Liverpool   (0) 3

Match 30

Saturday, 15th January 1994, Boundary Park   Att.: 14,573

OLDHAM ATHLETIC

13	Jon	HALLWORTH
2	Craig	FLEMING
22	Chris	MAKIN
23	Richard	GRAHAM
5	Richard	JOBSON
6	Steve	REDMOND
11	Paul	BERNARD
8	Andy	RITCHIE
14	Graeme	SHARP
17	*Darren*	*BECKFORD (+59)*
25	Rick	HOLDEN

Subs

15	Andy	BARLOW
1	Paul	GERRARD (gk)
21	*Sean*	*McCARTHY (+59)*

LIVERPOOL

1	Bruce	GROBBELAAR
2	Rob	JONES
3	Julian	DICKS
4	Steve	NICOL
15	Jamie	REDKNAPP
25	Neil	RUDDOCK
7	Nigel	CLOUGH
23	Robbie	FOWLER
10	*John*	*BARNES (†85)*
9	Ian	RUSH
17	Steve	McMANAMAN

16	*Michael*	*THOMAS (†85)*
13	David	JAMES (gk)
20	Stig	BJORNEBYE

Match Facts

- Julian Dicks' first goal for Liverpool.
- Michael Thomas's first appearance in over a year.

Score Sheet

J. DICKS 47 min – 0-1
R. FOWLER 54 min – 0-2
J. REDKNAPP 81 min – 0-3

Referee:
Mr. J. Lloyd (Wrexham)

FA Carling Premiership League

Pos	Team	P	W	D	L	F	A	Pts
4th	Leeds Utd	25	11	10	4	38	26	43
5th	Newcastle Utd	24	12	6	6	42	22	42
6th	**Liverpool**	**25**	**11**	**7**	**7**	**42**	**31**	**40**
7th	Norwich City	24	10	8	6	37	27	38
8th	Sheff Wed	26	9	10	7	46	35	37

Result of this Season's Fixture

No Fixture

79

Liverpool in Space

Oldham gave Liverpool the freedom of the Boundary Park pitch and it was a liberty which the Reds found very welcome. This was about as one-sided a match as you can get in the Premiership and if it hadn't been for Liverpool's continuing defensive uncertainties the Latics might not have had a chance to call their own.

At the other end Liverpool spent most of the first half besieging Hallworth's goal but without making the shot that counts. Clough shot wide, Barmes came close to scoring on a couple of occasions and somehow Steve McManaman hoofed one over the bar from within the six yard box.

The second half followed much the same pattern but Oldham's luck couldn't and didn't hold and it was just a couple of minutes after the break that Julian Dicks broke the deadlock with his first goal for Liverpool. It was quite a goal at that. About thirty yards from goal he latched onto a cross from Steve McManaman and sent a searing shot whistling past Hallworth and into the Oldham net. Fowler followed it up a few minutes later dancing free of Jobson to meet a Nigel Clough cross which he sent through Hallworth's legs.

The Liverpool midfield dominated as they built on the confidence earned in the Man Utd game. Clough and Redknapp combined well while Barnes' play led a frustrated Joe Royle to admit that *"we couldn't get the ball off him."* Hallworth had to fish the ball from his net one more time when Redknapp finished off another fluid Liverpool strike with a precision side-footed drive from outside the area that careered in off the post and sealed the game. The last five minutes saw a welcome appearance from long term absentee Michael Thomas who has been recovering from a ruptured Achilles tendon.

League Records

	P	W	D	L	F	A	Pts	Pos
93-94 Premiership Record	25	11	7	7	42	31	40	6th
All-time Premiership Record	67	27	18	22	104	86	99	–
All-time League Record	3591	1677	869	1045	6175	4611	5898	–

	Home	Away	Total
League Attendances	489,177	312,758	801,935

Bristol City (0) 1
Liverpool (0) 1

Wednesday, 19th January 1994, Ashton Gate   Att.: 21,718

BRISTOL CITY

1	Keith	WELCH
2	Andy	LLEWELLYN
3	Martin	SCOTT
4	Mark	SHAIL
5	Stuart	MUNRO
6	Bryan	TINNION – *Booked*
7	Dave	MARTIN – *Booked*
8	Junior	BENT
9	Liam	ROBINSON
10	Wayne	ALLISON
11	Rob	EDWARDS

Subs

12	Glenn	PENNYFATHER
14	Leroy	ROSENIOR
13	Andy	LEANING (gk)

LIVERPOOL

1	Bruce	GROBBELAAR
2	Rob	JONES – *Booked*
3	Julian	DICKS
4	Steve	NICOL
15	Jamie	REDKNAPP
17	Steve	McMANAMAN – *Booked*
7	Nigel	CLOUGH
23	*Robbie*	FOWLER (†67)
9	Ian	RUSH
10	John	BARNES
25	Neil	RUDDOCK – *Booked*

6	Don	HUTCHISON
13	David	JAMES (gk)
20	*Stig*	BJORNEBYE (†67)

Match Facts

- Ian Rush's 36th goal in the FA Cup.

Score Sheet

I. RUSH 62 min – 0-1

W. ALLISON 72 min – 1-1

Referee:
Mr M Bodenham (Looe)

81

A Sense of Deja Vu

One-all at Ashton Gate with Wayne Allison's goal cancelling out Ian Rush's earlier effort. Am I imagining things or does this have a familiar flavour to it?

The first attempt at settling this tie had ended with Liverpool very much on top before the plug was pulled thanks to floodlight failure. On this occasion it was Bristol City who left the pitch feeling disgruntled. For all their efforts they had failed to capitalise on home advantage and they let Liverpool off the hook with a scarcely deserved one-all draw.

The game was a scrappy affair and Liverpool failed to settle but, while they kept the score level they looked content to take the match back to Anfield for the replay. City had other ideas and they showed more enterprise and created several opportunities that gave lie to their lowly status in the First Division. But they lacked confidence in front of goal and Bent hit shots wide on a couple of occasions and both Edwards and Robinson also squandered chances. Liverpool's first main chance came in the second half when Julian Dicks took a free-kick deep into the City half. He floated a cross to the far post where Neil Ruddock fielded setting up Ian Rush for his 36th goal in the Cup.

A less spirited team than Bristol might have given up at this point but they continued to take the game to their higher division rivals. Ten minutes on Bent fired in a cross which could have been meant for any one of three Bristol players but it was Wayne Allison who found himself in the right place at the right time to apply the finishing touch. City continued to push forward not being overly anxious to face the prospect of a visit to Anfield but when the final whistle came they had only managed to draw.

FA Cup Record

	P	W	D	L	F	A
93-94 FA Cup Record	1	0	1	0	1	1
All-time FA Cup Record	348	180	82	86	555	331

	Home	Away	Total
FA Cup Attendances	–	21,718	21,718

Liverpool
Manchester City

(1) 2
(1) 1

Saturday, 22nd January 1994, Anfield   Att.: 41,872

LIVERPOOL

1	Bruce	GROBBELAAR
2	Rob	JONES
3	Julian	DICKS
4	Steve	NICOL
7	Nigel	CLOUGH
9	Ian	RUSH
10	John	BARNES
11	Mark	WALTERS
15	Jamie	REDKNAPP
17	Steve	McMANAMAN
25	Neil	RUDDOCK – *Booked*

Subs

6	Don	HUTCHISON
20	Stig	BJORNEBYE
13	David	JAMES

MANCHESTER CITY

1	Tony	COTON
22	Richard	EDGHILL
3	Terry	PHELAN
12	Ian	BRIGHTWELL
15	Alan	KERNAGHAN
6	Michael	VONK
7	David	ROCASTLE – *Booked*
10	Gary	FLITCROFT
11	Carl	GRIFFITHS
26	Kare	INGEBRIGTSEN
21	Steven	LOMAS

8	Mike	SHERON
28	Carl	SHUTT
25	Andy	DIBBLE (gk)

Match Facts

- Liverpool have now totalled over 100 Premiership points.

Score Sheet

C. GRIFFITHS 3 min – 0-1

I. RUSH 22 min – 1-1

I. RUSH 91 min – 2-1

Referee:
Mr. R. Milford (Bristol)

FA Carling Premiership League

Pos	Team	P	W	D	L	F	A	Pts
3rd	Arsenal	27	12	10	5	31	14	46
4th	Newcastle Utd	26	13	6	7	45	25	45
5th	**Liverpool**	**26**	**12**	**7**	**7**	**44**	**32**	**43**
6th	Leeds Utd	25	11	10	4	38	26	43
7th	Sheffield Wed	27	10	10	7	49	36	40

Result of this Season's Fixture

Liverpool

Manchester City

Daylight Robbery

Brian Horton clearly thought that some sort of crime had been committed. Was this why the police were in close attendance to the Manchester City manager so soon after his team's defeat at Anfield? No. They were there to restrain him from approaching the match referee Roger Milford who had done something to incense him. Exactly what, Mr Horton refused to say. The real culprit was in all probability fate which had intervened for the second time this season in matches between the two clubs. They met at Maine Road in October when an Ian Rush goal in the 88th minute had snatched a point for the Reds. They meet again at Anfield and what happens? An even later Ian Rush goal snatches victory for Liverpool. On this occasion Brian Horton had rather less to complain about and indeed he admitted that Manchester City had *"got what we deserved – nothing."*

Liverpool are not without problems of their own. Robbie Fowler is the latest to wear the plaster cast but his absence gave greater freedom to John Barnes who gave Liverpool time to work in.

Despite City taking an early lead Liverpool always looked in charge and appeared capable of winning the game at any time. Perhaps they were just trying to make it more exciting by leaving it so late.

The first goal came when Tony Coton's long goal kick was headed on by Flitcroft and Ruddock fluffed his lines. If Carl Griffiths was startled to find himself unchallenged with the ball in so promising a position he didn't let it affect him and he lobbed the approaching Grobbelaar to put City ahead. In the absence of Jamie Fowler Liverpool are fortunate to have another useful goalscorer, name of Ian Rush, to poach goals when required. Half way through the first half Coton parried a Jamie Redknapp shot into Ian Rush's path: 1-1.

Liverpool created chances galore but lacked the finishing touch and Coton was in sublime form in the City goal. But the winning goal eventually came in the dieing seconds of the game. Ian Rush ran in to meet a high cross, heading home at the far post.

League Records

	P	W	D	L	F	A	Pts	Pos
93-94 Premiership Record	26	12	7	7	44	32	43	5th
All-time Premiership Record	68	28	18	22	106	87	102	–
All-time League Record	3592	1678	869	1045	6177	4612	5900	–

	Home	Away	Total
League Attendances	531,049	312,758	843,807

Liverpool
Bristol City

(0) 0
(0) 1

Tuesday, 25th January 1994, Anfield   Att.: 36,720

LIVERPOOL

1	Bruce	GROBBELAAR – *Booked*
2	Rob	JONES
25	Neil	RUDDOCK
4	Steve	NICOL
22	Steve	HARKNESS
17	Steve	McMANAMAN
15	*Jamie*	*REDKNAPP (+45)*
7	Nigel	CLOUGH
11	Mark	WALTERS
9	Ian	RUSH
10	John	BARNES

BRISTOL CITY

1	Keith	WELCH
2	Andy	LLEWELLYN
3	Martin	SCOTT
4	Mark	SHAIL
5	Stuart	MUNRO
6	Bryan	TINNION – *Booked*
7	Dave	MARTIN
8	*Junior*	*BENT (+81)*
9	Liam	ROBINSON
10	Wayne	ALLINSON
11	Rob	EDWARDS

Subs

6	*Don*	*HUTCHISON (+45)*
13	David	JAMES (gk)
20	Stig	BJORNEBYE

12	*Glenn*	*PENNYFATHER (+81)*
13	Andy	LEANING (gk)
14	Leroy	ROSENIOR

Match Facts

- Liverpool knocked out of the FA Cup in the third round, at home, by a team from a lower division for the second year running.
- First Liverpool defeat in thirteen games.
- No Merseyside teams through to the Fourth Round of the FA Cup.

Score Sheet

B. TINNION 66 min – 0-1

Referee:
Mr M. Bodenham (Looe)

85

Power Failure

It's easy to see where the plan failed when you've got the benfit of hindsight. The idea was that Liverpool would go to Ashton Gate, grab a draw, bring the game back to Anfield and knock the stuffing out of Bristol City. Simple. It's a scheme of this kind that Liverpool have employed many times over the years against opposition from lower divisions. You may remember that the plan came rather unstuck this time last year when Bolton Wanderers refused to read the script and won the replay knocking Liverpool – the Cup holders no less – out of the Cup in the third round. This time, at least, we had the satisfaction of knowing that Liverpool wouldn't – couldn't – make the same mistake twice.

They did. The game was a nightmare. Bristol City played with more conviction and belief than Liverpool, never letting the home team settle. The visitors had chances in the first few minutes that demanded good saves from Grobbelaar and the Liverpool defence never looked comfortable. The attack never looked up to much either and there was an air of inevitability to Bristol's goal midway through the second half. Wayne Allison shrugged off a couple of challenges and knocked the ball on to Bryan Tinnion who fired in from the edge of the area.

The goal finally spurred Liverpool into action but by then the cause had already been lost. For all their effort Liverpool could only manage to create a few shots from long range which didn't trouble Welch unduly.

At the end of the game the Kop cheered the Bristol City team from the pitch but had nothing but criticism for their own side. And inevitably there were calls for the resignation of Graeme Souness...

FA Cup Record

	P	W	D	L	F	A
93-94 FA Cup Record	2	0	1	1	1	2
All-time FA Cup Record	349	180	82	87	555	332

	Home	Away	Total
FA Cup Attendances	36,720	21,718	58,438

Norwich City (1) 2
Liverpool (0) 2

Saturday, 5th February 1994, Carrow Road   Att.: 19,746

NORWICH CITY

1	Bryan	GUNN – *Sent Off*
5	Ian	CULVERHOUSE
8	Colin	WOODTHORPE
3	Rob	NEWMAN
10	John	POLSTON
11	Jeremy	GOSS
4	Ian	CROOK
9	Gary	MEGSON
2	Mark	BOWEN
22	Chris	SUTTON
7	Efan	EKOKU

Subs

20	Darren	EADIE
13	Scott	HOWIE
17	Ian	BUTTERWORTH

LIVERPOOL

1	Bruce	GROBBELAAR
2	Rob	JONES
3	Julian	DICKS
11	Mark	WALTERS
5	Mark	WRIGHT
17	Steve	McMANAMAN
21	Dominic	MATTEO
7	Nigel	CLOUGH
12	Ronnie	WHELAN
9	Ian	RUSH
10	John	BARNES

13	David	JAMES
6	Don	HUTCHISON
19	Torben	PIECHNIK

Match Facts

- Liverpool's first game with Roy Evans as manager.
- Ronnie Whelan's first game since September.

Score Sheet

C. SUTTON 12 min – 1-0

CULVERHOUSE 53 min (og) – 1-1

C. SUTTTON 63 min – 2-1

J. BARNES 76 min – 2-2

Referee:
Mr. D. Gallagher (Banbury)

FA Carling Premiership League

Pos	Team	P	W	D	L	F	A	Pts
3rd	Arsenal	27	12	10	5	31	14	46
4th	Newcastle Utd	26	13	6	7	45	25	45
5th	**Liverpool**	**27**	**12**	**8**	**7**	**46**	**34**	**44**
6th	Sheffield Wed	28	11	10	7	52	37	43
7th	Leeds Utd	26	11	10	5	39	28	43

Result of this Season's Fixture

Norwich City
Liverpool

Thank 'Eavens it's Evans

Following Liverpool's defeat in the previous game – at home to Bristol City – manager Graeme Souness resigned. His position had become untenable after repeated calls in all the local media for him to leave. His successor was announced within days – Roy Evans. Evans was Souness's assistant and was the man advocated for the post by Bob Paisley no less.

"Apart from the first half, I thought we were magnificent." It's not quite a Colemanball perhaps, but as an attempt to look on the positive side of things Roy Evans' first post-match analysis takes some beating. And what a first half it was.

Sutton and Ekoku bewildered a reorganised Liverpool defence that missed Ruddock absent through suspension. Norwich's first goal came when Sutton pounced on a muffed clearance by Mark Wright that was typical of Liverpool's uncertainty. But for all their elegant play Norwich could not capitalise any further in the first half leaving a relieved Liverpool to leave the field only one goal down. The Reds were much more composed in the second half and it was not long before Ian Rush dispossessed the Norwich defence and sent in a firm cross. Walters failed to make contact but the charitable Culverhouse prodded the ball into his own net; to be fair he was unsighted. Norwich went ahead again through a coolly taken shot from 20 yards out by the supremely talented Sutton but afterwards it was Liverpool who took charge. The second equaliser came after Julian Dicks chipped into the Norwich penalty area for Ian Rush. Challenged by Gunn the ball fell to John Barnes who calmly stroked the ball home. Liverpool nearly clinched the game in the dying minutes when Gunn ran from his area to challenge Steve McManaman and handballed the ensuing lob. Gunn was sent off but the Norwich substitute goalkeeper Scott Howie proved his worth with a fine save from Julian Dicks' free-kick. In the end a point apiece was a fair result for both sides.

League Records

	P	W	D	L	F	A	Pts	Pos
93-94 Premiership Record	27	12	8	7	46	34	44	5th
All-time Premiership Record	69	28	19	22	108	89	103	–
All-time League Record	3593	1678	870	1045	6179	4614	5901	–

	Home	Away	Total
League Attendances	531,049	332,504	863,553

Southampton (3) 4
Liverpool (0) 2

Monday, 14th February 1994, The Dell   Att.: 18,306

SOUTHAMPTON			LIVERPOOL		
1	Dave	BEASANT	1	Bruce	GROBBELAAR
2	Jeff	KENNA	2	Rob	JONES
18	Steve	WOOD	5	Mark	WRIGHT
6	Ken	MONKOU	4	Steve	NICOL
11	Francis	BENALI	3	Julian	DICKS
10	Neil	MADDISON	17	Steve	McMANAMAN
4	Jim	MAGILTON	12	Ronnie	WHELAN
14	Simon	CHARLTON	7	*Nigel*	*CLOUGH (*57)*
9	Iain	DOWIE	11	Mark	WALTERS
8	Craig	MASKELL	10	John	BARNES
7	Matthew	Le TISSIER	9	Ian	RUSH

Subs

			15	*Jamie*	*REDKNAPP (*57)*

Match Facts

- First defeat for Roy Evans as Liverpool manager.
- First Liverpool defeat in 10 Premiership games.
- Craig Maskell's debut game for Southampton.

Score Sheet

M. LE TISSIER 1 min – 1-0
C. MASKELL 6 min – 2-0
LE TISSIER 43 min Pen – 3-0
LE TISSIER 50 min Pen – 4-0
J. DICKS 68 min Pen – 4-1
I. RUSH 86 min – 4-2

Referee:
Mr. P. Foakes

FA Carling Premiership League

Pos	Team	P	W	D	L	F	A	Pts
3rd	Arsenal	28	12	11	5	32	15	47
4th	Newcastle Utd	27	13	6	8	47	29	45
5th	**Liverpool**	**28**	**12**	**8**	**8**	**48**	**38**	**44**
6th	Aston Villa	27	12	8	7	36	27	44
7th	Sheffield Wed	28	11	10	7	52	37	43

Result of this Season's Fixture

Southampton
Liverpool

It's Snow Fun

When Le Tissier blasted home his first goal after just 28 seconds of play there only looked like there was going to be one result to this game: a St Valentine's Day Massacre. For the Reds it was a night to forget as a revitalised Southampton team ran rings round the Liverpool defence. Nigel Clough had a terrible game and it was only when he was replaced by Jamie Redknapp in the second half that Liverpool began to show some form of their own. By that point though, the cause was lost as Southampton were already 4-0 up. Liverpool did snatch two late goals by way of consolation to add a measure of dignity to the scoreline but the night belonged to the Saints.

Le Tissier's first goal was an absolute stunner. Steve Nicol headed the ball out from the Liverpool defence but only as far as the Saints striker who sent a first time shot straight past Grobbelaar. Before the Liverpool defence had time to settle – something which looked like taking a long time anyway – Southampton had scored again. A Southampton corner found Dowie on the far post. He headed back across the goal to debutant Craig Maskell who drove the ball home.

As the snow fall thickened maybe the visibility worsened too. After all there has to be some excuse for Mr Foakes' bizarre penalty decisions that followed. Just before half time Dicks was deemed to have fouled Maskell and five minutes after the break Mark Wright was penalised for handball. Both decisons appeared harsh and both penalties wer converted by Le Tissier for his hat-trick.

The defence may be shiping goals too frequently for comfort but the attack is still capable of creating the odd goal. Liverpool's first came when Monkou brought down Rush inside the box, Dicks converting the penalty. Then with just a few minutes of play remaining Dave Beasant could only parry a long-range effort from Dicks. Inevitably it was Ian Rush who popped up to score on the rebound.

League Records

	P	W	D	L	F	A	Pts	Pos
93-94 Premiership Record	28	12	8	8	48	38	44	5th
All-time Premiership Record	70	28	19	23	110	93	103	–
All-time League Record	3594	1678	870	1046	6181	4618	5901	–

	Home	Away	Total
League Attendances	531,049	350,810	891,295

Leeds United
Liverpool

(1) 2
(0) 0

Saturday, 19th February 1994, Elland Road   Att.: 40,053

LEEDS UNITED

1	John	LUKIC
22	Gary	KELLY
6	David	O'LEARY (*86)
5	Chris	FAIRCLOUGH – B'ked
18	David	WETHERALL
3	Tony	DORIGO
7	Gordon	STRACHAN
10	Gary	McALLISTER
11	Gary	SPEED
19	Ray	WALLACE (+74)
9	Brian	DEANE

Subs

4	David	WHITE (+74)
16	Jon	NEWSOME (*86)
13	Mark	BEENEY (gk)

LIVERPOOL

1	Bruce	GROBBELAAR (+88)
2	Rob	JONES
5	Mark	WRIGHT
25	Neil	RUDDOCK
3	Julian	DICKS
17	Steve	McMANAMAN
15	Jamie	REDKNAPP – B'ked
12	Ronnie	WHELAN
21	Dominic	MATTEO (*65)
10	John	BARNES
9	Ian	RUSH

11	Mark	WALTERS (*65)
13	David	JAMES (+88)
7	Nigel	CLOUGH

Match Facts

- No win in 3 games for Roy Evans as Liverpool manager.
- Ian Rush's 400th League appearance for Liverpool.
- Leeds Utd's biggest Premiership gate ever and highest for 15 years, 10,000 up on last season's corresponding fixture.

Score Sheet

D. WETHERALL 10 min – 1-0
G. McALLISTER 87 min – 2-0

Referee:
Mr. G. Poll (Berkshire)

FA Carling Premiership League

Pos	Team	P	W	D	L	F	A	Pts
6th	Newcastle Utd	28	13	6	9	47	30	45
6th	Aston Villa	27	12	8	7	36	27	44
8th	**Liverpool**	**29**	**12**	**8**	**9**	**48**	**40**	**44**
9th	Sheffield Wed	28	11	10	7	52	37	43
10th	Norwich City	28	10	12	6	46	36	42

Result of this Season's Fixture

Leeds United
Liverpool

Liverpool All at Sea

The man in the hot seat may have changed but the team hasn't. Liverpool lost to Leeds United and after three games in charge Roy Evans' Reds are still without a win. The problem was the same as it has been all season – Liverpool's expensive defence giving far too many opportunities to their opponents. For all their indiviual skills the Liverpool back four of Jones, Wright, Ruddock and Dicks never played as a unit and Leeds took great pleasure in the freedom of movement they were allowed.

At the other end Steve McManaman was in sparkling form and had several chances but without that smidgin of luck whilst Ian Rush, in his 400th league outing for the club, ran tirelessly but without much supply from the midfield.

Liverpool were slow to get started and by the time they had found their feet they also found themselves a goal down. An early period of Leeds pressure saw Grobbelaar forced into a couple of save before McAllister floated in a free kick from the right touchline. The keeper managed to punch the ball away but only as far as Wetherall. The Leeds defender hid his surprise and buried his chance with a hard low shot. Liverpool survived a couple more strikes, notably when Deane headed spectacularly wide and even had a few chances of their own, what looked like John Barnes' knee provoking a diving save from Lukic but it was little surprise when McAllister sealed victory in the 87th minute. White sent McAllister through the Reds defence and he took his opportunity well. A minute later Grobbelaar hobbled off with a hamstring injury but Roy Evans felt that that was the least of his worries, reorganising Liverpool's leaky defence will cause him a much greater headache. After the game he said *"We keep matching teams but you can't keep saying you're unlucky."*

League Records

	P	W	D	L	F	A	Pts	Pos
93-94 Premiership Record	29	12	8	9	48	40	44	7th
All-time Premiership Record	71	28	19	24	110	95	103	–
All-time League Record	3595	1678	870	1047	6181	4620	5901	–

	Home	Away	Total
League Attendances	531,049	390,863	921,912

Liverpool
Coventry City

(1) 1
(0) 0

Saturday, 26th February 1994, Anfield   Att.: 38,547

LIVERPOOL			**COVENTRY CITY**		
13	David	JAMES	1	Steve	OGRIZOVIC
2	Rob	JONES	2	Brian	BORROWS
5	Mark	WRIGHT	3	Steve	MORGAN
25	Neil	RUDDOCK – *Booked*	6	David	RENNIE
3	Julian	DICKS	4	Peter	ATHERON
17	Steve	McMANAMAN	12	Peter	NDLOVU – *Booked*
12	Ronnie	WHELAN	25	Julian	DARBY
15	Jamie	REDKNAPP	18	Sean	FLYNN (+74)
11	*Mark*	*WALTERS (*81)*	16	Willie	BOLAND
10	John	BARNES	15	Paul	WILLIAMS
9	Ian	RUSH	10	Mick	QUINN

Subs

27	Mark	GAYLE	24	*Ally*	*PICKERING (+74)*
4	Steve	NICOL	23	Jonathan	GOULD
7	*Nigel*	*CLOUGH (*81)*	14	David	BUSST

Match Facts

- Home debut and first victory for Roy Evans as Liverpool manager.
- First full game of the season for David James.

Score Sheet

I. RUSH 2 min – 1-0

Referee:
Mr. D. Elleray (Harrow)

FA Carling Premiership League

Pos	Team	P	W	D	L	F	A	Pts
3rd	Arsenal	30	13	12	5	34	16	51
4th	Newcastle Utd	29	14	6	9	51	30	48
5th	**Liverpool**	**30**	**13**	**8**	**9**	**49**	**40**	**47**
6th	Leeds United	28	12	10	6	41	29	46
7th	Aston Villa	28	12	9	7	36	27	45

Result of this Season's Fixture

Liverpool
Coventry City

Hands off Rush

Talk in the papers recently was all about Manchester City putting in a £1,500,000 bid for Ian Rush. The bid was rejected for two reasons. Firstly because Rush doesn't want to play for Manchester City – who can blame him? – and secondly because his own club need him so much. Yet again his was the only name on the score sheet.

Phil Neal, the new Coventry City manager, needs no introduction to Liverpool fans and he was clearly looking forward to visiting his old stamping ground. The game plan, he explained afterwards, was for Coventry to make an explosive start to the game and poach an early goal. Sadly for him, someone got the scripts muddled up because it was Liverpool who started explosively with Ian Rush scoring in the second minute. Redknapp took the ball off Boland in the Coventry defence and pulled the defence one way before crossing to Ian Rush on the edge of the box. Rush slotted the ball home beautifully, 1-0. After that Liverpool spent much of the rest of the first half dissecting the Coventry defence with sharp accurate passes only to run out of steam before completing the move. Ogrizovic was in sparkling form in the Coventry goal and kept his team in the match. Liverpool should have sewn up the game before half time as chances were created for Jones, McManaman and Rush but a second goal never arrived.

If Liverpool had played the first half with customary majesty, they played the second in a fashion which has been familiar more recently. Again the defence was at sixes and sevens and too much space was given to Quinn and Darby. In the dieing seconds of the game, Coventry came close to snatching an undeserved equaliser when Morgan struck his free-kick against the upright. Luckily for Liverpool it was not to be.

League Records

	P	W	D	L	F	A	Pts	Pos
93-94 Premiership Record	30	13	8	9	49	40	47	5th
All-time Premiership Record	72	29	19	24	111	95	106	–
All-time League Record	3596	1679	870	1047	6182	4620	5903	–

	Home	Away	Total
League Attendances	569,596	390,863	960,459

Blackburn Rovers (1) 2
Liverpool (0) 0

Saturday, 5th March 1994, Ewood Park   Att.: 20,831

BLACKBURN ROVERS

26	Tim	FLOWERS
20	Henning	BERG
6	Graeme	LE SAUX – *Booked*
2	David	MAY
21	*Kevin*	*MORAN (*45)*
7	Stuart	RIPLEY
23	David	BATTY
12	Nicky	MARKER
11	Jason	WILCOX
9	Alan	SHEARER
4	Tim	SHERWOOD

LIVERPOOL

13	David	JAMES
2	Rob	JONES
5	Mark	WRIGHT
25	Neil	RUDDOCK
3	Julian	DICKS
17	Steve	McMANAMAN
12	Ronnie	WHELAN – *Booked*
15	Jamie	REDKNAPP
7	*Nigel*	*CLOUGH (†79)*
10	John	BARNES
9	Ian	RUSH

Subs

1	Bobby	MIMMS
5	*Colin*	*HENDRY (*45)*
22	Mark	ATKINS

11	*Mark*	*WALTERS (†79)*
27	Mark	GAYLE
22	Steve	HARKNESS

Match Facts

- Ewood Park's highest Premiership attendance.
- Roy Evans' third successive away defeat.
- Blackburn complete Premiership double over Liverpool.
- Tim Sherwood's first league goal this season.

Score Sheet

J. WILCOX 17 min – 1-0

T. SHERWOOD 65 min – 2-0

Referee:
Mr. G. Ashby (Worcester)

FA Carling Premiership League

Pos	Team	P	W	D	L	F	A	Pts
4th	Newcastle Utd	30	15	6	9	52	30	51
5th	Leeds United	30	12	12	6	42	30	48
6th	**Liverpool**	**31**	**13**	**8**	**10**	**49**	**42**	**47**
7th	Aston Villa	29	12	10	7	37	28	46
8th	Sheffield Wed	30	11	11	8	53	31	44

Result of this Season's Fixture

Blackburn Rvrs
Liverpool

Liverpool Need A Finishing School

Blackburn Rovers still have realistic hopes of winning this season's championship and it shows; Liverpool don't and it hurts. The three points they gained boosted Blackburn Rovers' slim chance of taking the league title but Liverpool are going to have a fight on their hands if they want to qualify for Europe.

The match was an indication of the troubles that Liverpool are facing at the moment. They dominated play for much of the game and yet came home with nothing. Blackburn, in contrast, had few chances but scored twice.

In Dicks and Ruddock Liverpool have two defenders who aren't frightened of pushing forward to increase the team's attacking options. The downside of this was demonstrated in the 17th minute when a Blackburn counter attack found them out of position. Ripley exploited this to the full and drew James out of position before crossing back for Wilcox to tap in a simple goal. At the other end chances went begging as first Barnes, then Clough and McManaman twice missed opportunites to level the score.

The second half was more of the same with Clough shooting wide and Redknapp heading against the post before Blackburn finally broke out of their own half and promptly scored.

2-0 made it Roy Evans' third consecutive away defeat as manager but for those members of the Clutching at Straws School of Optimism it wasn't all gloom. Liverpool seem to have regained their knack of dominating games, stringing together neat accurate passes and holding onto possession for long periods. All they need is that killer touch in front of goal and an end to those defensive abberations. Isn't that what everyone says?

League Records

	P	W	D	L	F	A	Pts	Pos
93-94 Premiership Record	31	13	8	10	49	42	47	6th
All-time Premiership Record	73	29	19	25	111	97	106	–
All-time League Record	3597	1679	870	1048	6182	4622	5903	–

	Home	Away	Total
League Attendances	569,596	411,694	981,290

Liverpool
Everton

(2) 2
(1) 1

Sunday, 13th March 1994, Anfield   Att.: 44,281

LIVERPOOL

13	David	JAMES
2	Rob	JONES
3	Julian	DICKS – *Booked*
25	Neil	RUDDOCK
5	Mark	WRIGHT
9	Ian	RUSH
10	*John*	*BARNES (+64)*
12	Ronnie	WHELAN
15	Jamie	REDKNAPP
17	Steve	McMANAMAN
23	Robbie	FOWLER

EVERTON

1	Neville	SOUTHALL
2	Matthew	JACKSON – *Booked*
3	Andy	HINCHCLIFFE
4	Ian	SNODIN
5	Dave	WATSON
14	John	EBBRELL
8	Graham	STUART
16		*PREKI (+77)*
11	Peter	BEAGRIE
9	Tony	COTTEE
22	Brett	ANGELL (*64)

Subs

16	*Michael*	*THOMAS (+64)*
27	Mark	GAYLE
21	Dominic	MATTEO

15	*Paul*	*RIDEOUT (*64)*
10	Barry	*HORNE (+77)*
13	Jason	KEARTON

Match Facts

- The final derby in front of the Kop.
- 150th league meeting between the two clubs.
- Liverpool unbeaten in the league at Anfield for over six months.
- Neville Southall's 34th derby appearance equals Bruce Grobbelaar's record.

Score Sheet

D. WATSON 22 min – 0-1
I. RUSH 22 min – 1-1
R. FOWLER 43 min – 2-0

Referee:
Mr. K. Cooper (Pontypridd)

FA Carling Premiership League

Pos	Team	P	W	D	L	F	A	Pts
3rd	Newcastle Utd	31	16	6	9	59	31	54
4th	Arsenal	31	14	12	5	39	17	54
5th	**Liverpool**	**32**	**14**	**8**	**10**	**51**	**43**	**50**
6th	Leeds United	31	12	13	6	44	32	49
7th	Aston Villa	31	13	10	8	38	29	49

Result of this Season's Fixture

Liverpool
Everton

The Kop's Last Derby

The Kop comes down at the end of the season to make way for an all-seater stand. This then was the last derby game to appear in front of it. It wasn't a derby game to rank with some of the classics but neither was it lacking in excitement. Both clubs were with new managers since their previous encounter and both looking to start with a clean slate.

Everton went ahead after 22 minutes with Dave Watson rising to meet a cross from Preki and head home past James. From the restart it took Liverpool just nine seconds to level the score. Julian Dicks saw Ian Rush making a run and launched a 50 yard pass to the Welshman. Rush ran past Snodin and volleyed home to silence the stunned Everton fans.

Ian Rush has scored a record 25 goals in 32 derby appearances and has been a continual nightmare for Everton with his habit of scoring on vital occasions – Cup finals, that sort of thing. If Everton will be glad to see the back of Ian Rush they look like having to face another tormentor in the shape of 18 year old Robbie Fowler. Fowler scored in his first match back after a seven week absence through injury. Rather than looking out of practice he just looks better with every game he plays. He scored the winning goal two minutes before half-time.

John Barnes had been giving the appearance of having an off game, drifting around rather aimlessly when he threaded a ball through the Everton defence for Fowler to run clear. It was a sharp angle but Fowler gave himself time to shoot before curling a drive past Southall. Two-One it stayed but Everton will rue their missed opportunity in the final minute when Beagrie's fierce volley was deflected towards the top corner of James' goal. The stand-in keeper was up to the challenge pulling off a magnificent save just to let Bruce Grobbelaar know that his place in the side isn't automatic.

League Records

	P	W	D	L	F	A	Pts	Pos
93-94 Premiership Record	32	14	8	10	51	43	50	5th
All-time Premiership Record	74	30	19	25	113	98	109	–
All-time League Record	3598	1680	870	1048	6184	4623	5905	–

	Home	Away	Total
League Attendances	613,877	411,694	1,025,571

Liverpool
Chelsea

(2) 2
(0) 1

Saturday, 19th March 1994, Anfield   Att.: 38,629

LIVERPOOL

13	David	JAMES
2	Rob	JONES
5	Mark	WRIGHT
25	Neil	RUDDOCK
3	Julian	DICKS
10	*John*	*BARNES (+70)*
12	Ronnie	WHELAN
15	Jamie	REDKNAPP
17	Steve	McMANAMAN
23	Robbie	FOWLER
9	Ian	RUSH

Subs

16	*Michael*	*THOMAS (+70)*
1	Bruce	GROBBELAAR
21	Dominic	MATTEO

CHELSEA

1	Dimitri	KHARINE
12	Steve	CLARKE
26	*Andy*	*DOW (*67)*
5	Erland	JOHNSEN
35	Jakob	KJELDBJERG
24	Craig	BURLEY
18	Eddie	NEWTON
20	Glenn	HODDLE
10	Gavin	PEACOCK
19	Neil	SHIPPERLEY
11	Dennis	WISE

27	*David*	*HOPKIN (*67)*
13	Kevin	HITCHCOCK
17	Nigel	SPACKMAN

Match Facts

- Roy Evans' first unchanged squad.

Score Sheet

I. RUSH 8 min – 1-0
C. BURLEY 18 min (og) – 2-0
C. BURLEY 50 min – 2-1

Referee:
Mr. R. Gifford (Llanbradach)

FA Carling Premiership League

Pos	Team	P	W	D	L	F	A	Pts
4th	Arsenal	32	15	12	5	43	17	57
5th	Leeds United	33	14	13	6	47	32	55
6th	**Liverpool**	**33**	**15**	**8**	**10**	**53**	**44**	**53**
7th	Aston Villa	33	13	10	10	39	33	49
8th	QPR	31	13	8	10	49	41	47

**Result of this
Season's Fixture**

Chelsea
Liverpool

Still Everything to Play for...

Liverpool started the game with the same line-up that has been so successful against Everton the week before and indeed the result was the same too: victory by two goals to one. Liverpool started the game at full pelt and were two-nil up inside twenty minutes but failed to wrap the game up and, with several chances going begging, did not increase the score. The second half saw Chelsea get back into the match with a goal of their own while forcing several acrobatic saves from David James and making the Liverpool defence look vulnerable once more.

The game was brought alive by some sparkling play from Steve McManaman down the right wing. He was expertly supplied by Rob Jones, the two of them managing to turn Chelsea's defence inside out, both hitting shots against the Chelsea woodwork. Liverpool's first goal came after Robbie Fowler chipped into the area towards Mark Wright. The Chelsea keeper only parried the ball as far as Ian Rush who buried it. The second came from a McManaman cross deep into the box. Several players challenged for it but Craig Burley got there first to head expertly home into his own net. As so often happens it was the player who scored the own goal who scored for his own side too. Burley had to wait until the second half for his opportunity. Whe it arrived it was a spectacular effort from 25 yards out which left James with no chance.

With UEFA considering three places for English teams in next season's UEFA Cup Liverpool need to be in third place to get back into Europe. With the teams above them playing so well at the moment and having a game in hand that's a tall order but Liverpool's remaining fixtures include games against Arsenal and Newcastle. Everything, as they say, to play for.

League Records

	P	W	D	L	F	A	Pts	Pos
93-94 Premiership Record	33	15	8	10	53	44	53	6th
All-time Premiership Record	75	31	19	25	115	99	112	–
All-time League Record	3599	1681	870	1048	6186	4624	5907	–

	Home	Away	Total
League Attendances	652,506	411,694	1,064,200

Arsenal
Liverpool

(1) 1
(0) 0

Saturday, 26th March 1994, Highbury

Att. 35,556

ARSENAL

1	David	SEAMAN
2	Lee	DIXON
14	Martin	KEOWN
23	Ray	PARLOUR
12	Steve	BOULD
5	Andy	LINIGHAN
17	*John*	*JENSEN (*66)*
8	*Ian*	*WRIGHT (+80)*
7	Kevin	CAMPBELL
10	Paul	MERSON
22	Ian	SELLEY

Subs

21	*Steve*	*MORROW (*66)*
9	*Alan*	*SMITH (+80)*
13	Alan	MILLER

LIVERPOOL

13	David	JAMES
2	Rob	JONES
3	Julian	DICKS
5	*Mark*	*WRIGHT (*28)*
25	Neil	RUDDOCK
15	Jamie	REDKNAPP
17	Steve	McMANAMAN
12	Ronnie	WHELAN
9	Ian	RUSH
23	*Robbie*	*FOWLER (+71)*
10	John	BARNES

4	*Steve*	*NICOL (*28)*
1	Bruce	GROBBELAAR
16	*Michael*	*THOMAS (+71)*

Match Facts

- Roy Evans' fourth consecutive away defeat as manager.
- Arsenal unbeaten in nine games.
- Paul Merson's fourth goal in four Premiership starts.
- Liverpool have conceded 100 Premiership goals.

Score Sheet

P. MERSON 47 mins – 1-0

Referee:
Mr. R. Hart (Darlington)

FA Carling Premiership League

Pos	Team	P	W	D	L	F	A	Pts
4th	Newcastle Utd	33	18	6	9	65	33	60
5th	Leeds United	34	14	13	7	47	33	55
6th	**Liverpool**	**34**	**15**	**8**	**11**	**53**	**45**	**53**
7th	QPR	32	14	8	10	52	42	50
8th	Aston Villa	33	13	10	10	39	33	49

Result of this Season's Fixture

Arsenal

Liverpool

Winning Away Looks A Long Way Away

With England coach Terry Venables in the crowd this was a game which gave the opportunity for players from both sides to boost their claims for an England place. Venables will have left Highbury with only one name to add to his list of possible contenders: Arsenal's Paul Merson.

With George Graham resting four key players ahead of their Cup Winners Cup semi-final game against Paris St Germain on the following Wednesday this looked like a golden opportunity for the Liverpool team to put an end to manager Roy Evand' dismal away record of three defeats in three games. It was not to be and a fourth game was added to that sequence. The culprit according to Evans was his team's most un-Liverpool like lack of belief in their ability to win away. As Evans pointed out after the game Liverpool only ever looked like they were in contention after they had gone the goal down. That came shortly after the interval when a through ball from Selley set Merson free and his shot left James with no chance. Was he offside? The linesman didn't seem to think so but there were plenty of Liverpool fans at Highbury who did.

It wasn't the first time in the game that Arsenal had the ball in the back of the Liverpool net. After only ten minutes it was Merson who latched onto the end of a Kevin Campbell shot but that time the linesman had no doubt about raising his flag.

Robbie Fowler had Liverpool's best first half chance after Rob Jones put him through but he had to watch as his shot took a deflection off an Arsenal shirt and headed towards safety.

Paul Merson's goal in the second half proved to be the rather unwelcome spark that Liverpool needed to try and get back into the match and the last twenty minutes of the game were all Liverpool. Jamie Redknapp came closest to levelling the scores but his shot cannoned off David Seaman's legs. Robbie Fowler was substituted by Michael Thomas in the 71st minute and he made a difference putting Ian Rush through on two occasions but for once the Welsh goalscoring supremo could not provide the telling touch. There were one or two long range efforts but although the Arsenal defence was not up to its usual tightfistedness, the Liverpool attack never looked like breaching its final line.

League Records

	P	W	D	L	F	A	Pts	Pos
93-94 Premiership Record	34	15	8	11	53	45	53	6th
All-time Premiership Record	76	31	19	26	115	100	112	–
All-time League Record	3600	1681	870	1049	6186	4625	5907	–

	Home	Away	Total
League Attendances	652,506	447,250	1,099,756

Manchester United (1) 1
Liverpool (0) 0

Tuesday, 29th March 1994, Old Trafford   Att: 44,751

MANCHESTER UNITED

1	Peter	SCHMEICHEL
2	Paul	PARKER
3	Denis	IRWIN
4	Steve	BRUCE
6	Gary	PALLISTER
5	Lee	SHARPE (†66)
7	Eric	CANTONA (+73)
8	Paul	INCE
16	Roy	KEANE
10	Mark	HUGHES
14	Andrei	KANCHELSKIS

Subs

11	Ryan	GIGGS (†66)
12	Bryan	ROBSON (+73)
13	Les	SEALEY

LIVERPOOL

13	David	JAMES
2	Rob	JONES
3	Julian	DICKS
25	Neil	RUDDOCk
4	Steve	NICOL
17	Steve	McMANAMAN
15	Jamie	REDKNAPP
12	Ronnie	WHELAN
9	Ian	RUSH (Booked)
10	John	BARNES
16	Michael	THOMAS (†81)

23	Robbie	FOWLER (†81)
1	Bruce	GROBBELAAR
7	Nigel	CLOUGH

Match Facts

- No Manchester United players were sent off (after four in the last five matches).
- Highest ever Premiership gate (by one).
- Liverpool's fifth consecutive away defeat.

Score Sheet

P. INCE 37 min – 1-0

Referee:
Mr. K. Hackett (Sheffield)

FA Carling Premiership League

Pos	Team	P	W	D	L	F	A	Pts
4th	Arsenal	34	16	13	5	46	19	61
5th	Leeds United	34	14	13	7	47	33	55
6th	**Liverpool**	**35**	**15**	**8**	**12**	**53**	**46**	**53**
7th	QPR	32	14	8	10	52	42	50
8th	Aston Villa	34	13	11	10	39	33	50

Result of this Season's Fixture

Manchester Utd
Liverpool

You Can Stop Whingeing Now

It is particularly galling that at a time when Liverpool are going through hard times that it should be Manchester United who have been the team of the moment. For a time this season it looked as though the Manchester team were going to make a clean sweep of all three domestic trophies but, having lost to Aston Villa in the League Cup final, they have had to come to terms with their own mortality. Still a League and FA Cup double is on the cards but if they achieve it it won't be to the popular acclaim that you might expect given their flowing, attacking football.

Chief culprit has been manager Alex Ferguson who has been a source of constant complaint. The World is against him and his beloved team, the BBC commentary team are all members of the Liverpool Supporters Club and Jimmy Hill is a prat. These are just some of the gems he has dreamed up and they haven't won him any friends.

Maybe after this game he will be satisfied because there was a moment of controversy and this time it went in Man Utd's favour. A goal down but pushing forward, Liverpool were having the better of a disappointing second half when Andrei Kanchelskis brought down Michael Thomas inside the United penalty area. A simple decision you might think but, after a penalty looked the only outcome, referee Keith Hackett continued his love affair with controversy by soliciting the opinion of a linesman who was fifty yards away at the time. 'No penalty' was the verdict and it proved something of a turning point. United's defensive vulnerability ceased and although the Manchester team never looked like finding a way past Liverpool's five man midfield Liverpool didn't look like scoring either.

League Records

	P	W	D	L	F	A	Pts	Pos
93-94 Premiership Record	35	15	8	12	53	46	53	6th
All-time Premiership Record	77	31	19	27	115	101	112	–
All-time League Record	3601	1681	870	1050	6186	4626	5907	–

	Home	Away	Total
League Attendances	652,506	492,001	1,144,507

Liverpool
Sheffield United

(1) 1
(0) 2

Match 43

Saturday, 2nd April 1994, Anfield   Att: 36,642

LIVERPOOL

13	David	JAMES
2	Rob	JONES
5	Mark	WRIGHT
25	Neil	RUDDOCK
3	Julian	DICKS
10	John	BARNES (†70)
12	Ronnie	WHELAN
15	Jamie	REDKNAPP
17	Steve	McMANAMAN
23	Robbie	FOWLER
9	Ian	RUSH

Subs

16	*Michael*	*THOMAS (†70)*
1	Bruce	GROBBELAAR
21	Dominic	MATTEO

SHEFFIELD UNITED

13	Simon	TRACEY
4	John	GANNON
5	Brian	GAYLE
7	Franz	CARR
8	Paul	ROGERS
9	Adrian	LITTLEJOHN
12	Jostein	FLO
14	David	TUTTLE
17	Carl	BRADSHAW – *B"ked*
18	Dane	WHITEHOUSE
33	Roger	NILSEN

10	Glyn	HODGES
30	Nathan	BLAKE
31	Salvatore	BIBBO (gk)

Match Facts

- Sheffield United's first away win of the season.
- Liverpool's first home league defeat in over six months.
- Liverpool's third consecutive defeat.

Score Sheet

I. RUSH 4 min – 1-0
J. FLO 46 min – 1-1
J. FLO 73 min – 1-2

Referee:
Mr. T. Holbrook (Walsall)

FA Carling Premiership League

Pos Team	P	W	D	L	F	A	Pts
4th Arsenal	35	16	14	5	47	20	62
5th Leeds United	35	14	14	7	48	34	56
6th Liverpool	**36**	**15**	**8**	**13**	**54**	**48**	**53**
7th Sheffield Wed	35	13	12	10	63	49	51
8th Wimbledon	35	14	9	12	54	45	51

Result of this Season's Fixture

No Fixture

Sheffield Show Steel to Steal Show

As if winning games wasn't difficult enough by itself, Liverpool have now discovered the knack of getting on top of a game and then contriving to lose it. Sheffield United arrived in their familiar spring position of putting together a good run of results in a bid to escape relegation. On the evidence of this game they are going to find it a stiff task unless they find a few more sides in as generous mood as Liverpool.

This was a game where Liverpool scored early on, dominated play and then eased off. They eased off so much in the second half that Sheffield United netted a couple of goals and stole the game.

Ian Rush has retrieved his mantle of chief goal getter from an out of sorts Robbie Fowler and it was he who grabbed the goal. Jamie Redknapp is behind much of the inspiration at Anfield these days and in the fourth minute he crossed to Ian Rush who drove home with his familiar aplomb.

For a while the Reds sparkled but although they maintained more than their fair share of the possession they lacked a cutting edge and the possibility of a second goal was kept at bay by Simon Tracey in the Blades' goal.

The second half belonged to United. Jostein Flo scored within the first couple of minutes after Adrian Littlejohn accelerated past Nicol. Flo's first shot was blocked by James' feet but the rebound fell kindly and Flo knocked it in to level the scores. Flo put the final touch to Sheffield's second goal which earned them three points. Franz Carr crossed in from the left over Ruddock's head and onto Flo's. It didn't look like the ball went where Flo intended but a stranded James watched as it went where it counts – in the back of the net.

If there was an element of good fortune in both Sheffield goals the result was deserved as the Yorkshiremen had fought with greater conviction. They looked like they wanted to win and in the end they did.

League Records

	P	W	D	L	F	A	Pts	Pos
93-94 Premiership Record	36	15	8	13	54	48	53	6th
All-time Premiership Record	78	31	19	28	116	103	112	–
All-time League Record	3602	1681	870	1051	6187	4628	5907	–

	Home	Away	Total
League Attendances	689,148	492,001	1,181,149

Wimbledon
Liverpool

(0) 1
(0) 1

Monday, 4th April 1994, Selhurst Park
Att: 13,819

WIMBLEDON

1	Hans	SEGERS
2	*Warren*	*BARTON (†45)*
5	Dean	BLACKWELL – B'kd
8	Robbie	EARLE
9	John	FASHANU
10	Dean	HOLDSWORTH
15	John	SCALES
19	*Stewart*	*CASTLEDINE (+80)*
20	Marcus	GALE
24	Peter	FEAR
33	Gary	ELKINS

Subs

21	*Chris*	*PERRY (†45)*
36	*Gary*	*BLISSETT (+80)*
23	Neil	SULLIVAN

LIVERPOOL

13	David	JAMES
2	Rob	JONES
3	Julian	DICKS
4	Steve	NICOL
9	Ian	RUSH
10	John	BARNES
12	Ronnie	WHELAN
15	Jamie	REDKNAPP
17	Steve	McMANAMAN
23	Robbie	FOWLER
25	Neil	RUDDOCK

16	Michael	THOMAS
1	Bruce	GROBBELAAR
14	Jan	MOLBY

Match Facts

- Liverpool have not beaten Wimbledon in the Premiership.
- Fourth draw between the two teams this season.
- Roy Evans still without an away win as manager.

Score Sheet

J. REDKNAPP 64 min – 0-1

G. ELKINS 90 min – 1-1

Referee:
Mr. J. Borrett (Moseley)

FA Carling Premiership League

Pos	Team	P	W	D	L	F	A	Pts
5th	Leeds United	36	15	14	7	52	34	59
6th	Sheffield Wed	36	14	12	10	64	49	54
7th	**Liverpool**	**37**	**15**	**9**	**13**	**55**	**49**	**54**
8th	Wimbledon	36	14	10	12	55	46	52
9th	Aston Villa	36	13	12	11	39	36	51

Result of this Season's Fixture

Wimbledon

Liverpool

107

'A Pain in the Arse'

Unbeaten in his ten confrontations with the Reds – four of them this season – Joe Kinnear proclaimed himself 'a pain in the arse' to Liverpool. Few Liverpool fans will disagree.

LIverpool looked like gaining a well deserved first away victory for new manager Roy Evans right until to the last minute of the game. It was then that Fashanu gave Nicol a shove just outside the Liverpool box and the referee made a bizarre decision and awarded Wimbledon the free kick. Elkins stepped up hit the ball against the Liverpool wall and watched as the ball took a fortunate deflection and bounced into the net. That levelled the score and gave the London team a scarce deserved draw.

Liverpool made all the running and set off at an impressive pace with Robbie Fowler having three shots at goal within the first ten minutes. The first effort went wide, the second demanded a spectacular save from Segers and the third – an acrobatic diving header – hit the post. McManaman then had a stab at putting his name on the score sheet for the first time since August but fired wide.

As has happened so many times recently Liverpool relaxed their grip on the game and, around half-time, Wimbledon had their own chances. James was called on to make a couple of saves, notably when Nicol's backpass almost let Fashanu through and Jones needed to clear the ball of the line shortly after. Just when you wondered whether Liverpool would ever score Rob Jones broke free on the right hand side. He squared the ball to Jamie Redknapp who let fly from 25 yards out. His effort cleared Segers and went in off the post. Liverpool could have wrapped up the game a quarter of an hour later but somehow the Wimbledon defence kept the ball from crossing the line. It looked like staying a Liverpool victory right up until the very last.

League Records

	P	W	D	L	F	A	Pts	Pos
93-94 Premiership Record	37	15	9	13	55	49	54	7th
All-time Premiership Record	79	31	20	28	117	104	113	–
All-time League Record	3603	1681	871	1051	6188	4629	5908	–

	Home	Away	Total
League Attendances	689,148	505,820	1,194,968

Liverpool
Ipswich Town

(0) 1
(0) 0

Saturday, 9th April 1994, Anfield

Att: 30,485

LIVERPOOL

13	David	JAMES
2	Rob	JONES
3	Julian	DICKS
4	Steve	NICOL
9	Ian	RUSH
10	John	BARNES
12	Ronnie	WHELAN
15	Jamie	REDKNAPP
17	Steve	McMANAMAN
23	Robbie	FOWLER
25	Neil	RUDDOCK

Subs

6	Don	HUTCHISON
16	Michael	THOMAS
1	Bruce	GROBBELAAR

IPSWICH TOWN

1	Craig	FORREST
2	Michael	STOCKWELL
5	John	WARK
6	David	LINIGHAN
7	Geraint	WILLIAMS
8	Gavin	JOHNSON
11	Chris	KIWOMYA
15	*Phil*	WHELAN (†80) – B'ked
16	Eddie	YOUDS Booked
18	Steve	PALMER
21	Stuart	SLATER

9	*Bontcho*	GUENTCHEV (†80)
4	Paul	MASON
13	Clive	BAKER

Match Facts

- Most boring match of the season.

Score Sheet

J. DICKS 75 min – 1-0

Referee:
Mr. D. Gallagher (Banbury)

FA Carling Premiership League

Pos	Team	P	W	D	L	F	A	Pts
5th	Leeds United	36	15	14	7	52	34	59
6th	Sheffield Wed	37	15	12	10	67	50	57
7th	**Liverpool**	**38**	**16**	**9**	**13**	**56**	**49**	**57**
8th	Wimbledon	36	14	10	12	55	46	52
9th	Aston Villa	36	13	12	11	39	36	51

Result of this Season's Fixture

Liverpool
Ipswich Town

Not Singing In The Rain

The game kicked off early so that it did not clash with the Grand National scheduled for later on in the afternoon. In the circumstances there was a healthily sized crowd quite undeserved by such a game.

Ipswich started the game with 41 points – just above the relegation zone – and had obviously calculated that the one point a draw would give them would be enough. They defended in numbers and with a solidity that Liverpool found nigh on impossible to break down. It was not a pretty sight to watch.

But it would be flattering to Ipswich to suggest that they had much say in stifling Liverpool's initiative. Blame it on the morning start, blame it on the filthy weather – we had sleet at one point – but whatever the excuse Liverpool's passing was awful. When they did manage to get past the massed ranks of Ipswich defenders, they played virtually with a back nine for much of the game, the keeper Craig Forrest was alwasy up to the challenge. A goal finally arrived a quarter of an hour before the end. A rush of blood to the head and Phil Whelan dragged substitute Don Hutchison to the ground in the Ipswich penalty area. Julian Dicks took the penalty kick and made no mistake. Whelan was lucky to stay on the pitch as he had been booked only five minutes beforehand for a near identical challenge on Rob Jones. The penalty was enough to give Liverpool their first win in five games with their first clean sheet in eight which was also James' first clean sheet of the season. Liverpool hadn't played too well but Ipswich went home with exactly what they deserved – nothing.

The only real entertainment was provided by Bruce Grobbelaar. He wasn't even playing but he's not the sort to let a small detail like that make any difference. He came from the substitutes bench to conduct a little bit of Kop singing but there wasn't really that much to sing about.

League Records

	P	W	D	L	F	A	Pts	Pos
93-94 Premiership Record	38	16	9	13	56	49	57	7th
All-time Premiership Record	80	32	20	28	118	104	116	–
All-time League Record	3604	1682	871	1051	6189	4629	5910	–

	Home	Away	Total
League Attendances	719,633	505,820	1,225,453

Liverpool
Newcastle United

(0) 0
(1) 2

Match 46

Saturday, 16th April 1994, Anfield   Att: 44,601

LIVERPOOL			NEWCASTLE UNITED		
13	David	JAMES	1	Pavel	SRNICEK
2	Rob	JONES	3	John	BERESFORD
4	Steve	NICOL	2	*Barry*	*VENISON (†89)*
25	Neil	RUDDOCK	15	Darren	PEACOCK
3	Julian	DICKS	20	Alan	NEILSON
17	*Steve*	*McMANAMAN (+71)*	5	Ruel	FOX
15	Jamie	REDKNAPP	7	Robert	LEE
12	Ronnie	WHELAN	4	Paul	BRACEWELL
10	John	BARNES	11	Scott	SELLARS
9	Ian	RUSH	9	Andy	COLE
23	*Robbie*	*FOWLER (†60)*	8	*Peter*	*BEARDSLEY (+90)*

Subs

6	*Don*	*HUTCHISON (†60)*	12	*Mark*	*ROBINSON (†89)*
16	*Michael*	*THOMAS (+71)*	14	*Alec*	*MATHIE (+90)*
1	Bruce	GROBBELAAR	30	Mike	HOOPER

FA Carling Premiership League

Pos	Team	P	W	D	L	F	A	Pts
5th	Leeds United	36	15	14	7	52	34	59
6th	Sheffield Wed	38	15	13	10	68	51	58
7th	**Liverpool**	**39**	**16**	**9**	**14**	**56**	**51**	**57**
8th	Wimbledon	37	15	10	12	44	46	55
9th	Aston Villa	38	14	12	12	41	38	54

Result of this Season's Fixture

Liverpool
Newcastle Utd

Just Like The Liverpool Of Old

Anfield's biggest gate of the season turned out on the fifth anniversary of the Hillsborough Disaster to greet Kevin Keegan's Newcastle United in what promised to be a thrilling encounter between Liverpool boys old and new. The capacity crowd were treated to a display of the most delightful passing play and simple one-touch football that for years has been the hallmark of great Liverpool sides.

The only disappointment for the home crowd was that it was the men in black and white who were providing the entertainment. Roy Evans paid the Newcastle manager the highest footballing accolade in saying that Kevin Keegan was keeping the Shankly tradition alive. Liverpool by contrast were made to look pedestrian and when they did engineer moves of their own they tended to overelaborate. Most Liverpool forays broke down under the burden of their own complexity rather than through the efforts of the Newcastle defence.

The first goal came through a sharp flick on from Cole which put Lee into space. James reacted and came racing from his line to narrow the angle but was not quick enough. Lee slotted the ball inside the post for Newcastle's first goal. A second looked likely throughout the first half but it wasn't until the 56th minute that the Magpies made the game safe. A Liverpool move broke down and a swift counter-attack involving Lee and Fox found Cole with room to send in his 39th goal of the season. Beardsley had an excellent chance to make it three later on that half when he volleyed a Srnicek clearance only a few feet wide of James' upright. Two-nil it stayed to complete a miserable run in which Liverpool have won just one of their last six games. In the last two months Liverpool have faced the top five teams – Manchester United, Blackburn Rovers, Newcastle United , Arsenal and Leeds United – and lost each game. It is a measure of the work that remains to be done before Liverpool can regain their rightful place at the top of the heap. Despite this the mood at Anfield remains one of optimism and the feeling is that Roy Evans has his team's confidence to turn things round.

League Records

	P	W	D	L	F	A	Pts	Pos
93-94 Premiership Record	39	16	9	14	56	51	57	7th
All-time Premiership Record	81	32	20	29	118	106	116	–
All-time League Record	3605	1682	871	1052	6189	4631	5910	–

	Home	Away	Total
League Attendances			

West Ham United (1) 1
Liverpool (1) 2

Saturday, 23rd April 1994, Upton Park   Att.: 26,096

LIVERPOOL

13	David	JAMES
22	Steve	HARKNESS
4	Steve	NICOL
25	Neil	RUDDOCK
3	Julian	DICKS
6	Don	HUTCHISON
15	Jamie	REDKNAPP
7	Nigel	CLOUGH
10	John	BARNES
9	Ian	RUSH
23	*Robbie*	*FOWLER (†60)*

Subs

1	Bruce	GROBBELAAR
21	Dominic	MATTEO
18	Phil	CHARNOCK

WEST HAM UNITED

1	Ludek	MIKLOSKO
2	Tim	BREACKER
4	Steve	POTTS
6	Martin	ALLEN
9	Trevor	MORLEY
12	Tony	GAYLE
14	*Ian*	*BISHOP (†73)*
16	Matthew	HOLMES
28	Matthew	RUSH
33	David	BURROWS
34	Mike	MARSH

25	*Lee*	*CHAPMAN (†73)*
13	Gary	KELLY (gk)
15	Kenny	BROWN

Match Facts

• Roy Evans' first away win as manager.

• Liverpool pass last season's points total of 59.

Score Sheet

M. ALLEN 1 min – 1-0
R. FOWLER 14 mins – 1-1
I. RUSH 87 mins – 1-2

Referee:
Mr. S. Lodge (Barnsley)

FA Carling Premiership League

Pos	Team	P	W	D	L	F	A	Pts
5th	Leeds United	38	16	15	7	56	35	63
6th	Sheffield Wed	39	16	13	10	73	51	61
7th	**Liverpool**	**40**	**17**	**9**	**14**	**58**	**52**	**60**
8th	Wimbledon	39	16	11	12	49	49	59
9th	QPR	37	15	9	13	57	55	54

Result of this Season's Fixture

West Ham Utd
Liverpool

Liverpool Get Away from it All

It was a fine win and the first away from Anfield since Roy Evans took charge at Liverpool in January. But neither Liverpool nor West Ham went into this match with much to play for. Liverpool's dreams of European football next season have been relegated to the realms of fantasy football while West Ham's fears of relegation could only result from the most freakish nightmare of mathematics. In which case the match and the club's league standings are true to form: Liverpool were the better team but aren't good enough for European football and West Ham were beaten here but are worth their place in the top flight.

West Ham took the lead in this game so early that the Liverpool defence might have been caught asleep. That would be their best excuse as West Ham's first attack left them bewildered. Morley and Holmes were the architects exchanging passes before freeing Martin Allen who caught an indecisive James wandering from his line with a perfectly judged lob.

With a side showing several changes from the previous match it took Liverpool a while to gel. It was left to John Barnes, now playing the role of occasional provider, who took a chip from Nicol, turned from his marker and crashed the ball across the goal against the upright. The rebound fell kindly for Robbie Fowler who followed up to bag the equaliser. It was the sort of opportunist's goal that Ian Rush once made his hallmark but he struggled in this game to find any sort of form. On the half hour a cross from Don Hutchison found him unmarked in the six-yard area. Time was when that set of circumstances automatically meant a goal but this was not the Ian Rush of yesteryear. He lunged at the ball, mistimed it and Miklosko picked up the rebound of his legs. Again in the second half he headed over from the same distance when the net was begging to be filled.

Finally he got it right. With only a few minutes remaining Tony Gale undercued his back pass and Rush raced in. He rounded the keeper and tapped the ball home to give Roy Evans his first away win as manager and to give himself some satisfaction on an otherwise frustrating day.

League Records

	P	W	D	L	F	A	Pts	Pos
93-94 Premiership Record	40	17	9	14	58	52	60	7th
All-time Premiership Record	82	33	20	29	120	107	119	–
All-time League Record	3606	1683	871	1052	6191	4632	5912	–

	Home	Away	Total
League Attendances	764,234	531,916	1,296,150

Liverpool
Norwich City

(0) 0
(1) 1

Saturday, 30th April 1994, Anfield · · · Att.: 44,339

LIVERPOOL

13	David	JAMES
2	Rob	JONES
4	Steve	NICOL
25	Neil	RUDDOCK
3	Julian	DICKS
15	Jamie	REDKNAPP
7	*Nigel*	*CLOUGH (†71)*
12	Ronnie	WHELAN
10	John	BARNES
23	*Robbie*	*FOWLER (†60)*
9	Ian	RUSH

Subs

6	*Don*	*HUTCHISON (†71)*
1	Bruce	GROBBELAAR
22	*Steve*	*HARKNESS (†60)*

NORWICH CITY

1	Bryan	GUNN
2	Mark	BOWEN
5	Ian	CULVERHOUSE
8	Colin	WOODTHORPE
10	John	POLSTON
27	Spencer	PRIOR
18	Robert	ULLATHORNE
11	Jeremy	GOSS
4	Ian	CROOK
7	Efan	EKOKU
22	Chris	SUTTON

12	Mark	ROBINS
21	David	SMITH
13	Scott	HOWIE

Match Facts

- Last game in front of a standing Kop.
- Second highest attendance at Anfield this season.

Score Sheet

J. GOSS 35 min – 0-1

Referee:
Mr. B. Hill (Kettering)

FA Carling Premiership League

Pos	Team	P	W	D	L	F	A	Pts
6th	Wimbledon	41	18	11	12	54	50	65
7th	Sheffield Wed	40	16	14	10	73	51	62
8th	**Liverpool**	**41**	**17**	**9**	**15**	**58**	**53**	**60**
9th	QPR	40	15	11	14	60	60	56
10th	Aston Villa	41	14	12	15	44	49	54

Result of this Season's Fixture

Norwich City
Liverpool

115

Norwich Spoil The Party

On the Monday after the game the bulldozers moved in. The Kop had had its last stand. But from the moment that Jeremy Goss scored Norwich's first half winner you could not but speculate whether Roy Evans would be taking a bulldozer to the Liverpool squad.

For the Liverpool fans the highlight came before the kick-off when names from the past were introduced such as Joe Fagan, the wives of Bill Shankly and Bob Paisley, Tommy Smith, Billy Liddell and most acclaimed of them all, Kenny Dalglish.

Such a parade of great names reminded the crowd of the glory days at Anfield. It also served to highlight the inadequacies of the Liverpool team on the field. Where once had played the Champions of Europe now saw a squad of league also-rans. Not a poor team by any means but not one fit to grace the home of legends.

Norwich again proved that they are a team to be taken seriously and turned on the style for the party. If there was an element of good fortune about the goal that won the match, the greater part of the good fortune belonged to Liverpool. James in goal was the barrier between Norwich and more goals as the Liverpool outfield players played, but not as a team. The goal came after 35 minutes when Jeremy Goss latched onto a clearance. With the rest of the Norwich players running from the Kop to stay onside, he fired in a terrific rising drive that gave James no chance. It was a goal of the sort of quality that has become synonymous with football at Anfield but, not for the first time in recent seasons, the Kop had to look to the visitors to provide the entertainment.

League Records

	P	W	D	L	F	A	Pts	Pos
93-94 Premiership Record	41	17	9	15	58	53	60	8th
All-time Premiership Record	83	33	20	30	120	108	119	–
All-time League Record	3607	1683	871	1053	6191	4633	5912	–

	Home	Away	Total
League Attendances	808,573	531,916	1,340,489

Aston Villa (0) 2
Liverpool (1) 1

Saturday, 7th May 1994, Villa Park   Att.: 45,347

ASTON VILLA

13	Mark	BOSNICH
2	Earl	BARRETT
3	Steve	STAUNTON
5	Paul	McGRATH
6	Kevin	RICHARDSON
7	Ray	HOUGHTON
9	Dean	SAUNDERS
11	*Tony*	*DALEY (†45)*
14	Andy	TOWNSEND
16	Ugo	EHIOGU
19	*Stefan*	*BEINLICH (+45)*

Subs

23	*Bryan*	*SMALL (†45)*
18	*Dwight*	*YORKE (+45)*
30	Michael	OAKES

LIVERPOOL

13	David	JAMES
2	Rob	JONES
3	Julian	DICKS
4	Steve	NICOL
25	Neil	RUDDOCK
12	*Ronnie*	*WHELAN (+79)*
6	Don	HUTCHISON
15	Jamie	REDKNAPP
10	John	BARNES
9	Ian	RUSH
23	Robbie	FOWLER

22	*Steve*	*HARKNESS (+79)*
7	Nigel	CLOUGH
1	Bruce	GROBBELAAR

Match Facts

- Premiership record attendance of 45,347.
- Liverpool's third consecutive defeat.

Score Sheet

R. FOWLER 35 min – 0-1

D. YORKE 65 min – 1-1

D. YORKE 81 min – 2-1

Referee:
Mr. K. Burge (Tonypandy)

FA Carling Premiership League

Pos Team	P	W	D	L	F	A	Pts
6th Wimbledon	42	18	11	13	56	53	65
7th Sheffield Wed	42	16	16	10	76	54	64
8th Liverpool	**42**	**17**	**9**	**16**	**59**	**55**	**60**
9th QPR	42	16	12	14	62	61	60
10th Aston Villa	42	15	12	15	46	50	57

Result of this Season's Fixture

Aston Villa

Liverpool

Sometimes Good, Sometimes Bad

The 93-94 Premiership season came to a frustrating end for Liverpool. A final league placing of eighth place is the lowest in over thirty years and that, coupled to early exits from the League Cup and FA Cup and an undignified changing of manager, have meant a disappointing time for all associated with the club.

The game against Villa in many ways encapsulated much that has gone wrong at the club.

Liverpool played so well in the first half that Roy Evans felt it was the best they had played since he took over. Ian Rush and Don Hutchison both had shots blocked early on. In the seventeenth minute Fowler played a one-two with Rush and swept the return past Bosnich. The same two could have wrapped the game up just before the interval when Robbie Fowler laid the ball off to Ian Rush only for Bosnich to pull off a one-handed stop.

Ron Atkinson made an inspired double substitution at half-time with Dwight Yorke making only his third appearance of the season. It worked. Villa returned to the pitch fired up and Yorke was the beneficiary of a Saunders pass to level the scores. Liverpool hopes of restoring their lead floundered when Fowler was dumped to the ground by Bosnich. Finally Yorke pinched the game for the home team in their last home game in front of a terraced Holte End. Liverpool had shown much promise in the first half and then blew the game in the second. What everyone wants is for the team to play well all the time.

League Records

	P	W	D	L	F	A	Pts	Pos
93-94 Premiership Record	42	17	9	16	59	55	60	8th
All-time Premiership Record	84	33	20	31	121	110	119	–
All-time League Record	3608	1683	871	1054	6192	4635	5912	–

	Home	Away	Total
League Attendances	808,573	577,263	1,385,836

Liverpool
Player by Player

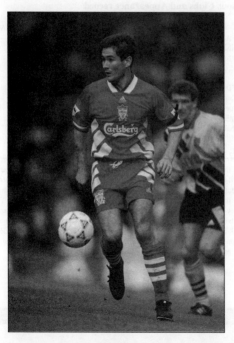

Bruce Grobbelaar

Date of Birth: 16th October 1957, Durban, South Africa

Signed: March 1981   Fee: £250,000
Liverpool Debut: Wolverhampton Wanderers (Molyneux), August 29th 1981
First Liverpool Goal: None

International Details – Zimbabwe

1993 Apperances: 15
Goals: –

Previous Clubs and Appearance record

| Club | Signed | Fee | Appearances | | | | Goals | | | |
			Lge	FLC	FAC	Oth	Lge	FLC	FAC	Oth
Crewe Alexandra	1979	–	24	–	–	–	–	–	–	–
Vancouver (Canada)	5/80									
Stoke City	3/93	loan	4	–	–	–	–	–	–	–
Liverpool	3/81	£250,000	440	70	62	7	–	–	–	–

Liverpool Honours

FA Cup Winner: 1986, 1989, 1992
League Championship: 1981/82, 1982/83. 1983/84, 1985/86, 1987/88, 1989/90
European Cup: 1984
Football League Cup :   1981, 1982, 1983, 1984

Ooh, aah, Grobbelaar

One of the most popular Anfield characters in recent years, Bruce Grobbelaar had the hard task of taking over the goalkeeping responsibilities from Ray Clemence. His reputation for clowning and the occasional condemnation for being erratic tend to hide the fact that he has been one of the most gifted keepers in the game. You certainly don't win the trophies he has amassed through sporadic play. In a season when the Liverpool defence has been plagued with uncertainty Grobbelaar was a bedrock and kept the team in games where lesser talents would have failed. His final appearance was against Leeds United when he had to withdraw through hamstring trouble. The first player ever to walk on his hands at Wembley.

Estimated value: £1,600,000

Rob Jones

Date of Birth: 5th November 1971, Wrexham

Signed: December 1988   Fee: £300,000
Liverpool Debut: v Manchester United (Old Trafford), 6th October 1991
First Liverpool Goal: none

International Details – England
Debut: 1992 v France
Played: 4

Previous Clubs and Appearance record

Club	Signed	Fee	Appearances				Goals			
			Lge	FLC	FAC	Oth	Lge	FLC	FAC	Oth
Crewe Alexandra	12/88	–	69/16	9	0/3	–	2	–	–	–
Liverpool	10/91	£300,000	97	7/1	13	4/1	–	–	–	–

Liverpool Honours
FA Cup Winner: 1992

Rob Jones

A skilled defender signed in 1991 from Crewe Alexandra. He has been on the
fringes of England selection for two years but has suffered from unavailability
through injury. Has been first choice for Terry Venables in his first games in charge
of the national squad. The 93-94 season saw him as an automatic choice for full-
back for both Graeme Souness and Roy Evans.
Not surprisingly goals are something of a rarity but he has combined well with
Steve McManaman to launch many an attack on the right hand flank.

Estimated value: £1,800,000

Julian Dicks

Date of Birth: 8th August 1968, Bristol

Signed: September 1993   Fee: swap estimated at £1,600,000
Liverpool Debut: v Everton (a) 18/09/93
First Liverpool Goal: v Oldham Athletic (a) 15/1/94

International Details – none

Previous Clubs and Appearance record

| Club | Signed | Fee | Appearances | | | | Goals | | | |
			Lge	FLC	FAC	Oth	Lge	FLC	FAC	Oth
Birmingham City	4/86	–	83/6	5/1	5	–	1	–	–	–
West Ham United	3/88	£300,000	159	19	14	–	29	5	–	–
Liverpool	9/93	£1.6m	24/3	3	1	–	3	–	–	–

Liverpool Honours

Julian Dicks

Julian Dicks was signed from West Ham United in September 93 in an effort by manager Graeme Souness to shore up an uncertain Liverpool defence. There was technically no transfer fee but Dicks was bought in an exchange deal for David Burrows and Mike Marsh. The estimated value of the deal was £1,600,000. Sadly Dicks' addition to the Liverpool squad has not wrought the transformation that was sought as the Reds have continued to leak goals at an alarming rate. Dicks had a comparatively good strike rate for West Ham but has so far only scored three goals for Liverpool – two of which have been penalties.

Estimated value: £1,800,000

Mark Wright

Date of Birth: 1st August 1961, Dorchester on Thames

Signed: July 1991   Fee: £2,200,000
Liverpool Debut: v Oldham Athletic (Anfield) D1, 17/8/91
First Liverpool Goal: v Southampton (Anfield) PL, 7/9/92

International Details – England

Debut: 1984 v Wales
Played: 40/3

Previous Clubs and Appearance record

Club	Signed	Fee	Appearances				Goals			
			Lge	FLC	FAC	Oth	Lge	FLC	FAC	Oth
Oxford United	8/80	–	–	1	–	–	–	–	–	–
Southampton	3/82	£80,000	170	25	17	–	7	2	1	–
Derby County	8/87	£760,000	144	12	6	–	10	–	–	–
Liverpool	7/91	£2.2m	84/4	3/2	14	7	3	1	–	1

Liverpool Honours

FA Cup Winners: 1992

Mark Wright

One of the star players from England's successes in the World Cup in Italy in 1990.
Mark Wright was signed from Derby County for £2,200,000 for the start of the
91/92 by Graeme Souness but has so far failed to produce the very best
performances of which he is capable.

He scored a face-saving goal for Liverpool to earn them a home draw against
bottom placed Swindon Town which made up for his own goal howler against
Sheffield Wednesday a week earlier. Made 36 appearances in all competitions for
the Reds in the 1993-94 season.

Estimated value: £1,200,000

Don Hutchison

Date of Birth: 9th May 1971, Gateshead

Signed: December 1990   Fee: £175,000
Liverpool Debut: v Notts County (h) D1 31/3/92
First Liverpool Goal: v Chesterfield (h) LC 22/9/92

International Details – none

Previous Clubs and Appearance record

Club	Signed	Fee	Appearances Lge	FLC	FAC	Oth	Goals Lge	FLC	FAC	Oth
Hartlepool United	3/90	–	19/5	1/1	2	–	3	–	–	–
Liverpool	12/90	£175,000	33/12	7/1	1/2	3	7	2	–	1

Liverpool Honours

Don Hutchinson

Don Hutchinson made almost as many appearances for Liverpool during the 1993-94 season as a substitute as he made starts. He made 8 starts in all and 7 appearances as sub. Not the way that the possessor of the number 6 shirt would want the season to have progressed. However, some solid performances towards the end of the 1993-94 season meant a brighter finish to the season than most.

Estimated value: £600,000

Nigel Clough

Date of Birth: March 19th 1966, Sunderland

Signed: August 1993   Fee: £2,275,000
Liverpool Debut: v Sheffield Wednesday (h), 14/8/93
First Liverpool Goal: v Sheffield Wednesday (h), 14/8/93

International Details – England

Debut: 1989 v Chile
Played: 10/4

Previous Clubs and Appearance record

			Appearances				Goals			
Club	Signed	Fee	Lge	FLC	FAC	Oth	Lge	FLC	FAC	Oth
Nottingham Forest	9/84	–	265/4	41	24	–	91	25	5	–
Liverpool	8/93	£2.275m	24/1	2	2	–	7	1	–	–

Liverpool Honours

We've all been making plans for Nigel

Son of that most famous of managers, Brian Clough, the one-time Nottingham
Forest 'number 9' is another Liverpool player looking to establish himself at the top
of the game. Picked by Graham Taylor on several occasions he has yet to make
himself an automatic choice for either an England or Liverpool shirt. His form at
Anfield has been patchy with injury not exactly helping but his goalscoring touch
has not failed him when most needed – he was the inspiration behind the fine
Liverpool fightback against Manchester United at Anfield when he bagged a brace
of goals. He also scored twice on his debut but it has been made clear that he will
have to fight for his place in the team.

Estimated value: £1,900,000

Paul Stewart

Date of Birth: October 10th 1964, Manchester

Signed: Fee: £1,700,00
Liverpool Debut: v Nottingham Forest (a) PL, 16/8/92
First Liverpool Goal: v Sheffield United (h) PL, 19/8/92

International Details – England

Debut: 1992 v Germany
Played: 0/3

Previous Clubs and Appearance record

Club	Signed	Fee	Appearances Lge	FLC	FAC	Oth	Goals Lge	FLC	FAC	Oth
Blackpool	10/81	–	188/3	11	7	–	56	3	2	–
Manchester City	3/87	£200,000	51	6	4	–	27	2	1	–
Tottenham Hotspur	6/88	£1.7m	126/23	–	9	–	28	7	2	–
Liverpool	–	–	28/4	6	1	2	1	–	–	2

Liverpool Honours

Paul Stewart

Paul Stewart has had a thin time at Anfield. Relations between him and Graeme Souness were reported to be difficult and he was the source of much criticism from the fans. Much was expected of him after his £1.9 million move from Tottenham but somehow it didn't quite work out.

In the latter part of the 93-94 season he played on loan at Crystal Palace where he fitted into the squad beautifully and was an instrumental in helping the London side win the Endsleigh League First Division championship and regain their place in the Premiership.

Expect to see him playing in the Premiership in 94/95 – just don't expect him to be wearing a Liverpool shirt. Paul was England substitute on three occasions.

Estimated value: £1,200,000

126

Ian Rush

Date of Birth: October 20th 1961, St Asaph

Signed: April 1981, August 1988   Fee: £300,000, £2,200,000
Liverpool Debut: v Stoke City (h) D1, 3/4/81
First Liverpool Goal: v Oulu Palloseura (h) EC, 30/9/81

International Details – Wales

Debut: 1980 v Scotland
Played: 57/3

Previous Clubs and Appearance record

| Club | Signed | Fee | Appearances | | | | Goals | | | |
			Lge	FLC	FAC	Oth	Lge	FLC	FAC	Oth
Chester City	7/79	–	33/1	–	5	–	14	–	3	–
Liverpool	4/81	£300,000								
Juventus	6/87	£3.8m								
Liverpool	8/88	£2.2m	401/11	69	48/2	33/1	211	41	36	21

Liverpool Honours

FA Cup Winner: 1986, 1989, 1992
League Championship: 1981-82, 1982-83, 1983-84, 1985-86, 1989-90
European Cup: 1984
Football League Cup: 1981, 1982, 1983, 1984

More records than John Peel

Liverpool's all-time highest goalgetter. He has scored from just about every
position possible but his speciality has always been the unspectacular tap-in goal
from only a few yards out. This uncanny knack of being in exactly the right place at
the right time has seen him score over 200 league goals for the Reds and set
numerous records on the way. Superb in situations when *"there's only the keeper to
beat"* he scored 48 goals in all competitions in the 83-84 season making defences'
lives a misery wherever he went. He is Liverpool's all-time top scorer, the Welsh
all-time top scorer, the top scorer in the FA Cup, the top scorer in Merseyside
derbies and top scorer in the league in several seasons.

Estimated value: £2,100,00

John Barnes

Date of Birth: 7th November 1963, Jamaica

Signed: June 1987   Fee: £900,000
Liverpool Debut: v Arsenal (a) D1, 15/8/87
First Liverpool Goal: v Oxford United (h) D1, 12/9/87

International Details – England

Debut:	1983 v Northern Ireland
Played:	60/13

Previous Clubs and Appearance record

			Appearances				Goals			
Club	Signed	Fee	Lge	FLC	FAC	Oth	Lge	FLC	FAC	Oth
Watford	7/81	–	232/1	21	31	–	65	7	11	–
Liverpool	6/87	£900,000	202/3	14	36	1	70	3	14	–

Liverpool Honours

FA Cup Winner:	1989
League Championship:	1987-88, 1989-90

"There's only one way to beat them – get round the back..."

One of the most gifted players of his generation, John Barnes has turned so many
games for Liverpool that his supposed comparative lack of success in an England
shirt has been the cause of some disappointment, not least for the man himself. Yet
he will be best remembered for a blazing solo goal scored for England against
Brazil and several other spectacular strikes from set pieces.

His skill on the ball and unruffled ease in possession gives his team mates time to
regroup and is often used as a springboard from which to launch an attack. An
absolute pain to mark for any defender as his acceleration, strength and ability to
turn with the ball is second to none. The only doubts concern his fitness and
whether he still has the necessary speed. Has also 'scored' a number one in the pop
charts with England/New Order's 1990 Italia World Cup song "World in Motion..."

Estimated value: £1,800,000

Mark Walters

Date of Birth: June 2nd 1964, Birmingham

Signed: August 1991   Fee: £1,250,000
Liverpool Debut: v Oldham Athletic (h) D1, 17/8/91
First Liverpool Goal: v Notts County (a) D1, 7/9/91

International Details – England

Debut: 1991 v New Zealand
Played: 1

Previous Clubs and Appearance record

Club	Signed	Fee	Appearances				Goals			
			Lge	FLC	FAC	Oth	Lge	FLC	FAC	Oth
Aston Villa	5/82		168/13	21/2	11/1	–	39	6	1	–
Rangers	12/87	£500,000	106				32			
Liverpool	8/91	£1.25m	51/25	9/2	4/1	7/1	14	4	–	1

Liverpool Honours

Mark Walters

Mark Walters was one of Graeme Souness's signings being bought from Rangers – where Souness had previously been manager – for £1.25 million. 1993-94 was a frustrating season for the one-time England international. He has been continually on the fringe of the Liverpool squad but without ever getting a full crack at the job. In all he managed 8 appearances and a further 12 as substitute. Most worryingly of all he failed to find the net.

Estimated value: £1,400,000

David James

Date of Birth: August 1st 1970, Welwyn Garden City

Signed: June 1992   Fee: £1,000,000
Liverpool Debute: v Nottingham Forest (a) PL, 16/8/92
First Liverpool Goal: none

International Details – none

Previous Clubs and Appearance record

Club	Signed	Fee	Appearances				Goals			
			Lge	FLC	FAC	Oth	Lge	FLC	FAC	Oth
Watford	7/88	–	89	6	2	–	–	–	–	–
Liverpool	6/92	£1m	42/1	1	–	1	–	–	–	–

Liverpool Honours

David James

David James was signed from Watford at the start of the 92-93 season for
£1,000,000 and played 30 games for Liverpool in his first season. However, some
inconsistencies meant he failed to make himself the automatic choice between the
sticks as goalkeeping responsibilities were shared with Bruce Grobbelaar and Mike
Hooper. Lost the Number 1 shirt to Grobbelaar for the start of the 93-94 season and
was an ever-present on the substitutes bench until Grobbelaar's injury after which
he showed considerable flair in the remaining games when Grobbelaar has stayed
on the bench. He has always looked vulnerable to high crosses into the box
sometimes appearing uncertain as to whether to come out or stay back. The main
problem seems to be one of confidence not ability and it is hoped that he can find
his feet at this higher level. His strongest assets are the stunning reflex saves he has
made which, with his height, can make him very difficult to beat.

Estimated value: £1,300,000

Ronnie Whelan

Date of Birth: September 25th 1961, Dublin

Signed: October 1979   Fee: £ -
Liverpool Debut: v Stoke City (h) D1, 3/4/81
First Liverpool Goal: v Stoke City (h) D1, 3/4/81

International Details – Republic of Ireland

Debut: 1981 v Czechoslovakia
Played: 38/11

Previous Clubs and Appearance record

Club	Signed	Fee	Appearances				Goals			
			Lge	FLC	FAC	Oth	Lge	FLC	FAC	Oth
Liverpool	10/79	–	351/12	47/4	40/1	22/1	45	14	7	6

Liverpool Honours

FA Cup Winner: 1986, 1989
League Championship: 1981-82, 1982-83, 1983-84, 1985-86, 1987-88, 1989-90
European Cup: 1984
Football League Cup: 1982, 1983, 1984

Mr Trophy Cabinet

Son of another Republic of Ireland international, Ronnie Whelan has been a
Liverpool regular for a decade and a half. His strength in midfield has made him a
key component in many successful Liverpool sides but he also gets involved in the
goal scoring.

His strength with his left foot and in the air has helped add an extra dimension to
the overall strength of the side and presented further options in attack. 23 Liverpool
appearances in total during the 1993-94 season and just the one goal – during the
thumping of Swindon Town at the start of the season.

His Republic of Ireland apperances shown above do not include any made during
the 1994 World Cup.

Estimated value: £600,000

Jan Molby

Date of Birth: 7th July 1963, Jutland Denmark

Signed: August 84   Fee: £575,000
Liverpool Debut: v Norwich City (a) D1, 25/8/84
First Liverpool Goal: v Chelsea (a) D1, 1/12/84

International Details – Denmark
Played: 25 games while with Liverpool starting in 1984 v Austria

Previous Clubs and Appearance record

Club	Signed	Fee	Appearances				Goals			
			Lge	FLC	FAC	Oth	Lge	FLC	FAC	Oth
Ajax, Netherlands										
Liverpool	8/84	£575,000	183/21	22	3	25/4	7	42	10	4	1

Liverpool Honours
FA Cup Winner: 1986, 1992
League Championship: 1989-90

Multi-purpose Molby mixes roles

An intelligent gifted player who has been able to adapt to a variety of roles. His is
the sort of skill which provokes descriptions along the lines of *thoughtful*, *refined* or
cultured and which has made him a favourite with the fans.

He has a great ability to read a game and is expert at creating openings with a well
weighted pass. He is not afraid to follow up after an attacking move and has scored
many goals for Liverpool and has proved to be a deadly marksman from the penalty
spot.

His 93-94 season was blighted by injury and fitness problems leaving him with just
13 Liverpool appearances in all competitions.

Estimated value: £1,400,000

Jamie Redknapp

Date of Birth: 25th June 1973, Barton-on-Sea

Signed: June 1990   Fee: £350,000
Liverpool Debut: v Southampton (a) 7/12/91
First Liverpool Goal: v Southampton (a) 7/12/91

International Details – none

Previous Clubs and Appearance record

Club	Signed	Fee	Appearances				Goals			
			Lge	FLC	FAC	Oth	Lge	FLC	FAC	Oth
Bournemouth	6/90	–	6/7	3	3	–	–	–	–	–
Liverpool	1/91	£350,000	61/9	10	5	5/1	7	1	–	–

Liverpool Honours

Jamie and his magic touch

For all its trials and tribulations 1993-94 was the season that Jamie Redknapp established himself as an automatic choice for a red shirt. He played 35 games in all competitions and a further 6 as substitute. His goals tally was just four and in a better season he will be looking to get into goalscoring positions more often.

Estimated value: £2,100,000

Jamie Redknapp in typical hair-raising action.

Michael Thomas

Date of Birth: 24th August 1967, Lambeth

Signed: December 1991   Fee: £1,500,000
Liverpool Debut: v Tottenham Hotspurs (a) 18/12/91
First Liverpool Goal: v Oldham Athletic (a) 18/1/92

International Details – England

Debut: 1989 v Saudi Arabia
Played: 3

Previous Clubs and Appearance record

Club	Signed	Fee	Appearances				Goals			
			Lge	FLC	FAC	Oth	Lge	FLC	FAC	Oth
Arsenal	12/84	–	149/1	42	2/2	14/3	–	24	5	–	–
Portsmouth	12/86	loan	3	–	–	–	–	–	–	–
Liverpool	12/91	£1.5m	23/9	1	7	1	4	–	2	–

Liverpool Honours

FA Cup Winner: 1992

Taking the Michael

Whatever he succeeds at Anfield it is unlikely that Michael Thomas will ever score
a more important goal than the one he scored there at the end of the 88/89 season to
clinch the title – for Arsenal. The Gunners came to Anfield needing to win the
game by two goals to win the championship and Michael Thomas's strike in the
dieing minutes of the game ensured that they did just that. Unfortunately Michael
Thomas has been a long term absentee from the Liverpool team through injury and
has struggled to command a place to justify his £1,500,000 transfer.
He managed one appearance in the 1993-94 season – against Manchester United –
and no less than six as substitute.

Estimated value: £800,000

Steve McManaman

Date of Birth: 11th February 1972, Bootle

Signed: February 1990   Fee: £ -
Liverpool Debut: v Sheffield United (h) 15/12/90
First Liverpool Goal: v Manchester City (a) 21/8/91

International Details – none

Previous Clubs and Appearance record

Club	Signed	Fee	Appearances				Goals			
			Lge	FLC	FAC	Oth	Lge	FLC	FAC	Oth
Liverpool	2/90	–	82/11	11	1/1	11	11	5	3	1

Liverpool Honours

FA Cup Winner: 1992

The main man McManaman

The 1993/94 season may well have been the one when Steve McManaman finally came of age. As his confidence has grown he has helped destroy many Premiership defences with searing runs down the right wing. He has built up a strong rapport with Rob Jones and the combination has to be fancied for use in a future England line-up. Despite such attacking play and 32 games for Liverpool this season he only managed two goals both of them in the 5-0 defeat of Swindon right at the start of the season. Since then he has peppered the opposition woodwork on many occasions and torn defences asunder but without getting another goal. They'll come.

Ronny Rosenthal

Date of Birth: 4th October 1963, Haifa, Israel

Signed: March 1990   Fee: £1,000,000
Liverpool Debut: v Southampton (h) D1, 31/3/90
First Liverpool Goal: v Charlton Athletic, 3 (a) D1, 11/4/90

International Details – Israel

Ronny Rosenthal made 7 appearances for Israel in the 1993-94 season.

Previous Clubs and Appearance record

Club	Signed	Fee	Appearances Lge	FLC	FAC	Oth	Goals Lge	FLC	FAC	Oth
Liverpool	3/90	£1m	32/40	2/7	5/2	1/4	21	1	–	–

Liverpool Honours

"Rosie" by any other name

Ronny Rosenthal managed a grand total of 3 appearances during the 1993-94 season before being sold to Tottenham Hotspur for £250,000. He helped Spurs avoid relgation but the highlight of his season must have been a World Cup group match which saw Israel defeat France thus setting up the French for one of the major shocks of the qualifying rounds.

Torben Piechnik

Date of Birth: 21st May 1963, Copenhagen

Signed: September 1992   Fee: £500,000
Liverpool Debut: v Aston Villa (a) 19/9/92
First Liverpool Goal: none

International Details – Denmark

Previous Clubs and Appearance record

Club	Signed	Fee	Lge	FLC	FAC	Oth	Lge	FLC	FAC	Oth
			Appearances				Goals			
Liverpool	9/92	£0.5m	16/1	5	2	–	–	–	–	–

Liverpool Honours

Torben, or not Torben, that is the question

Just one appearance for Torben Piechnik during the 1993-94 season and even then
it wasn't the happiest of experiences. He played in the first half of Liverpool's away
defeat by Newcastle United, a period which saw the Reds concede three goals.
Torben was substituted at half-time and has only been seen once since then – as a
non-playing substitute in the game away to Norwich City in February.

Stig Bjornebye

Date of Birth: 11th December 1969, Elvcrum, Norway

Signed: December 1992   Fee: £600,000
Liverpool Debut: v Coventry City (a) 19/12/92
First Liverpool Goal: none

International Details – Norway

Stig Bjornebye made nine appearances for Norway during the 1993-94 season.

Previous Clubs and Appearance record

Club	Signed	Fee	Appearances				Goals			
			Lge	FLC	FAC	Oth	Lge	FLC	FAC	Oth
Rosenborg, Norway										
Liverpool	12/92	£0.6m	17/3	–	2/1	–	–	–	–	–

Liverpool Honours

Bonjour Bjornebye

The Norwegian international has been in and out of the Liverpool side since his £600,000 signing from Rosenborg in the middle of the 1992-93 season. He has not made any appearances since Roy Evans took over.
His successes have been mainly in a Norwegian shirt. The statistics above do not include any appearances for the 1994 World Cup.

Mike Marsh

Date of Birth: 21st July 1967, Liverpool

Signed: August 1987   Fee: £ -
Liverpool Debut: v Charlton Athletic (h) 1/3/89
First Liverpool Goal: v Sheffield United (h) 11/11/92

International Details – none

Previous Clubs and Appearance record

Club	Signed	Fee	Appearances				Goals			
			Lge	FLC	FAC	Oth	Lge	FLC	FAC	Oth
Liverpool	8/87	–	42/27	10/1	6/2	11/1	2	3	–	1

Liverpool Honours

League Championship: 1989-90

There's no bogging down Mike Marsh

Mike Marsh was one of three Liverpool players involved in a swap with West Ham United near the start of the 1993-94 season. Basically Mike Marsh + David Burrows = Julian Dicks = £1,600,000 (you can take your pick over the relative values of Marsh and Burrows). In terms of strike record for the Reds' season Mike Marsh has to be at the top with one goal from about 40 minutes of play.

Estimated value: see above

Dominic Matteo

Date of Birth: 28th April 1971, Dumfries

Signed: Fee: £ -
Liverpool Debut: v Manchester City (a) 23/10/93
First Liverpool Goal: none

International Details – none

Previous Clubs and Appearance record

Club	Signed	Fee	Appearances				Goals			
			Lge	FLC	FAC	Oth	Lge	FLC	FAC	Oth
Liverpool		–	9	2	–	–	–	–	–	–

Liverpool Honours

Dominic Matteo

1993-94 was the debut season for Dominic Matteo who was brought into the side by Graeme Souness. He is still searching for a first goal and tried claiming one in the 2-0 victory over West Ham United in November. The goal was eventually deemed to be an own goal having taken too much of a deflection to be credited to the Liverpool midfielder.

Estimated value: £600,000

Steve Harkness

Date of Birth: 27th August 1971, Carlisle

Signed: July 1989   Fee: £75,000
Liverpool Debut: v Queens Park Rangers (h) 27/8/91
First Liverpool Goal: v Tottenham Hotspur (h) 8/5/93

International Details – none

Previous Clubs and Appearance record

Club	Signed	Fee	Appearances				Goals			
			Lge	FLC	FAC	Oth	Lge	FLC	FAC	Oth
Carlisle United	3/89	–	12/1	–	–	–	–	–	–	–
Liverpool	8/89	£75,000	27/5	3/2	2	3/2	1	–	–	–

Liverpool Honours

Harken to Harkness

Steve Harkness played the rather unfortunate role in the 1993-94 season as the spare defender, stepping into the side when others were out of the team due to injury or suspension. He spent some of the early part of the season on loan at Huddersfield Town. However he did feature in the Liverpool squads for the last three games of the season and there are signs that with increased maturity we may be seeing more of him in the future.

Robbie Fowler

Date of Birth: 9th April 1975, Liverpool

Signed: Fee: £
Liverpool Debut: v Fulham (a) LC, 22/09/93
First Liverpool Goal: v Fulham (a) LC, 22/09/93

International Details – none

Previous Clubs and Appearance record

			Appearances				Goals			
Club	Signed	Fee	Lge	FLC	FAC	Oth	Lge	FLC	FAC	Oth
Liverpool	–	–	27/1	5	1	–	11	6	–	–

Liverpool Honours

Fowler ingredients sparkle of the real thing

Robbie Fowler made about as much impact that a new player can possibly dream of. He scored on his debut which was against Fulham in the second round of the Coca-Cola Cup in the Autumn of 93 and then followed it up by bagging all five in the return leg.

A member of England's successful under-18 squad and given a place in the under-21 team it can only be a matter of time before he claims a place in the full international squad.

He possesses all the right ingredients to make a truly great striker and can only benefit from being in the same team as Ian Rush. He shares many of the same talents such as the ability to be in the right place at the right time and being able to keep a cool head under pressure.

Estimated value: £3,200,000

Neil Ruddock

Date of Birth: 9th May 1968, Wandsworth

Signed: July 1993   Fee: £2,500,000
Liverpool Debut: v Sheffield Wed (h) PL, 14/08/93
First Liverpool Goal: v Swindon Town (a) PL, 22/08/93

International Details – none

Previous Clubs and Appearance record

Club	Signed	Fee	Appearances				Goals			
			Lge	FLC	FAC	Oth	Lge	FLC	FAC	Oth
Millwall	3/86	–	–	–	–	–	–	–	–	–
Tottenham	4/86	£50,000	7/2	–	1/1	–	–	–	–	–
Millwall	6/88	£0.3m	0/2	2	–	–	1	3	–	–
Southampton	2/89	£0.25m	100/7	14/1	10	–	9	1	3	–
Tottenham	5/92	£0.75m	38	4	5	–	3	–	–	–
Liverpool	7/93	£2.5m	39	5	2	–	3	1	–	–

Liverpool Honours

Hard times with "Razor" Ruddock

At the time a controversial signing from beleaguered Tottenham Hotspur Neil "Razor" Ruddock was an automatic choice in the Liverpool defence during the 1993-94 season. Always popular with opposing supporters for his smooth-tackling style, he likes to make the occasional foray forward and has scored several important goals. No international appearances yet although he has been tipped several times.

Estimated value: £2,100,000

Steve Nicol

Date of Birth: 1st December 1961, Irvine

Signed: October 1981   Fee: £300,000
Liverpool Debut: v Birmingham City (a) D1, 31/8/82
First Liverpool Goal: v Queens Park Rangers (a)D1, 22/10/83

International Details – Scotland

Debut: v Yugoslavia (1985)
Played: 27

Previous Clubs and Appearance record

			Appearances				Goals			
Club	Signed	Fee	Lge	FLC	FAC	Oth	Lge	FLC	FAC	Oth
Ayr United	1979	–	70				7			
Liverpool	–	£0.3m	317/13	41	51	17/2	37	4	3	2

Liverpool Honours

FA Cup Winner: 1986, 1989, 1992
League Championship: 1983-84, 1985-86, 1987-88,1989-90

Coming to the end of the road?

Are we coming to the end of an Anfield era with Steve Nicol? He has been with the club since 1981and has seen the Reds amass a number of trophies in that time. Now at 32 there have been suggestions that time is running out for the former Scottish international. But, with so many players stretching their careers into the mid-30s why not Nicol? His experience and reliability could prove invaluable if the Reds are to experiment with new sides in the times ahead.

Estimated value: £800,000

David Burrows

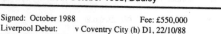

Date of Birth: 25th October 1968, Dudley

Signed: October 1988   Fee: £550,000
Liverpool Debut: v Coventry City (h) D1, 22/10/88
First Liverpool Goal: v Everton (h) D1, 31/8/91

International Details – none

Previous Clubs and Appearance record

Club	Signed	Fee	Appearances				Goals			
			Lge	FLC	FAC	Oth	Lge	FLC	FAC	Oth
West Bromwich Albion	10/86	–	37/9	3/2	2	–	1	–	–	–
Liverpool	10/88	£550,000	135/11	16	16/1	11	3	–	–	–

Liverpool Honours

FA Cup Winner: 1992
League Championship: 1989-90

Digging deep for Burrows

David Burrows formed half of the exchange deal at the start of the 1993-94 season when he and Mike Marsh went to West Ham United and Julian Dicks came to Anfield. The deal was worth an estimated £1,600,000.

Estimated value: see above

Season's Records 1993/94

HOME GAMES

44,601	v	Newcastle United	0-2	16/04/94
44,339	v	Norwich City	0-1	30/04/94
44,281	v	Everton	2-1	13/03/94
44,068	v	Leeds United	2-0	28/08/93
44,004	v	Sheffield Wednesday	2-0	14/04/93
42,795	v	Manchester United	3-3	04/01/94
42,750	v	Arsenal	0-0	02/10/93
42,456	v	Tottenham Hotspur	1-2	25/08/93
42,254	v	West Ham United	2-0	06/11/93
41,872	v	Manchester City	2-1	22/01/94
38,629	v	Chelsea	2-1	19/03/94
38,547	v	Coventry City	1-0	26/02/94
38,484	v	Aston Villa	2-1	28/11/93
37,355	v	Blackburn Rovers	0-1	12/09/93
36,642	v	Sheffield United	1-2	02/04/94
32,818	v	Southampton	4-2	30/10/93
32,739	v	Swindon Town	2-2	12/12/93
32,661	v	Oldham Athletic	2-1	17/10/93
32,232	v	Wimbledon	1-1	28/12/93
30,485	v	Ipswich Town	1-0	09/04/94
24,561	v	Queens Park Rangers	3-2	07/12/93

808,573	*Total*
38,503	*Average*

AWAY GAMES

45,347	v	Aston Villa	1-2	07/05/94
44,751	v	Manchester United	0-1	29/03/94
40,053	v	Leeds United	0-2	19/02/94
38,157	v	Everton	0-2	18/09/93
36,374	v	Newcastle United	0-3	20/11/93
35,556	v	Arsenal	0-1	26/03/94
32,177	v	Sheffield Wednesday	1-3	04/12/93
31,394	v	Tottenham Hotspur	3-3	18/12/93
31,271	v	Chelsea	0-1	25/09/93
30,403	v	Manchester City	1-1	23/10/93
26,096	v	West Ham United	2-1	23/04/94
22,932	v	Sheffield United	0-0	26/12/93

22,355	v	Ipswich Town	2-1	02/01/94
20,831	v	Blackburn Rovers	0-2	05/03/94
19,746	v	Norwich City	2-2	05/02/94
19,365	v	Queens Park Rangers	3-1	19/08/93
18,306	v	Southampton	2-4	14/02/94
17,017	v	Swindon Town	5-0	22/08/93
16,740	v	Coventry City	0-1	01/09/93
14,573	v	Oldham Athletic	3-0	15/01/94
13,819	v	Wimbledon	1-1	04/04/94

| 577,263 | *Total* |
| 27,489 | *Average* |

ALL PREMIERSHIP
| 1,385,836 | Total |
| 32,996 | Average |

1993/94 Attendances – *FA Cup*

HOME
| 36,720 | v | Bristol City | 0-1 | 25/01/94 |

AWAY
| 21,718 | v | Bristol City | 1-1 | 19/01/94 |

1993/94 Attendances – *Coca-Cola Cup*

HOME
19,290	v	Wimbledon	1-1	01/12/93
19,058	v	Ipswich Town	3-2	27/10/93
12,541	v	Fulham	5-0	06/10/93

AWAY
| 13,599 | v | Fulham | 3-1 | 23/09/93 |
| 11,343 | v | Wimbledon | 2-2 | 14/12/93 |

Total Attendances

1,520,105 from 49 matches at an average of 31,022 per game

Bookings and Dismissals 93-94

19th August	v	Queens Park Rangers	A	Stig Bjornebye	
22nd August	v	Swindon Town	A	Rob Jones	
28th August	v	Leeds United	H	David Burrows	
1st September	v	Coventry City	A	Rob Jones	‡
				Neil Ruddock	
				Ronnie Whelan	
12th September	v	Blackburn Rovers	H	Rob Jones	
18th September	v	Everton	A	Ronnie Whelan	
				Jamie Redknapp	
				Nigel Clough	
25th September	v	Chelsea	A	Neil Ruddock	
				Paul Stewart	
				Jamie Redknapp	
2nd October	v	Arsenal	H	Mark Wright	
				Paul Stewart	
17th October	v	Oldham Athletic	H	Don Hutchison	
23rd October	v	Manchester City	A	Mark Walters	
27th October	v	Ipswich Town	H	Mark Wright	
6th November	v	West Ham United	H	Mark Wright	
				Ian Rush	
20th November	v	Newcastle United	A	Steve Nicol	
28th November	v	Aston Villa	H	Neil Ruddock	
4th December	v	Sheffield Wednesday	A	Jan Molby	
7th December	v	Queens Park Rangers	H	Neil Ruddock	
18th December	v	Tottenham Hotspur	A	Steve Harkness	
4th January	v	Manchester United	H	Nigel Clough	
19th January	v	Bristol City	A	Rob Jones	
				Steve McManaman	
				Neil Ruddock	
22nd January	v	Manchester City	H	Neil Ruddock	
25th January	v	Bristol City	H	Bruce Grobbelaar	
19th February	v	Leeds United	A	Jamie Redknapp	
26th February	v	Coventry City	H	Neil Ruddock	
5th March	v	Blackburn Rovers	A	Ronnie Whelan	
13th March	v	Everton	H	Julian Dicks	
29th March	v	Manchester United	A	Ian Rush	

‡ – Sent off

Sendings off by Number

1	Rob Jones

Bookings by Number

7	Neil Ruddock
4	Rob Jones
3	Jamie Redknapp, Ronnie Whelan, Mark Wright
2	Nigel Clough, Ian Rush, Paul Stewart
1	Stig Bjornebye, David Burrows, Julian Dicks, Bruce Grobbelaar, Steve Harkness, Don Hutchison, Steve McManaman, Jan Molby, Steve Nicol, Mark Walters

Transfers

Player	From	To	Fee
Neil Ruddock	Tottenham	Liverpool	£2,500,000
Nigel Clough	Nottingham Forest	Liverpool	£2,275,000
Istvan Kozma	Liverpool	Ujpesti Te	free
Julian Dicks	West Ham	Liverpool	£1,600,000
Mike Hooper	Liverpool	Newcastle United	£550,000
Mike Marsh	Liverpool	West Ham United	swap
David Burrows	Liverpool	West Ham United	swap
Agent Sawu	Zimbabwe	Liverpool	trial
Ronny Rosenthal	Liverpool	Tottenham Hotspur	£250,000

Loans

Player	From	To
Steve Harkness	Liverpool	Huddersfield Town
Phil Jones	Liverpool	Crewe Alexandra
Paul Stewart	Liverpool	Crystal Palace
Mark Walters	Liverpool	Stoke City

1993/94 Goalscorers

Scorer	Prem	FA Cup	Lge Cup	Total
Rush	14	1	4	19
Fowler	12	-	6	18
Clough	7	-	1	8
Redknapp	4	-	-	4
Ruddock	3	-	1	4
Barnes	3	-	-	3
Dicks	3 (2 pen)	-	-	3 (2 pen)
Molby	2 (2 pen)	-	1 (1 pen)	3 (3 pen)
McManaman	2	-	-	2
Marsh	1	-	-	1
Nicol	1	-	-	1
Whelan	1	-	-	1
Wright	1	-	-	1
Opposition	5	-	1	6
Total	59	1	14	74

1993/94 Premiership Scores by Number

HOME GAMES		AWAY GAMES		ALL GAMES	
2-1	5	0-1	4	2-1	7
2-0	3	2-1	2	0-1	6
1-0	2	1-1	2	2-0	3
0-1	2	0-2	2	0-2	3
1-2	2	3-0	1	1-1	3
3-2	1	3-1	1	1-2	3
4-2	1	5-0	1	1-0	2
0-0	1	0-0	1	0-0	2
1-1	1	2-2	1	2-2	2
2-2	1	3-3	1	3-3	2
3-3	1	1-2	1	3-0	1
0-2	1	0-3	1	3-1	1
		1-3	1	3-2	1
		2-4	1	4-2	1
				5-0	1
				0-3	1
				1-3	1
				2-4	1

Appearances – *FA Carling Premiership*

Match No.	1	2	3	4	5	6	7	8	9	10	11	12	13
Bruce Grobbelaar	•	•	•	•	•	•	•	•	•	•	•	•	•
Rob Jones	•	•	•	•	•	•	–	•	•	•	•	•	•
Stig Bjornebye	•	•	•73	–	–	–	•58	–	–	–	–	–	–
Steve Nicol	•	•	•	•	•	•	•	•	•	•	•	•	•
Mark Wright	•	•	•	•	•	•	•	•	•	•	•	•	•
Neil Ruddock	•	•	•76	•	•	•	•	•	•	•	•	•	•
Nigel Clough	•	•72	•	•	•	•	•	•	•	•	•	•	•
Jan Molby	•74	•	•	•	•	•	•	•					
Ian Rush	•	•	•	•	•	•	•80	•	•	•	•	•	•
Ronnie Whelan	•	•	•	•	•	•	•	–	–	–	S	S	–
Mark Walters	•	–	–	58	S	68	–	•52	–	–	–	–	61
Jamie Redknapp	74	72	–	–	–	–	80	•	•67	•	–	–	•
Steve McManaman	S	•	•	•	•	•	•	•64	67	66	S	S	•
Mike Hooper	S	S	S	S	S	S	S	S	–	–	–	–	–
David Burrows	–	S	73	•58	•	•68	–	–	–	–	–	–	–
Mike Marsh	–	–	76	S	64	–	–	–	–	–	–	–	–
Don Hutchison	–	–	–	–	•64	S	–	–	•	•66	•	•	•46
Ronny Rosenthal	–	–	–	–	–	–	58	52	–	–	–	–	–
Robbie Fowler	–	–	–	–	–	–	–	–	•	•	•	•	•
Torben Piechnik	–	–	–	–	–	–	–	–	S	–	–	–	–
Steve Harkness	–	–	–	–	–	–	–	–	–	–	–	–	–
Paul Stewart	–	–	–	–	–	–	–	64	•	•	•	•	•
David James	–	–	–	–	–	–	–	–	S	S	S	S	S
Julian Dicks	–	–	–	–	–	–	–	•	•	•	•	•	•61
John Barnes	–	–	–	–	–	–	–	–	–	–	–	–	–
Dominic Matteo	–	–	–	–	–	–	–	–	–	–	–	–	–
Michael Thomas	–	–	–	–	–	–	–	–	–	–	–	–	–
Mark Gayle	–	–	–	–	–	–	–	–	–	–	–	–	–
Phil Charnock	–	–	–	–	–	–	–	–	–	–	–	–	–

Key

•	Played for the full duration of the game
•73	Started game but substituted in 73rd minute
73	Came on as substitute in 73rd minute
S	Non-playing substitute
–	No appearance

Appearances – *FA Carling Premiership*

Match No.	14	15	16	17	18	19	20	21	22	23	24	25	26
Bruce Grobbelaar	•	•	•	•	•	•	•	•	•	•	•	•	•
Rob Jones	•	•	•	•18	–	–	–	•	•	•	•	•	•
Stig Bjornebye	•	–	•46	–	–	–	–	–	–	–	–	–	–
Steve Nicol	•	•	•	•86	•	•	–	•77	72	78	•	•	•
Mark Wright	•	•	•	•	•	•	•	•	•	•	•	•	•
Neil Ruddock	•	•	•	•	•	•	•	•	•	•	–	•	•
Nigel Clough	–	S	S	•	•	S	S	•	S	–	–	46	•
Jan Molby	–	–	–	–	–	•80	•	•	•	•	•34	–	–
Ian Rush	•	•	•	•	•	•	•	S	•	•	•	•	•82
Ronnie Whelan	–	–	–	–	–	–	–	–	–	–	–	–	–
Mark Walters	•52	–	–	–	S	80	77	77	–	S	34	83	82
Jamie Redknapp	52	–	–	18	•	•	•	•	•	•	•	•	•
Steve McManaman	–	–	–	–	–	–	–	•	•	•	•	•	•
Mike Hooper	–	–	–	–	–	–	–	–	–	–	–	–	–
David Burrows	–	–	–	–	–	–	–	–	–	–	–	–	–
Mike Marsh	–	–	–	–	–	–	–	–	–	–	–	–	–
Don Hutchison	71	72	–	–	–	–	–	–	–	–	–	–	–
Ronny Rosenthal	–	–	46	–	–	–	–	–	–	–	–	–	–
Robbie Fowler	•	•	•	•	•	•	•	•	•	•	•	•	•
Torben Piechnik	–	–	–	–	•46	–	–	–	–	–	–	–	–
Steve Harkness	–	•72	•	•	•	•	•	•	•	•78	25	•	–
Paul Stewart	•71	•	•	•	•	–	–	–	–	–	–	–	–
David James	S	S	S	S	S	S	S	S	S	S	S	S	S
Julian Dicks	–	•	–	–	–	–	–	–	–	–	–	–	•
John Barnes	–	–	–	–	46	•	•77	•	•72	•	•	•46	–
Dominic Matteo	•	•	•	•	•	•	•	•	–	–	–	–	S
Michael Thomas	–	–	–	–	–	–	–	–	–	–	–	–	–
Mark Gayle	–	–	–	–	–	–	–	–	–	–	–	–	–
Phil Charnock	–	–	–	–	–	–	–	–	–	–	–	–	–

Key

- •   Played for the full duration of the game
- •73   Started game but substituted in 73rd minute
- 73   Came on as substitute in 73rd minute
- S   Non-playing substitute
- –   No appearance

Appearances – *FA Carling Premiership*

Match No.	27	28	29	30	31	32	33	34	35	36	37	38	39
Bruce Grobbelaar	•	•	•	•	•	•	•	•	•	•89	–	–	–
Rob Jones	•	•	•	•	•	•	•	•	•	•	•	•	•
Stig Bjornebye	–	29	77	S	67	S	S	–	–	–	–	–	–
Steve Nicol	•79	–	S	•	•	•	•	–	•	–	S	–	–
Mark Wright	•	•	•	•	•	•	•	•	•	•	•	•	•
Neil Ruddock	•	•	•	•	•	•	•	–	–	•	•	•	•
Nigel Clough	•	•	•	•	•	•	•	•	•58	S	S	•74	–
Jan Molby	–	–	–	–	–	–	–	–	–	–	–	–	–
Ian Rush	•	•	•	•	•	•	•	•	•	•	•	•	•
Ronnie Whelan	•	•	•	•	•	•	•	•	•	•	•	•	•
Mark Walters	79	•	•	•	•	•	•	•	•	65	•	74	–
Jamie Redknapp	•	•	•	•	•	•	•46	–	58	•	•	•	•
Steve McManaman	•	•76	•77	•	•	•	•	•	•	•	•	•	•
Mike Hooper	–	–	–	–	–	–	–	–	–	–	–	–	–
David Burrows	–	–	–	–	–	–	–	–	–	–	–	–	–
Mike Marsh	–	–	–	–	–	–	–	–	–	–	–	–	–
Don Hutchison	–	–	–	–	S	S	46	S	–	–	–	–	–
Ronny Rosenthal	–	–	–	–	–	–	–	–	–	–	–	–	–
Robbie Fowler	•	•	•	•	•67	–	–	–	–	–	–	–	•
Torben Piechnik	–	–	–	–	–	–	–	S	–	–	–	–	–
Steve Harkness	S	•	–	–	–	–	•	–	–	–	–	S	–
Paul Stewart	–	–	–	–	–	–	–	–	–	–	–	–	–
David James	S	S	S	S	S	S	S	S	S	89	•	•	•
Julian Dicks	–	–	•	•	•	•	–	•	•	•	•	•	•
John Barnes	–	76	•	•85	•	•	•	•	•	•	•	•	•64
Dominic Matteo	–	•29	–	–	–	–	–	•	S	•65	–	–	S
Michael Thomas	–	–	–	85	–	–	–	–	–	–	–	–	64
Mark Gayle	–	–	–	–	–	–	–	–	–	–	S	S	S
Phil Charnock	–	–	–	–	–	–	–	–	–	–	–	–	–

Key

•	Played for the full duration of the game
•73	Started game but substituted in 73rd minute
73	Came on as substitute in 73rd minute
S	Non-playing substitute
–	No appearance

Roy Evans takes over from Graeme Souness

Appearances – *FA Carling Premiership*

Match No	40	41	42	43	44	45	46	47	48	49
Bruce Grobbelaar	S	S	S	S	S	S	S	S	S	S
Rob Jones	•	•	•	•	•	•	•	−	•	•
Stig Bjornebye	−	−	−	−	−	−	−	−	−	−
Steve Nicol	S	28	−	−	−	−	−	−	•	•
Mark Wright	•	•28	−	−	−	−	−	−	−	−
Neil Ruddock	•	•	•	•	•	•	•	•	•	•
Nigel Clough	−	−	S	−	−	−	−	•	•71	S
Jan Molby	−	−	−	−	S	−	−	−	−	−
Ian Rush	•	•	•	•	•	•	•	•	•	•
Ronnie Whelan	•	•	•	•	•	•	•	−	•	•78
Mark Walters	−	−	−	−	−	−	−	−	−	−
Jamie Redknapp	•	•	•	•	•	•	•	•	•	•
Steve McManaman	•	•	•	•	•	•	•71	−	−	−
Mike Hooper	−	−	−	−	−	−	−	−	−	−
David Burrows	−	−	−	−	−	−	−	−	−	−
Mike Marsh	−	−	−	−	−	−	−	−	−	−
Don Hutchison	−	−	−	76	−	72	60	•	71	•
Ronny Rosenthal	−	−	−	−	−	−	−	−	−	−
Robbie Fowler	•	•71	81	•	•	•72	•60	•	•	•
Torben Piechnik	−	−	−	−	−	−	−	−	−	−
Steve Harkness	−	−	−	−	−	−	−	•	S	78
Paul Stewart	−	−	−	−	−	−	−	−	−	−
David James	•	•	•	•	•	•	•	•	•	•
Julian Dicks	•	•	•	•	•	•	•	•	•	•
John Barnes	•69	•	•	•76	•	•	•	•	•	•
Dominic Matteo	−	−	−	−	−	−	−	S	−	−
Michael Thomas	69	71	•81	74	S	S	71	−	−	−
Mark Gayle	−	−	−	−	−	−	−	−	−	−
Phil Charnock	−	−	−	−	−	−	S	−	−	−

Key

- •   Played for the full duration of the game
- •73   Started game but substituted in 73rd minute
- 73   Came on as substitute in 73rd minute
- S   Non-playing substitute
- −   No appearance

General Records

Longest Runs – All Competitions

Home Wins:	21	29/1/72 to 30/12/72
Away Wins:	6	24/09/04 to 19/11/04
		31/12/04 to 11/03/05
		27/02/82 to 24/04/82
Home Matches Undefeated:	63	25/02/78 to 31/01/81
Away Matches Undefeated:	16	02/09/1893 to 03/09/1894
		09/05/87 to 16/03/88
Defeats:	9	29/04/1899 to 21/10/1899
Without Home Win:	10	13/10/51 to 22/03/52
Without Away Win:	24	21/02/53 to 07/04/54

Records

Football League Champions:	18 times – a record
Football League Cup Winners:	4 times – a record
FA Cup Winners:	5 times
European Champions:	4 times
UEFA Cup Winners:	2 times
Charity Shield Winners:	12 times:
	8 times outright, 4 times jointly – a record
Points Scoring Records:	68 points in season – a record

68 points in the 1978-79 season was a record under the two points for a win system with 42 games played.

Fortress Anfield

1948-49 is the only season in Liverpool's 90 years of league competition when Liverpool have lost more home league games than they have won. Liverpool have managed nine league seasons undefeated at home.

They are: 1893-94, 1895-96, 1904-05, 1961-62, 1970-71, 1976-77, 1978-79, 1979-80 and 1987-88.

It took Liverpool four visits to the second division before they lost a home game – that was in 1954.

Lancashire League

Biggest Home Win:	8-0 v Higher Walton	03/09/1892
Biggest Away Win:	5-0 v Higher Walton	22/10/1892
Biggest Home Defeat:	0-2 v Blackpool	17/12/1892
Biggest Away Defeat:	0-3 v Blackpool	05/11/1892
	v Bury	11/02/1893
Highest Home Attendance:	4,000 v Blackpool (0-2)	17/12/1892
	v Bury (4-0)	24/09/1892
Lowest Home Attendance:	200 v Higher Walton	03/09/1892
Most Appearances:	22 A. Hannah	
	D. McLean	
	Wyllie	
Leading Goalscorer:	Miller 22 goals	
Most Goals in a Game:	5 Miller v Fleetwood R (7-0)	03/12/1892
Most Consecutive Wins:	6 18/02/1893 to 15/04/1893	
Longest Unbeaten Run:	7 games to end of season 1893	18/02/1893

Football League

Biggest Home Win:	10-1 v Rotherham Town (Div 2)	18/02/1896
	9-0 v Crystal Palace (Div 1)	12/09/89
Biggest Away Win:	7-0 v Burton Swifts (Div 2)	29/02/1896
	v Crewe Alexandra (Div 2)	28/03/1896
	6-0 v Wolves (Div 1)	28/09/69
Biggest Home Defeat:	0-6 v Sunderland (Div 1)	19/04/30
Biggest Away Defeat:	1-9 v Birmingham City (Div 2)	11/12/54
	0-8 v Huddersfield Town (Div 1)	10/11/34
Highest Home Attendance:	58,757 v Chelsea (2-2)	27/12/49
Highest Away Attendance:	78,599 v Everton (1-1)	18/09/48
Most Appearances:	Ian Callaghan (1959-78)	
	637 plus 3 as substitute	
Leading Goal Scorer:	245 goals Roger Hunt	
Most Goals in a Season:	41 Roger Hunt	1962-63
Most Goals in a Game:	5 A. McGuigan v Stoke City (7-0)	04/01/02
	Ian Rush v Luton Town (6-0)	29/10/83
Most Consecutive Wins:	11 09/03/82 to 03/05/82	
Most Consecutive Defeats:	9 29/04/1899 to 21/10/1899	

| **Longest Unbeaten Run:** | 31 | 04/05/87 to 20/03/88 |
| | 30 | 02/09/1893 to 08/09/1894 |

(Liverpool's first 30 games in the Football League, the unbeaten run stretches to 37 games if 7 from the end of the previous season in the Lancashire League are included)

	23	11/03/78 to 28/10/78
		09/03/82 to 02/10/78
Longest Run Without a Win:	14	12/12/53 to 03/04/54
Consecutive Draws:	6	19/02/75 to 22/03/75

FA Premiership

Biggest Home Win:	5-0 v	Crystal Palace	28/11/92
Biggest Away Win:	5-0 v	Swindon Town	22/08/93
Biggest Home Defeat:	0-2 v	Arsenal	22/08/92
	0-2 v	Newcastle United	16/04/94
Biggest Away Defeat:	5-1 v	Coventry City	19/12/92
Highest Home Attendance:	44,619 v Everton (1-0)		20/03/93
Most Appearances:	73/1	Ian Rush	
Leading Goal Scorer:	Ian Rush	28 goals	
Most Goals in a Season:	14	Ian Rush	1992/93
	14	Ian Rush	1993/94
Most Goals in a Game:	3	M. Walters v Coventry City	17/04/93
	3	R. Fowler v Southampton	30/10/93
Most Consecutive Wins:	4	07/11/92 to 01/12/92
	4	08/05/93 to 25/08/93
Most Consecutive Defeats:	4	01/09/93 to 02/10/93
Longest Unbeaten Run:	10	08/12/93 to 14/02/94
Longest Run Without a Win:	7	16/12/92 to 31/01/93

FA Cup

Biggest Home Win:	9-0 v	Newton (2nd Qual. Rnd)	29/10/1892
	8-0 v	Swansea City (3rd Round)	09/01/90
Biggest Away Win:	6-2 v	Yeovil & Petters (3rd Rnd)	12/01/35
	4-0 v	Nantwich (1st Qual. Rnd)	15/10/1892
	v	Everton (4th Round)	29/01/55
	v	Swansea City (3rd Round)	02/01/82
	v	Barnsley (6th Round)	10/03/85
	v	Manchester City (6th Rnd)	13/03/88

Biggest Home Defeat:	1-5 v Derby Co. (3rd Rnd replay)	02/03/1898
Biggest Away Defeat:	0-5 v Bolton Wand. (4th Rnd, 1st leg)	21/01/46
Highest Home Attendance:	61,905 v Wolves (4th Round, 2-1)	02/02/52
Most Appearances:	77 Ian Callaghan	
Leading Goal Scorer:	37 Ian Rush	
Most Goals in a Season:	8 Tony Hateley	1967-68
Most Goals in a Game:	4 H. Barton v Chesterfield (4th Rnd, 4-2)	23/01/32
	Alf Arrowsmith v Derby Co. (3rd Rnd, 5-0)	04/01/64
	Tony Hateley v Walsall (4th Rnd Rep, 5-2)	19/02/68
Games Without Defeat:	12 07/01/89 to 08/04/90	
Games Without a Win:	5 08/02/02 to 13/01/06	

Football League Cup

Biggest Home Win:	10-0 v Fulham (2nd Round)	23/09/86
Biggest Away Win:	6-0 v Exeter City (2nd Round)	28/10/81
Biggest Home Defeat:	1-2 v Southampton (3rd Round)	16/11/60
	0-1 v Middlesbrough (4th Rnd)	12/11/74
	v Everton (3rd Round)	27/10/87
	(Liverpool's only home defeats in the competition)	
Biggest Away Defeat:	1-4 v West Ham Utd (4th Rnd)	30/12/88
Highest Home Attendance:	50,880 v Notts Forest (Semi-Final, 1-1)	12/02/81
Most Appearances:	70 Bruce Grobbelaar	
Leading Goal Scorer:	41 Ian Rush	
Most Goals in a Season:	8 Ian Rush	1982/82
	Ian Rush	1983/84
	Steve McMahon	1986/87
Most Goals in a Game:	5 R. Fowler v Fulham (2nd Rnd, 5-0)	6/10/93
Games Without Defeat:	24 02/09/80 to 15/02/83	

European Cup

Biggest Home Win:	10-1 *v* Oulu Pallouseura, Finland (1st Rnd)	17/09/80
Biggest Away Win:	5-0 *v* Reykjavik, Iceland (1st Rnd)	17/08/64
	v Crusaders, Northern Ireland (1st Rnd)	28/09/76
Biggest Home Defeat:	1-2 *v* Red Star Belgrade, Yug. (2nd Rnd)	06/11/73
	(Liverpool's only home defeat in the competition)	
Biggest Away Defeat:	1-5 *v* Ajax, Netherlands (1st Rnd)	07/12/66
Highest Home Attendance:	55,043 *v* St Etienne (3rd Round)	16/03/77
Most Appearances:	57 Phil Neal	
Leading Goal Scorers:	12 Terry McDermott Ian Rush	
Most Goals in a Season:	7 Roger Hunt	1964/65
Most Goals in a Game:	3 Graeme Souness *v* Oulu Pallouseura, Finland (10-1)	17/09/80
	Terry McDermott *v* Oulu Pallouseura, Finland (10-1)	17/09/80
	Graeme Souness *v* CSKA Sofia, Bulgaria (5-1)	04/03/81
	John Wark *v* Lech Poznan, Poland (4-0)	03/10/84
	Ian Rush *v* Benfica, Portugal (3-1)	24/10/84
Games Without Defeat:	14 17/09/80 to 17/03/82	
	13 16/03/83 to 07/11/84	

European Cup Winners Cup

Biggest Home Win:	11-0 *v* Stromsgodset Drammen, Norway (1st Round)	17/09/74
Biggest Away Win:	2-1 *v* Standard Liege, Belgium (1st Round)	15/12/65
	v Apollon Limassol, Cyprus (1st Rnd)	29/09/92

161

Biggest Home Defeat:	0-2 v	Spartak Moscow, Russia (2nd Round)	04/11/92
Biggest Away Defeat:	2-4 v	Spartak Moscow, Russia (2nd Round)	22/10/92
	1-3 v	Bayern Munich, West Germany (2nd Rnd)	03/11/71
Highest Home Attendance:	54,631 v	Honved, Rumania (2nd Round, 2-0)	08/03/66
Most Appearances:	17	Ian Callaghan	
Leading Goal Scorers:	5	Chris Lawler Ian Rush	
Most Goals in a Season:	5	Ian Rush	1992/93
Most Goals in a Game:	4	Ian Rush v Apollon Limassol, Cyprus	16/09/92
Games Without Defeat:	6	17/09/74 to 04/11/92	

UEFA Cup (includes European Fairs Cup)

Biggest Home Win:	10-0 v	Dundalk, Eire (1st Rnd)	16/09/69
Biggest Away Win:	4-0 v	Dundalk, Eire (1st Rnd)	30/09/69
Biggest Home Defeat:	1-2 v	Genoa, Italy (4th Rnd)	18/03/92
	0-1 v	Ferencvaros, Hungary (3rd Rnd)	09/01/68
	v	Leeds United (Semi-Final)	14/04/71
Biggest Away Defeat:	1-3 v	Bayern Munich, W Germany (2nd Rnd)	03/11/72
	0-2 v	Borussia Moenchengladbach, West Germany (Final) *(After Liverpool's 3-0 win in the first leg)*	23/05/73
	v	Auxerre, France	23/10/91
	v	Genoa, Italy	04/03/92
Highest Home Attendance:	55,104 v	Barcelona, Spain (Semi-Final, 1-1)	14/04/76
Most Appearances:	40 plus 1 as substitute	Ian Callaghan	
Leading Goal Scorer:	9	Dean Saunders	
Most Goals in a Season:	9	Dean Saunders	1991/92
Most Goals in a Game:	4	Dean Saunders v Kuusysil, Finalnd (1st Rnd, 6-1)	18/09/91
Games Without Defeat:	12	30/9/75 to 2/10/91	

World Club Championship

13/12/81   *v* Flamengo (Tokyo)   0-3   Att: 62,000
Team: Grobbelaar, Neal, Lawrenson, Thompson, R. Kennedy, Hansen, Dalglish, Lee, Johnston, McDermott (Johnson), Souness.

09/12/84   *v* Independiente (Tokyo)   0-1   Att: 62,000
Team: Grobbelaar, Neal, A. Kennedy, Gillespie, Nicol, Hansen, Dalglish, Molby, Rush, Johnston, Wark (Whelan).

European Super Cup

22/11/77   *v* SV Hamburg (A)   1-1   Att: 16,000
Team: Clemence, Neal, Jones (Smith), Thompson, R. Kennedy, Hughes, Dalglish, Case (Johnson), Heighway, **Fairclough,** Callaghan.

06/12/77   *v* SV Hamburg (H)   6-0   Att: 34,931
Team: Clemence, Neal, Smith, **Thompson,** R. Kennedy, Hughes, **Dalglish, McDermott (3),** Heighway (Johnson), **Fairclough,** Case.
(Liverpool won 7-1 on aggregate)

04/12/78   *v* Anderlecht (A)   1-3   Att: 35,000
Team: Clemence, Neal, A. Kennedy, Hughes, R. Kennedy, Hansen, Dalglish, **Case,** Johnson (Heighway), McDermott, Souness.

19/12/78   *v* Anderlecht (H)   2-1   Att: 23,598
Team: Ogrizovic, Neal, **Hughes,** Thompson, R. Kennedy, Hansen, Dalglish, Case, **Fairclough,** McDermott, Souness.
(Anderlecht won 4-3 on aggregate)

16/01/85   *v* Juventus   0-2   Att: 60,000
Team: Grobbelaar, Neal, A. Kennedy, Lawrenson (Gillespie), Nicol, Hansen, Walsh, Whelan, Rush, MacDonald, Wark.

Liverpool Football Club

Anfield Road, Liverpool L4 0TH

Following a dispute between Everton FC and its Anfield landlord over the level of rent, Everton quit Anfield to find their own ground and the landlord John Houlding formed his own club – Liverpol AFC. Refused admission to the Football League they spent their first year winning the Lancashire League championship and were then chosen to fill a vacancy in the Second Division of an expanded Football League.

Liverpool won their first Football League title in the 1900-01 season and established themselves as a major force in the game. A lean spell in the late 1950s was followed by over thirty years at the top of the English and European game.

Nickname: The Reds, 'Pool
Change: Racing Green/White Trim
Pitch: 110 yds x 75 yds

Colours: All Red/White Trim
All-Seater Capacity: 44,243

Officials

Chairman:	D.R. Moores
Chief Executive/General Secretary:	P.B. Robinson
Directors:	J.W. Smith, J.T. Cross, N. White, T.D. Smith, P.B. Robinson, T.W. Saunders, K.E.B. Clayton
Vice-Presidents:	C.J. Hill, H.E. Roberts, W.D. Corkish, R. Paisley
Manager:	Roy Evans

Honours

League Champions:	1900-01, 1905-06, 1921-22, 1922-23, 1946-47, 1963-64, 1965-66, 1972-73,1975-76, 1976-77, 1978-79, 1979-80, 1981-82, 1982-83, 1983-84, 1985-86, 1987-88, 1989-90
Runners-up:	1898-89, 1909-10, 1968-69, 1973-74, 1974-75, 1977-78, 1984-85, 1986-87, 1988-89, 1990-91
Division 2 Champions:	1893-94, 1895-96, 1904-05, 1961-62
FA Cup Winners:	1965, 1974, 1986, 1989, 1992
FA Cup Finalists:	1914, 1950, 1971, 1977, 1988
League Cup Winners:	1980-81, 1981-82, 1982-83, 1983-84
League Cup Finalists:	1977-78, 1986-87
Charity Shield:	1964, 1965, 1966, 1974, 1976, 1977, 1979,1980, 1982, 1986, 1988, 1989, 1990
League Super Cup Winners:	1985-86

International Honours

European Cup Winners:	1976-77, 1977-78, 1980-81, 1983-84
European Cup Finalists:	1984-85
UEFA Cup Winners:	1972-73, 1975-76
European Cup Winners Cup Finalists:	1965-66
European Super Cup Winners:	1977
European Super Cup Finalists:	1978, 1985
World Club Championship Finalists:	1981, 1984

Miscellaneous Records

Record Attendance:	61,905 v Wolverhampton Wanderers (2-1), FA Cup 4th Round, 2nd February 1952
Record League Attendance:	58,757 v Chelsea (2-2) 27th December 1949

League History

1892-93	Lancashire League		1904-05	Division Two
1893-94	Division Two		1905-54	Division One
1894-95	Division One		1954-62	Division Two
1895-96	Division Two		1963-92	Division One
1896-1904	Division One		1992-	FA Premiership

Managers

1892-96	John McKenna/ WE Barclay		1956-59	Phil Taylor
1896-1915	Tom Watson		1959-74	Bill Shankly
1920-23	David Ashworth		1974-83	Bob Paisley
1923-28	Matt McQueen		1983-85	Joe Fagan
1928-36	George Patterson		1985-91	Kenny Dalglish
1936-51	George Kay		1991-94	Graeme Souness
1951-56	Don Welsh		1994-	Roy Evans

Telephone Numbers

Clubcall:	0891 121184	Ticketcall:	0891 121584
Administration:	051 263 2361/2	Tickets (Credit Card):	051 263 5727
Souvenir Shop:	051 263 1760	Sales and Marketing:	051 263 9199
Public Relations and Museum visits:	051 263 2361	Development Association:	051 263 6391
Banqueting/Conference Suite:	051 263 7744	Fax:	051 260 8813
Match Information:	051 260 9999 (24 hours)		
Match Ticket Office:	051 620 8680 (office hours)		

Directions

From North: M6 junction 8 follow the A58 to Walton Hall Avenue. Pass Stanley Park before turning left into Anfield Road.

From South and East: Follow M62 to the end and then turn right onto the A5058, Queens Drive. After 3 miles take a left turn into Utting Avenue and after another mile turn right into Anfield Road.

From West: M53 through the Wallasey tunnel follow the signs for Preston before taking a right turn into Walton Hall Avenue. Take a right turn into Anfield Road just ahead of Stanley Park.

Nearest Station: Liverpool Lime Street, Kirkdale.

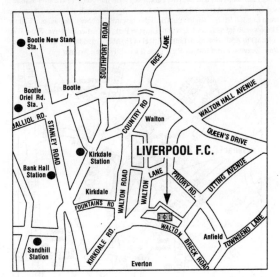

Arsenal

Arsenal Stadium, Highbury, London N5

Nickname: Gunners
Colours: Red/White sleeves, White, Red
All-seater Capacity: 39,497

Change: Yellow, Navy Blue, Yellow
Pitch: 110 yds x 71 yds

Directions:

From North: M1, J2 follow sign for the City. After Holloway Road station (c 6 miles) take third left into Drayton Park. Then right into Aubert Park after ¼ mile and 2nd left into Avenell Road. *From South:* Signs for Bank of England then Angel from London Bridge. Right at traffic lights towards Highbury roundabout. Follow Holloway Road then third right into Drayton Park, thereafter as above. *From West:* A40(M) to A501 ring road. Left at Angel to Highbury roundabout, then as above.
Rail: Drayton Park/Finsbury Park Tube (Piccadilly line): Arsenal

Telephone: 071-226 0304

Aston Villa

Villa Park, Trinity Rd, Birmingham, B6 6HE

Nickname: The Villains

Colours: Claret/Blue, White, Blue/Claret   **Change:** White, Black, White

All-seater Capacity: 40,530   **Pitch:** 115 yds x 75 yds

Directions:

M6 J6, follow signs for Birminham NE. 3rd exit at roundabout then right into Ashton Hall Rd after ½ mile.

Rail: Witton

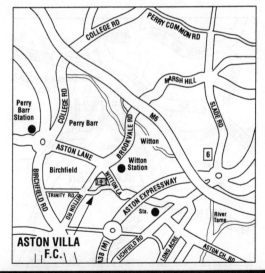

Blackburn Rovers

Ewood Park, Blackburn, BB2 4JF

Nickname: Blue and Whites
Colours: Blue/White, White, Blue   **Change:** Black/Red, Black, Black/Red
All-seater Capacity: 30,591   **Pitch:** 115yds x 76yds

Directions:

From North, South & West: M6 J31 follow signs for Blackburn then Bolton Road.
Turn left after 1½ miles into Kidder Street.
From East: A677 or A679 following signs for Bolton Road, then as above.
Rail: Blackburn Central

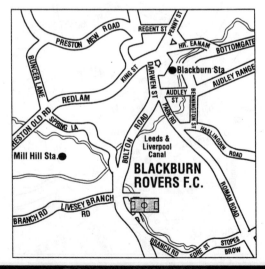

Telephone: (0254) 55432

170

Chelsea

Stamford Bridge, London SW6

Nickname: The Blues

Colours: Royal Blue, Royal Blue, White   **Change:** White/Red, Black, Black

All-seater Capacity: 41,050   **Pitch:** 110 yds x 72 yds

Directions:

From North & East: A1 or M1 to central London and Hyde Park corner. Follow signs for Guildford (A3) and then Knightsbridge (A4). After a mile turn left into Fulham Road. *From South:* A219 Putney Bridge then follow signs for West End joining A308 and then into Fulham Road. *From West:* M4 then A4 to central London. Follow A3220 to Westminster, after ³/₄ mile right at crossroads into Fulham Road.

Rail/Tube: Fulham Broadway (District line).

Telephone: 071-385 5545

Coventry City

Highfield Road Stadium, King Richard Street, Coventry, CV2 4FW

Nickname: Sky Blues
Colours: All Sky Blue
All-Seater Capacity: 24,021

Change: Yellow, Blue, Yellow
Pitch: 110 yds x 75 yds

Directions:

From North & West: M6 J3, after 3½ miles turn left into Eagle Street and straight on to Swan Lane. *From South & East:* M1 to M45 then A45 to Ryton-on-Dunsmore where 3rd exit at roundabout is A423. After 1 mile turn right into B4110. Left at T-junction then right into Swan Lane.
Rail: Coventry

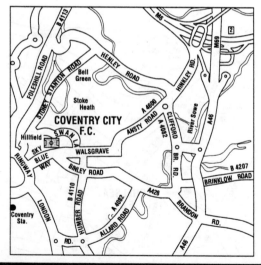

Telephone: (0203) 223535

172

Crystal Palace

Selhurst Park, London, SE25 6PU

Nickname: Eagles
Colours: Red/Blue, Red, Red
All-seater Capacity: 26,995

Change: Yellow, Light Blue, White
Pitch: 110 yds x 74 yds

Directions:

From North: M1 or A1 to A406 for Chiswick, then A205 to Wandsworth. A3 and then A214 for Streatham and then A23 to B273 for Whitehorse Lane.
From South: A23 and then B266. Turn right into High Street and then as above.
From East: A232 and then A215 to B266 for High Street and then as above.
From West: M4 to Chiswick and then as for the North.
Rail: Norwood Junction, Thornton Heath or Selhurst.

Everton

Goodison Park, Liverpool, L4 4EL

Nickname: The Toffees
Colours: Royal Blue, White, Blue   **Change:** Salmon/Dark Blue, Salmon, Salmon
All-seater Capacity: 40,160   **Pitch:** 112 yds x 78 yds

Directions:

From North: M6 J8 take A58 to A580 and follow into Walton Hall Avenue.
From South & East: M6 J21A to M62, turn right into Queen's Drive then, after 4 miles, left into Walton Hall Avenue.
From West: M53 through Wallasey Tunnel, follow signs for Preston on A580. Walton Hall Avenue is signposted.
Rail: Liverpool Lime Street, Kirkdale.

Ipswich Town

Portman Road, Ipswich, Suffolk, IP1 2DA

Nickname: Blues or Town
Colours: Blue/White, White, Blue **Change:** Red/Black, Black, Red/Black
All-seater Capacity: 22,823 **Pitch:** 112 yds x 70 yds

Directions:

Follow A45 and signs for Ipswich West. Through Post House traffic lights and turn
right at second roundabout into West End Road. Ground is situated on the left.
Rail: Ipswich

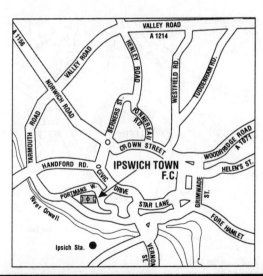

Telephone: (0473) 219211

175

Leeds United

Nickname: United
Colours: All White
All-seater Capacity: 39,176

Change: All Yellow
Pitch: 117 yds x 76 yds

Directions:

From North & East: A58, A61, A63 or A64 into city centre and then onto M621.
Leave Motorway after 1½ miles onto A643 and Elland Road.
From West: take M62 to M621 then as above.
From South: M1 then M621 then as above
Rail: Leeds City

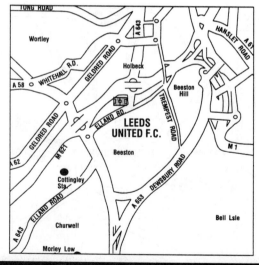

Leicester City

City Stadium, Filbert Street, Leicester, LE2 7FL

Nickname: The Filberts or Foxes

Colours: Blue, White, Blue   **Change:** Red, Black, Black

Capacity: 27,722   **Pitch:** 112 yds x 75 yds

Directions:

From North: Leave M1 at J22 or take A46, A607 to town centre. Towards Rugby via Almond Road, Sylestone Road and left into Walnut Street and Filbert Street. *From South:* M1 or M69 and then A46 to Upperton Road and Filbert Street. *From East:* A47 into town contre, right along Oxford Street to Aylestone Road and then as North. *From West:* M69 and A50 toAylestone Road and then as North. *Rail:* Leicester

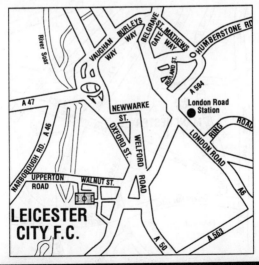

Manchester City

Maine Road, Moss Side, Manchester, M14 7WN

Nickname: Blues or City
Colours: Sky Blue, White, Sky Blue
All-seater Capacity: 45,053

Change: Purple/Candy stripe, Purple, Purple
Pitch: 117 yds x 77 yds

Directions:

From North & West: M61 to M63 J9. Follow signs into Manchester (A5103). Right after 3 miles into Claremont Road. Right after 400 yards into Maine Road.
From South: M6 J19 to A556 joining M56. Leave at J3 following A5103 as above.
From East: M62 J17 following signs for Manchester Airport (A56 and A57(M)). Then follow Birmingham signs to A5103. Left into Claremont Road after 1 mile then right into Maine Road. *Rail:* Manchester Piccadilly

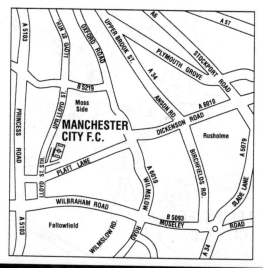

Manchester United

Old Trafford, Manchester, M16 0RA

Nickname: Red Devils
Colours: Red Shirts, White Shorts **Change:** All Black or Yellow/Green Halves
All-seater Capacity: 44,622 **Pitch:** 116 yds x 76 yds

Directions:

From North: M63 J4 follow signs for Manchester (A5081). Right after 2½ miles into Warwick Rd.
From South: M6 J19 follow A556 then A56 (Altrincham). From Altrincham follow signs for Manchester turning left into Warwick Rd after 6 miles.
From East: M62 J17 then A56 to Manchester. Follow signs South and then Chester. Turn right into Warwick Rd after 2 miles.
Rail: Manchester Victoria, Piccadilly, Old Trafford.

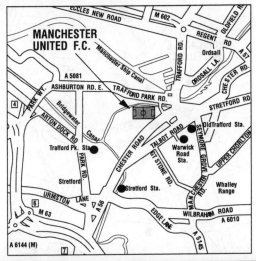

Telephone: 061-872 1661

Newcastle United

St James' Park, Newcastle-upon-Tyne, NE1 4ST

Nickname: Magpies
Colours: Black/White, Black, Black
All-seater Capacity: 36,401

Change: All Blue
Pitch: 115 yds x 75 yds.

Directions:

From South: Follow A1, A68 then A6127 to cross the Tyne. At roundabout, first exit into Moseley Street. Left into Neville Street, right at end for Clayton Street and then Newgate Street. Left for Leaze Park Road. *From West:* A69 towards city centre. Left into Clayton Street for Newgate Street, left again for Leaze Park Road. *From North:* A1 then follow signs for Hexham until Percy Street. Right into Leaze Park Road. *Rail:* Newcastle Central (½ mile).

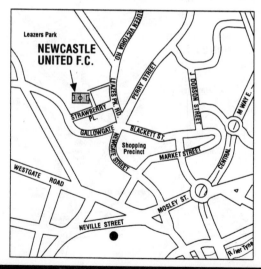

Telephone: 091-232 8361

Norwich City

Carrow Road, Norwich, NR1 1JE

Nickname: The Canaries
Colours: Yellow, Green, Yellow
All-seater Capacity: 25,000

Change: All White
Pitch: 114yds x 74 yds

Directions:

From North: A140 to ring road and follow signs for Yarmouth A47. Turn right at T junction after 3¹/₂ miles then left after ¹/₂ mile into Carrow Road.
From South & West: A11/A140 onto ring road. Follow signs for Yarmouith A47 etc as for North above.
From East: A47 into Norwich then left onto ring road.

Telephone: (0603) 612131

Nottingham Forest

City Ground, Nottingham, NG2 5FJ

Nickname: The Reds or Forest
Colours: Red, White, Red
All-seater Capacity: 30,500

Change: White, Black, White
Pitch: 115 yds x 78 yds

Directions:

From North: Leave the M1 J26 for the A610 and the A606. Left into Radcliffe
Road for the ground. *From South:* Leave the M1 J24 to Trent Bridge, turning right
into Radcliffe Road. *From East:* A52 to West Bridgeford and right for the ground.
From West: A52 to A606 and then as for the North.
Rail: Nottingham.

Telephone: (0602) 822202

Queens Park Rangers

South Africa Road, W12 7PA

Nickname: Rangers or Rs
Colours: Blue/White, White, White
All-seater Capacity: 19,300

Change: Red/Black, Black, Black
Pitch: 112 yds x 72 yds

Directions:

From North: M1 to north circular A406 towards Neasden. Left onto A404 for Hammersmith, past White City Stadium then right into South Africa Road. *From South:* A3 across Putney Bridge and signs for Hammersmith. A219 to Shepherds Bush and join A4020 towards Acton. Turn right after ¼ mile into Loftus Road. *From East:* From A40(M) towards M41 roundabout. Take 3rd exit at roundabout to A4020 then as above. *From West:* M4 to Chiswick then A315 and A402 to Shepherd's Bush joining A4020 then as for South. *Rail:* Shepherds Bush *Tube:* White City (Central Line)

Sheffield Wednesday

Hillsborough, Sheffield, S6 1SW

Nickname: The Owls
Colours: Blue/White, Blue, Blue   **Change:** All Black with Yellow/Grey trim
All-seater Capacity: 40,000   **Pitch:** 115 yds x 75 yds

Directions:

From North: M1 J34 then A6109 to Sheffield. At roundabout after 1½ miles take 3rd exit then turn left after 3 miles into Herries Road.

From South & East: M1 J31 or 33 to A57. At roundabout take Prince of Wales Road exit. A further 6 miles then turn left into Herries Road South.

From West: A57 to A6101 then turn left after 4 miles at T junction into Penistone Road.

Rail: Sheffield Midland

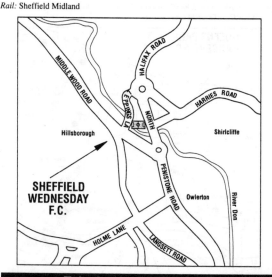

Southampton

The Dell, Milton Road, Southampton, SO9 4XX

Nickname: The Saints
Colours: Red/White, Black, Black   **Change:** Turquoise/Blue, Turquoise, Blue
All-seater Capacity: 15,288   **Pitch:** 110 yds x 72 yds

Directions:

From North: A33 into The Avenue then right into Northlands Road. Right at the end into Archer's Road. *From East:* M27 then A334 and signs for Southampton along A3024. Follow signs for the West into Commercial Road, right into Hill Lane then first right into Milton Road.

From West: Take A35 then A3024 towards city centre. Left into Hill Lane and first right into Milton Road.

Rail: Southampton Central

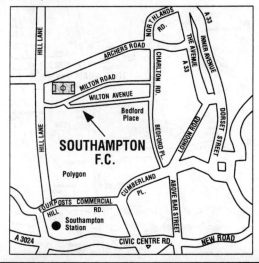

Telephone: (0703) 220505

Tottenham Hotspur

748 High Road, Tottenham, London, N17 0AP

Nickname: Spurs
Colours: White, Navy Blue, White
All-seater Capacity: 30,246

Change: All Yellow or all Sky Blue
Pitch: 110 yds x 73 yds

Directions:

A406 North Circular to Edmonton. At traffic lights follow signs for Tottenham along A1010 then Fore Street for ground.
Rail: White Hart Lane (adjacent)
Tube: Seven Sisters (Victoria Line) or Manor House (Piccadilly Line).

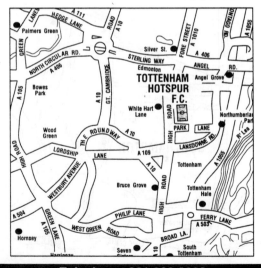

Telephone: 081-808 6666

West Ham United

Nickname: The Hammers
Colours: Claret, White, White
All-seater Capacity: 24,500

Change: All Blue
Pitch: 112 yds x 72 yds

Directions:

From North & West: North Circular to East Ham then Barking Rd for 1½ miles until traffic lights. Turn right into Green Street.
From South: Blackwall Tunnel then A13 to Canning Town. Then A124 to East Ham, Green Street on left after 2 miles.
From East: A13 then A117 and A124. Green Street on right after ¾ miles.
Rail/Tube: Upton Park (¼ mile)

Wimbledon

Selhurst Park, South Norwood, London E5

Nickname: The Dons
Colours: All Blue with Yellow trim   **Change:** All Red
All-seater Capacity: 26,995   **Pitch:** 110 yds x 74 yds

Directions:

From North: M1/A1 to North Circular A406 and Chiswick. Follow South Circular A205 to Wandsworth then A3 and A214 towards Streatham and A23. Then left onto B273 for 1 mile and turn left at end into High Street and Whitehorse Lane. *From South:* On A23 follow signs for Crystal Palace along B266 going through Thornton Heath into Whitehorse Lane. *From East:* A232 Croydon Road to Shirley joining A215, Norwood Road. Turn left after 2½ miles into Whitehorse Lane. *From West:* M4 to Chiswick then as above.
Rail: Selhurst, Norwood Junction or Thornton Heath.

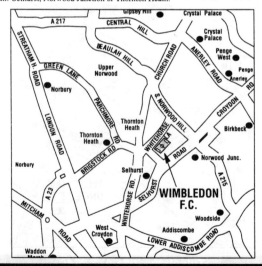

Telephone: 081-771 2233

188

All-time Records and Statistics

Liverpool Against Other Clubs – *Lancashire League*

Liverpool played just the one season in the Lancashire League – 1892/93 –
Liverpool's first season in existence. They won the Lancashire League and gained
entry to the second division of the Football League.

Club	P	W	D	L	F	A
Blackpool	2	0	0	2	0	5
Bury	2	1	0	1	4	3
Fairfield	2	2	0	0	9	1
Fleetwood R	2	2	0	0	11	1
Heywood Central	2	2	0	0	8	3
Higher Walton	2	2	0	0	13	0
Nelson	2	2	0	0	9	4
Rossendale Utd	2	2	0	0	4	1
South Shore	2	2	0	0	5	1
Southport Central	2	1	1	0	3	1
West Manchester	2	1	1	0	3	1
Total	22	17	7	3	66	19

Liverpool Against Other Clubs – *Football League*

Liverpool have played against 76 clubs during their 91 seasons in the Football
League. The following list gives their record against each of those clubs. Where
clubs have changed their names only the latest name is used but the list includes
all games against that club under either name – eg Small Heath became
Birmingham City – and so the record shown for games against Birmingham City
includes games against Small Heath. Records against Chelsea, Middlesbrough and
Sheffield United include one game at the start of the 1939-40 season which was
subsequently abandoned.

Club	P	W	D	L	F	A
Arsenal	136	54	33	49	195	181
Aston Villa	134	61	30	43	241	212
Barnsley	10	6	2	2	20	12
Birmingham City	86	44	17	25	145	121
Blackburn Rovers	92	37	27	28	169	132
Blackpool	40	18	9	13	72	62
Bolton Wanderers	92	35	25	32	139	117

Club	P	W	D	L	F	A
Bradford	6	3	1	2	10	8
Bradford City	22	15	2	5	39	20
Brentford	10	4	3	3	16	16
Brighton & Hove Albion	16	8	6	2	36	20
Bristol City	30	16	3	11	52	39
Bristol Rovers	16	10	1	5	32	21
Burnley	74	29	19	26	117	95
Burton Swifts	4	3	1	0	17	3
Burton United	2	1	0	1	3	2
Burton Wanderers	2	1	0	1	5	3
Bury	48	26	14	8	92	53
Cardiff City	26	8	2	16	35	51
Carlisle United	2	2	0	0	3	0
Charlton Athletic	40	21	5	14	66	54
Chelsea	99	48	21	30	169	140
Chesterfield	2	1	1	0	7	2
Coventry City	50	30	13	7	86	28
Crewe Alexandra	4	4	0	0	20	1
Crystal Palace	18	10	4	4	37	11
Darwen	2	1	1	0	4	0
Derby County	112	56	27	29	218	147
Doncaster Rovers	10	5	2	3	19	13
Everton	146	54	44	48	203	181
Fulham	28	15	9	4	54	30
Gainsborough Trinity	2	2	0	0	8	2
Glossop North End	4	3	1	0	11	5
Grimsby Town	36	18	10	8	87	47
Huddersfield Town	68	25	17	26	113	113
Hull City	6	5	1	0	15	7
Ipswich Town	50	23	16	11	90	52
Leeds United	76	37	21	18	116	78
Leicester City	72	29	15	28	124	107
Leyton Orient	14	9	2	3	37	15
Lincoln City	20	11	4	5	42	28
Loughborough Town	2	2	0	0	5	2
Luton Town	28	13	9	6	52	33
Manchester City	122	62	26	34	225	170
Manchester United	118	42	36	40	161	161
Middlesbrough	107	45	30	32	193	149
Middlesbrough Ironopolis	2	2	0	0	8	0
Millwall	4	3	1	0	6	3
Newcastle United	116	52	31	33	193	149

Club	P	W	D	L	F	A
Northampton Town	2	2	0	0	5	0
Northwich Victoria	2	2	0	0	7	2
Norwich City	38	19	10	9	67	40
Nottingham Forest	90	46	20	24	149	88
Notts County	60	34	12	14	110	63
Oldham Athletic	20	11	4	5	31	26
Oxford United	6	5	1	0	20	3
Plymouth Argyle	10	5	3	2	22	15
Portsmouth	46	17	12	17	81	78
Port Vale	12	7	3	2	38	20
Preston North End	64	26	17	21	114	99
Queens Park Rangers	32	22	5	5	55	27
Rotherham United	20	24	3	3	57	21
Scunthorpe United	8	6	2	0	17	8
Sheffield United	113	53	25	35	185	150
Sheffield Wednesday	100	45	22	33	170	149
Southampton	48	23	11	14	67	53
Stoke City	106	53	27	26	176	113
Sunderland	128	54	26	48	221	204
Swansea City	20	10	4	6	51	27
Tottenham Hotspur	98	46	24	28	153	111
Walsall	4	2	2	0	11	3
Watford	12	9	1	2	29	13
West Bromwich Albion	108	47	33	28	157	127
West Ham United	76	38	22	16	124	74
Wimbledon	12	6	4	2	19	14
Wolverhampton Wanderers	86	42	15	29	134	105
Total	3527	1652	851	1024	6077	4530

Liverpool Against Other Clubs – *FA Premiership*

In two years in the FA Premiership Liverpool have played against 24 different clubs.

Club	Home						Away					
	P	W	D	L	F	A	W	D	L	F	A
Arsenal	4	0	1	1	0	2	1	0	1	1	1
Aston Villa	4	1	0	1	3	3	0	0	2	3	6
Blackburn Rovers	4	1	0	1	2	1	0	0	2	1	6
Chelsea	4	2	0	0	4	2	0	1	1	0	1
Coventry City	4	2	0	0	5	0	0	0	2	1	6
Crystal Palace	2	1	0	0	5	0	0	1	0	1	1

Club	Home						Away				
	P	W	D	L	F	A	W	D	L	F	A
Everton	4	2	0	0	3	1	0	0	2	1	4
Ipswich Town	4	1	1	0	1	0	1	1	0	4	3
Leeds United	4	2	0	0	4	0	0	1	1	2	4
Manchester City	4	1	1	0	3	2	0	2	0	2	2
Manchester United	4	0	1	1	4	5	0	1	1	2	3
Middlesbrough	2	1	0	0	4	1	1	0	0	2	1
Newcastle United	2	0	0	1	0	2	0	0	1	0	3
Norwich City	4	1	0	1	4	2	0	1	1	2	3
Nottingham Forest	2	0	1	0	0	0	0	0	1	0	1
Oldham Athletic	4	2	0	0	3	1	1	0	0	5	3
Queens Park Rangers	4	2	0	0	4	2	2	0	0	4	1
Sheffield United	4	1	0	1	2	2	0	1	1	1	0
Sheffield Wednesday	4	2	0	0	3	0	0	1	1	2	4
Southampton	4	1	1	0	5	3	0	0	2	6	3
Swindon Town	2	0	1	0	2	2	1	0	0	5	0
Tottenham Hotspur	4	1	0	1	7	4	0	1	1	3	5
West Ham United	2	1	0	0	2	0	1	0	0	2	1
Wimbledon	4	0	1	1	3	4	0	1	1	1	3
Total	84	25	8	9	74	41	8	12	22	47	69

Full League Record

Season		Home					Away										
	P	W	D	L	F	A	W	D	L	F	A	Pts	Pos	%	FAC	LC	Eur
Lancashire League																	
1892-93	22	10	0	1	44	7	7	2	2	22	12	36	1	81.8	3q	–	–
Division Two																	
1893-94	28	14	0	0	46	6	8	6	0	31	12	50	1	89.3	3	–	–
Division One																	
1894-95	30	6	4	5	38	28	1	4	10	13	42	22	16	36.7	2	–	–
Division Two																	
1895-96	30	14	1	0	65	11	8	1	6	41	21	46	1	76.7	2	–	–
Division One																	
1896-97	30	7	6	2	25	10	5	3	7	21	28	33	5	55.0	SF	–	–
1897-98	30	7	4	4	27	16	4	2	9	21	29	28	9	46.7	3	–	–
1898-99	34	12	3	2	29	10	7	2	8	20	23	43	2	63.2	SF	–	–
1899-00	34	9	4	4	31	19	5	1	11	18	26	33	10	48.5	2	–	–
1900-01	34	12	2	3	36	13	7	5	5	23	22	45	1	66.2	1	–	–
1901-02	34	8	3	6	28	16	2	9	6	14	22	32	11	47.1	2	–	–
1902-03	34	11	3	3	48	21	6	1	10	20	28	38	5	55.9	1	–	–
1903-04	34	7	5	5	24	20	2	3	12	25	42	26	17	38.2	1	–	–

		Home					Away										
Season	P	W	D	L	F	A	W	D	L	F	A	Pts	Pos	%	FA	LC	Eur
Division Two																	
1904-05	34	14	3	0	60	12	13	1	3	33	13	58	1	85.3	1	–	–
Division One																	
1905-06	38	14	3	2	49	15	9	2	8	30	31	51	1	67.1	SF	–	–
1906-07	38	9	2	8	45	32	4	5	10	19	33	33	15	43.4	4	–	–
1907-08	38	11	2	6	43	24	5	4	10	25	37	38	8	50.0	3	–	–
1908-09	38	9	5	5	36	25	6	1	12	21	40	36	16	47.4	2	–	–
1909-10	38	13	3	3	47	23	8	3	8	31	34	48	2	63.2	1	–	–
1910-11	38	11	3	5	38	19	4	4	11	15	34	37	13	48.7	2	–	–
1911-12	38	8	4	7	27	23	4	6	9	22	32	34	17	44.7	2	–	–
1912-13	38	12	2	5	40	24	4	3	12	21	47	37	12	48.7	3	–	–
1913-14	38	8	4	7	27	25	6	3	10	19	37	35	16	46.1	F	–	–
1914-15	38	11	5	3	45	34	3	4	12	20	41	37	13	48.7	2	–	–
1919-20	42	12	5	4	35	18	7	5	9	24	26	48	4	57.1	4	–	–
1920-21	42	11	7	3	41	17	7	8	6	22	18	51	4	60.7	2	–	–
1921-22	42	15	4	2	43	15	7	9	5	20	21	57	1	67.9	2	–	–
1922-23	42	17	3	1	50	13	9	5	7	20	18	60	1	71.4	3	–	–
1923-24	42	11	5	5	35	20	4	6	11	14	28	41	12	48.8	4	–	–
1924-25	42	13	5	3	43	20	7	5	9	20	35	50	4	59.5	4	–	–
1925-26	42	9	8	4	43	27	5	8	8	27	36	44	7	52.4	4	–	–
1926-27	42	13	4	4	47	27	5	3	13	22	34	43	9	51.2	5	–	–
1927-28	42	10	6	5	54	36	3	7	11	30	51	39	16	46.4	4	–	–
1928-29	42	11	4	6	53	28	6	8	7	37	36	46	5	54.8	4	–	–
1929-30	42	11	5	5	33	29	5	4	12	30	50	41	12	48.8	3	–	–
1930-31	42	11	6	4	48	28	4	6	11	38	57	42	9	50.0	3	–	–
1931-32	42	13	4	4	56	38	6	2	13	25	55	44	10	52.4	6	–	–
1932-33	42	10	6	5	53	33	4	5	12	26	51	39	14	46.4	3	–	–
1933-34	42	10	6	5	52	37	4	4	13	27	50	38	18	45.2	5	–	–
1934-35	42	13	4	4	53	29	6	3	12	32	59	45	7	53.6	4	–	–
1935-36	42	11	4	6	43	23	2	8	11	17	41	38	19	45.2	4	–	–
1936-37	42	9	8	4	38	26	3	3	15	24	58	35	18	41.7	3	–	–
1937-38	42	9	5	7	40	30	6	6	9	25	41	41	11	48.8	5	–	–
1938-39	42	12	6	3	40	24	2	8	11	22	39	42	11	50.0	5	–	–
1939-40	3	2	0	0	5	1	0	0	1	1	2	4	–	–	–	–	–
1945-46	–	–	–	–	–	–	–	–	–	–	–	–	–	–	4	–	–
1946-47	42	13	3	5	42	24	12	4	5	42	28	57	1	67.9	SF	–	–
1947-48	42	9	8	4	39	23	7	2	12	26	38	42	11	50.0	4	–	–
1948-49	42	5	10	6	25	18	8	4	9	28	25	40	12	47.6	5	–	–
1949-50	42	10	7	4	37	23	7	7	7	27	31	48	8	57.1	F	–	–
1950-51	42	11	5	5	28	25	5	6	10	25	34	43	9	51.2	3	–	–
1951-52	42	6	11	4	31	25	6	8	7	26	36	43	11	51.2	5	–	–
1952-53	42	10	6	5	36	28	4	2	15	25	54	36	17	42.9	3	–	–
1953-54	42	7	8	6	49	38	2	2	17	19	59	28	22	33.3	3	–	–

Season	P	W	D	L	F	A	W	D	L	F	A	Pts	Pos	%	FAC	LC	Eur
Division Two																	
1954-55	42	11	7	3	55	37	5	3	13	37	59	42	11	50.0	5	–	–
1955-56	42	14	3	4	52	25	7	3	11	33	38	48	3	57.1	5	–	–
1956-57	42	16	1	4	53	26	5	10	6	29	28	53	3	63.1	3	–	–
1957-58	42	17	3	1	50	13	5	7	9	29	41	54	4	64.3	6	–	–
1958-59	42	15	3	3	57	25	9	2	10	30	37	53	4	63.1	3	–	–
1959-60	42	15	3	3	59	28	5	7	9	31	38	50	3	59.5	4	–	–
1960-61	42	14	5	2	49	21	7	5	9	38	37	52	3	61.9	4	–	–
1961-62	42	18	3	0	68	19	9	5	7	31	24	62	1	73.8	5	–	–
Division One																	
1962-63	42	13	3	5	45	22	4	7	10	26	37	44	8	52.4	SF	–	–
1963-64	42	16	0	5	60	18	10	5	6	32	27	57	1	67.9	6	–	–
1964-65	42	12	5	4	42	33	5	5	11	25	40	44	7	52.4	W†	–	EC-S
1965-66	42	17	2	2	52	15	9	7	5	27	19	61	1	72.6	3	–	CWC-F
1966-67	42	12	7	2	36	17	7	6	8	28	30	51	5	60.7	5	–	EC-2
1967-68	42	17	2	2	51	15	5	9	7	20	23	55	3	65.5	6	2	UEFA-3
1968-69	42	16	4	1	36	10	9	7	5	27	14	61	2	72.6	5	4	UEFA-1
1969-70	42	10	7	4	34	20	10	4	7	31	22	51	5	60.7	6	3	UEFA-2
1970-71	42	11	10	0	30	10	6	7	8	12	14	51	5	60.7	F†	3	UEFA-S
1971-72	42	17	3	1	48	16	7	6	8	16	14	57	3	67.9	4	4	CWC-2
1972-73	42	17	3	1	45	19	8	7	6	27	23	60	1	71.4	4	5	UEFA-W
1973-74	42	18	2	1	34	11	4	11	6	18	20	57	2	67.9	W	5	EC-2
1974-75	42	14	5	2	44	17	6	6	9	16	22	51	2	60.7	4	4	CWC-2
1975-76	42	14	5	2	41	21	9	9	3	25	10	60	1	71.4	4	3	UEFA-W
1976-77	42	18	3	0	47	11	5	8	8	15	22	57	1	67.9	F	2	EC-W
1977-78	42	15	4	2	37	11	9	5	7	28	23	57	2	67.9	3	F	EC-W
1978-79	42	19	2	0	51	4	11	6	4	34	12	68	1	81.0	SF	2	EC-1
1979-80	42	15	6	0	46	8	10	4	7	35	22	60	1	71.4	SF	SF	EC-1
1980-81	42	13	5	3	38	15	4	12	5	24	27	51	5	60.7	4	W*	EC-W
1981-82	42	14	3	4	39	14	12	6	3	41	18	87	1	72.6	5	W†	EC-Q
1982-83	42	16	4	1	55	16	8	6	7	32	21	82	1	69.0	5	W†	EC-Q
1983-84	42	14	5	2	50	12	8	9	4	23	20	80	1	66.7	4	W*	EC-W†
1984-85	42	12	4	5	36	19	10	7	4	32	16	77	2	65.5	SF	3	EC-F
1985-86	42	16	4	1	58	14	10	6	5	31	23	88	1	73.8	W	SF	–
1986-87	42	15	3	3	43	16	8	5	8	29	26	77	2	64.3	3	F	–
1987-88	40	15	5	0	49	9	11	7	2	38	15	90	1	80.0	F	3	–
1988-89	38	11	5	3	33	11	11	5	3	32	17	76	2	71.0	W	4	–
1989-90	38	13	5	1	38	15	10	5	4	40	22	79	1	73.7	SF	4	–
1990-91	38	14	3	2	42	13	9	4	6	35	27	76	2	69.7	5	3	–
1991-92	42	13	5	3	34	17	3	11	7	13	23	64	6	57.1	W	4	UEFA-Q

			Home				Away								
Season	P	W	D	L	F	A	W	D	L	F	A	Pts	Pos	%	FAC LC	Eur
FA Premiership																
1992-93	42	13	4	4	41	18	3	7	11	21	37	59	6	51.2	3 4	CWC-2
1993-94	42	12	4	5	33	23	5	5	11	26	32	60	8	51.2	3 4	–

† after extra time.   * replay after draw following extra time.
Percentages all calculated on the basis of two points for a win, one for a draw.

Liverpool Career Records

League appearances and goals. Entries include games played in the Lancashire League but not in the FA Premiership which has its own column. At the end of seasons 1893/94, 1894/95 and 1895/96 Liverpool were involved in several test matches to decide promotion and demotion. Appearances and goals scored in these matches have also been included in the League column. The chart does not include wartime games when innumerable players turned out for whichever club they were stationed closest to at the time.

Player	FAPL		League		FACup		LgeCup		Europe		Totals	
	App	Goals	App	Goals	App	Goals	App	Goals	App	Goals	App	Goals
A'Court, Alan (1952/65)	–	–	355	61	24	2	2	–	1	–	382	63
Ablett, Gary (1983/92)	–	–	103/6	1	16/2	–	10/1	–	6	–	135/9	1
Aitken (1930/31)	–	–	1	–	–	–	–	–	–	–	1	–
Aldridge, John (1986/90)	–	–	69/14	50	10	3	7/1	8	–	–	86/15	61
Allan, George (1895/99)	–	–	83	53	14	7	–	–	–	–	97	60
Allman, M (1908/09)	–	–	1	–	–	–	–	–	–	–	1	–
Anderson, Eric (1952-57)	–	–	73	21	3	–	–	–	–	–	76	21
Armstrong (1919/20)	–	–	1	–	–	–	–	–	–	–	1	–
Arnell, Alan (1952/61)	–	–	69	33	6	2	–	–	–	–	75	35
Arnold, Steve (1970/71)	–	–	1	–	–	–	–	–	–	–	1	–
Arrowsmith, Alf (1961/68)	–	–	43/4	20	6	4	–	–	1	–	50/4	24
Ashcroft, Charlie (1946/55)	–	–	87	–	2	–	–	–	–	–	89	–
Balmer, Jack (1935-52)	–	–	292	99	21	12	–	–	–	–	313	111
Bamber, John (1919/24)	–	–	72	2	8	–	–	–	–	–	80	2
Banks, Alan (1958/61)	–	–	8	6	–	–	–	–	–	–	8	6
Banks, William (1913-15)	–	–	26	6	–	–	–	–	–	–	26	6
Barkas, Ned (1930-32)	–	–	5	–	–	–	–	–	–	–	5	–
Barnes, John (1987/94)	50/3	8	152	62	36	14	14	3	1	–	253/3	87
Baron, Frederick (1924/27)	–	–	20	7	–	–	–	–	–	–	20	7
Baron, Kevin (1945/54)	–	–	140	32	12	1	–	–	–	–	152	33
Barton, Harold (1929/34)	–	–	100	25	6	4	–	–	–	–	106	29
Bartrop, Wilf (1914/15)	–	–	3	–	–	–	–	–	–	–	3	–
Battles, Ben (1895/98)	–	–	6	–	–	–	–	–	–	–	6	–
Beadles, Harold (1921/24)	–	–	17	6	–	–	–	–	–	–	17	6
Beardsley, Peter (1987/91)	–	–	120/11	46	22/3	11	13/1	1	–	–	155/15	58

Player	FAPL App	FAPL Goals	League App	League Goals	FACup App	FACup Goals	LgeCup App	LgeCup Goals	Europe App	Europe Goals	Totals App	Totals Goals
Becton, Frank (1894/98)	–	–	74	37	12	4	–	–	–	–	86	41
Beeby, A (1909/11)	–	–	16	–	–	–	–	–	–	–	16	–
Beglin, Jim (1984/87)	–	–	64	2	10	–	13	–	3	1	90	3
Bennett (1919/20)	–	–	1	–	–	–	–	–	–	–	1	–
Berry, Arthur (1907/13)	–	–	4	–	–	–	–	–	–	–	4	–
Bimpson, Louis (1952/60)	–	–	94	39	6	1	–	–	–	–	100	40
Bjornebye, Stig (1992/94)	17/3	–	–	–	2/1	–	–	–	–	–	19/4	–
Blanthorne, Robert (1906/07)	–	–	2	–	–	–	–	–	–	–	2	–
Blenkinsop, Ernie (1933/38)	–	–	71	–	–	–	–	–	–	–	71	–
Blore, Reg (1959/60)	–	–	1	–	–	–	–	–	–	–	1	–
Boersma, Phil (1969/76)	–	–	73/9	17	7/3	–	5/3	3	13/6	8	98/21	29
Bovill, John (1911/14)	–	–	27	7	2	–	–	–	–	–	29	7
Bowen, G (1901/02)	–	–	2	–	–	–	–	–	–	–	2	–
Bowyer, Sam (1907/12)	–	–	45	14	3	2	–	–	–	–	48	16
Bradley, James (1905/11)	–	–	2	–	–	–	–	–	–	–	2	–
Bradshaw, Harry (1893/1898)	–	–	124	49	14	5	–	–	–	–	138	54
Bradshaw, Tom (1929/38)	–	–	277	3	14	1	–	–	–	–	291	4
Bratley, Philip (1914/15)	–	–	13	–	–	–	–	–	–	–	13	–
Brierley, Ken (1947/53)	–	–	58	8	1	–	–	–	–	–	59	8
Brough, J (1910/11)	–	–	10	3	–	–	–	–	–	–	10	3
Brownbill, Derek (1973/74)	–	–	1	–	–	–	–	–	–	–	1	–
Bromilow, Tom (1919/30)	–	–	341	11	33	–	–	–	–	–	374	11
Browning, John (1934/39)	–	–	19	–	–	–	–	–	–	–	19	–
Bruton, Les (1931/33)	–	–	7	1	2	–	–	–	–	–	9	1
Buck, Frederick (1903/04)	–	–	13	1	–	–	–	–	–	–	13	1

Player	FAPL		League		FACup		LgeCup		Europe		Totals	
	App	Goals	App	Goals	App	Goals	App	Goals	App	Goals	App	Goals
Bull, B (1895/96)	–	–	1	1	–	–	–	–	–	–	1	1
Burkinshaw, Keith (1954/55)	–	–	1	–	–	–	–	–	–	–	1	–
Burrows, David (1988/93)	32/2	2	103/9	1	16/1	–	16	–	11	–	178	3
Busby, Matt (1935/40)	–	–	118	3	7	–	–	–	–	–	125	3
Bush, Tom (1933/47)	–	–	64	1	8	–	–	–	–	–	72	1
Buxton (1930/31)	–	–	–	–	–	–	–	–	–	–	–	–
Byrne, Gerry (1957/69)	–	–	273/1	2	29	–	5	–	22	1	329/1	3
Cadden, Joe (1950/52)	–	–	4	–	1	–	–	–	–	–	5	–
Callaghan, Ian (1959/78)	–	–	673/3	50	77/1	2	42	7	87/1	10	843/5	69
Cameron (1892/93)	–	–	8	3	–	–	–	–	–	–	8	3
Cameron, J (1894/95)	–	–	4	–	–	–	–	–	–	–	4	–
Campbell, Bobby (1959/61)	–	–	14	1	–	–	–	–	–	–	14	1
Campbell, Don (1953/59)	–	–	57	3	1	–	–	–	–	–	58	3
Campbell, Kenneth (1911/20)	–	–	125	–	17	–	–	–	–	–	142	–
Carlin, John (1902/07)	–	–	31	8	3	–	–	–	–	–	34	8
Carlin, Willie (1959/60)	–	–	1	–	–	–	–	–	–	–	1	–
Carney, Len (1946/48)	–	–	6	1	–	–	–	–	–	–	6	1
Carr, Lance (1933/36)	–	–	31	8	2	–	–	–	–	–	33	8
Carter (1990/91)	–	–	2/3	–	2	–	–	–	0/1	–	4/4	–
Case, Jimmy (1974/81)	–	–	170/16	23	20/2	7	21/1	3	25/6	12	236/25	45
Chadburn, John (1903/04)	–	–	2	–	–	–	–	–	–	–	2	–
Chadwick, Ernest (1902/04)	–	–	43	7	2	–	–	–	–	–	45	7
Chalmers (1924/25)	–	–	2	–	–	–	–	–	–	–	2	–
Chambers, Harry (1919/28)	–	–	310	135	28	16	–	–	–	–	338	151
Charlton (1931/31)	–	–	3	–	–	–	–	–	–	–	3	–

Player	FAPL App	FAPL Goals	League App	League Goals	FACup App	FACup Goals	LgeCup App	LgeCup Goals	Europe App	Europe Goals	Totals App	Totals Goals
Charnock (1992/93)	0/1	–	–	–	1	–	–	–	–	–	1/1	–
Checkland, F (1921/22)	–	–	5	–	–	–	–	–	–	–	5	–
Childs, Albert (1953/54)	–	–	2	–	–	–	–	–	–	–	2	–
Chisnall, Phil (1964/66)	–	–	6	1	–	–	–	–	2	1	8	2
Christie, Frank (1949/50)	–	–	4	–	–	–	–	–	–	–	4	–
Chorlton, Tom (1904/11)	–	–	118	8	4	–	–	–	–	–	122	8
Clarke, James (1927/31)	–	–	40	11	3	–	–	–	–	–	43	11
Cleghorn, Thomas (1895/99)	–	–	60	–	10	1	–	–	–	–	70	1
Clelland (1894/95)	–	–	1	–	–	–	–	–	–	–	1	–
Clemence, Ray (1968/81)	–	–	470	–	54	–	55	–	77	–	656	–
Clough, Nigel (1993/94)	24/1	7	–	–	2	–	2	1	–	–	28/1	8
Cockburn, Bill (1924/27)	–	–	63	–	4	–	–	–	–	–	67	–
Cohen, Avi (1979/81)	–	–	16/2	1	1	–	1	–	2/1	–	20/3	1
Collins (1935/37)	–	–	7	–	–	–	–	–	–	–	7	–
Colvin, R (1897/98)	–	–	3	–	–	–	–	–	–	–	3	–
Cooper, Tom (1934/39)	–	–	150	–	10	–	–	–	–	–	160	–
Cormack, Peter (1972/76)	–	–	119/6	21	14	2	20	1	15/3	2	168/9	26
Cotton, C (1903/04)	–	–	12	–	–	–	–	–	–	–	12	–
Cox, Jack (1897/1909)	–	–	327	72	33	8	–	–	–	–	360	80
Craik, H (1903/04)	–	–	1	–	–	–	–	–	–	–	1	–
Crawford (1932/33)	–	–	7	4	–	–	–	–	–	–	7	4
Crawford, Robert (1908/15)	–	–	108	1	6	–	–	–	–	–	114	1
Crossley, Russell (1950/54)	–	–	68	–	5	–	–	–	–	–	73	–
Cunliffe, Daniel (1897/98)	–	–	14	6	4	1	–	–	–	–	18	7
Cunningham, W (1920/22)	–	–	3	–	–	–	–	–	–	–	3	–

Player	FAPL		League		FACup		LgeCup		Europe		Totals	
	App	Goals	App	Goals	App	Goals	App	Goals	App	Goals	App	Goals
Curran, J (1894/96)	—	—	21	—	3	—	—	—	—	—	24	—
Dabbs, Benjamin (1933/38)	—	—	54	—	2	—	—	—	—	—	56	—
Dalglish, Kenny (1977/90)	—	—	342/13	118	36	13	57/2	27	46/1	10	481/15	168
Davidson, David (1928/30)	—	—	58	2	4	—	—	—	—	—	62	2
Davies, J (1900/03)	—	—	9	—	1	—	—	—	—	—	10	—
Dawson, J (1913/14)	—	—	13	3	1	—	—	—	—	—	14	3
Devlin, William (1926/28)	—	—	19	15	—	—	—	—	—	—	19	15
Dewhurst, G (1893/94)	—	—	1	—	—	—	—	—	—	—	1	—
Dick, D (1893/94)	—	—	10	2	—	—	—	—	—	—	10	2
Dicks, Julian (1993/94)	24/3	3	—	—	1	—	3	—	—	—	28/3	3
Dickson, Joe (1955/56)	—	—	6	3	—	—	—	—	—	—	6	3
Dines, J (1912/13)	—	—	1	—	—	—	—	—	—	—	1	—
Doig, James (1904/08)	—	—	51	—	2	—	—	—	—	—	53	—
Done, Cyril (1939/52)	—	—	94	33	15	4	—	—	—	—	109	37
Done, Robert (1926/35)	—	—	147	13	8	—	—	—	—	—	155	13
Donnelly, W (1896/97)	—	—	6	—	2	—	—	—	—	—	8	—
Drummond, John (1894/95)	—	—	15	—	3	1	—	—	—	—	18	1
Dunlop, Billy (1894/1909)	—	—	322	2	36	—	—	—	—	—	358	2
Durnin (1988/89)	—	—	—	—	0/1	—	—	—	—	—	0/1	—
Easdale, John (1946/47)	—	—	2	—	—	—	—	—	—	—	2	—
Eastham, Harry (1936/47)	—	—	63	3	6	1	—	—	—	—	69	4
Edmed, Dick (1926/31)	—	—	160	44	10	2	—	—	—	—	170	46
English, Sam (1933/35)	—	—	47	25	3	2	—	—	—	—	50	27
Evans, Alun (1968/72)	—	—	77/2	21	9/2	3	7	2	11/2	7	104/6	33
Evans, John (1953/57)	—	—	96	49	10	4	—	—	—	—	106	53

Player	FAPL		League		FACup		LgeCup		Europe		Totals	
	App	Goals	App	Goals	App	Goals	App	Goals	App	Goals	App	Goals
Evans, Roy (1969/74)	-	-	9	-	-	-	1	-	1	-	11	-
Fagan, Chris (1970/71)	-	-	1	-	-	-	-	-	-	-	1	-
Fagan, Willie (1937/52)	-	-	161	47	24	10	-	-	-	-	185	57
Fairclough, David (1975/83)	-	-	64/36	34	10/4	7	7/13	10	7/9	4	88/62	52
Fairfoul, Thomas (1913/15)	-	-	62	-	9	-	-	-	-	-	71	-
Ferguson, Robert (1912/15)	-	-	92	2	11	1	-	-	-	-	103	3
Ferns, Phil (1962/65)	-	-	27	1	1	-	-	-	-	-	28	1
Finney (1945/46)	-	-	-	-	2	-	-	-	-	-	2	-
Finnerhan, Patrick (1897/98)	-	-	5	1	3	-	-	-	-	-	8	1
Fitsimmon (1938/39)	-	-	-	-	1	-	-	-	-	-	1	-
Fitzpatrick, H (1907/08)	-	-	4	2	-	-	-	-	-	-	4	2
Fleming, George (1901/06)	-	-	79	5	4	1	-	-	-	-	83	6
Forshaw, Dick (1919/27)	-	-	266	117	21	7	-	-	-	-	287	124
Fowler, Robbie (1993/94)	27/1	11	-	-	1	-	5	6	-	-	33/1	17
Foxall, A (1899/1900)	-	-	1	-	-	-	-	-	-	-	1	-
Furnell, Jim (1961/64)	-	-	28	-	-	-	-	-	-	-	28	-
Gardner, Tom (1929/30)	-	-	5	-	-	-	-	-	-	-	5	-
Garner (1924/26)	-	-	5	-	-	-	-	-	-	-	5	-
Garside, James (1904/06)	-	-	5	-	-	-	-	-	-	-	5	-
Gayle, Howard (1980/81)	-	-	3/1	1	-	-	-	-	0/1	-	3/2	1
Geary, Fred (1895/99)	-	-	40	14	5	-	-	-	-	-	45	14
Gerhardi, Hugh (1952/53)	-	-	6	-	-	-	-	-	-	-	6	-
Gilhespy, Cyril (1921/25)	-	-	19	3	-	-	-	-	-	-	19	3
Gillespie, Gary (1983/91)	-	-	152/4	13	21/2	-	22	2	2/1	-	197/7	15
Gilligan, Sam (1910/13)	-	-	41	16	-	-	-	-	-	-	41	16

Player	FAPL		League		FACup		LgeCup		Europe		Totals	
	App	Goals	App	Goals	App	Goals	App	Goals	App	Goals	App	Goals
Givens, J (1893/95)	–	–	10	3	–	–	–	–	–	–	10	3
Glassey (1935/37)	–	–	9	4	–	–	–	–	–	–	9	4
Glover, John (1900/03)	–	–	59	–	1	–	–	–	–	–	60	–
Goddard, Arthur (1901/14)	–	–	388	75	27	5	–	–	–	–	415	80
Goldie, Archie (1895/1900)	–	–	130	1	20	–	–	–	–	–	150	1
Goldie, Bill (1897/1903)	–	–	158	6	16	–	–	–	–	–	174	6
Goode B (1908/10)	–	–	7	1	–	–	–	–	–	–	7	1
Gordon, Patrick (1893/95)	–	–	27	8	3	–	–	–	–	–	30	8
Gorman, James (1905/08)	–	–	19	–	4	1	–	–	–	–	23	1
Gracie, Thomas (1911/14)	–	–	1	–	–	–	–	–	–	–	1	–
Graham, Bobby (1964/72)	–	–	96/5	31	7/2	4	7/1	2	13	5	123/8	42
Gray, Alfred (1928/29)	–	–	–	–	–	–	–	–	–	–	–	–
Grayer, F (1913/14)	–	–	1	–	–	–	–	–	–	–	1	–
Green, T (1901/03)	–	–	7	1	–	–	–	–	–	–	7	1
Griffin, Michael (1907/09)	–	–	4	–	–	–	–	–	–	–	4	–
Griffiths, Harry (1905/08)	–	–	6	–	–	–	–	–	–	–	6	–
Grobbelaar, Bruce (1981/94)	34	–	406	–	62	–	70	–	7	–	579	–
Gunson, Gordon (1929/33)	–	–	81	24	6	2	–	–	–	–	87	26
Hafekost, C (1914/1915)	–	–	1	–	–	–	–	–	–	–	1	–
Haigh, Jack (11950/52)	–	–	11	3	–	–	–	–	–	–	11	3
Hall, Brian (1968/76)	–	–	140/13	15	17/2	3	12/1	1	27/8	2	196/24	21
Hancock (1931/32)	–	–	9	2	–	–	–	–	–	–	9	2
Hannah, Andrew (1892/95)	–	–	63	2	3	–	–	–	–	–	66	2
Hannah, Davy (1894/97)	–	–	31	12	2	1	–	–	–	–	33	13
Hansen, Alan (1977/90)	–	–	434/2	7	59/1	2	64	1	42/1	3	599/4	13

Player	FAPL App	FAPL Goals	League App	League Goals	FACup App	FACup Goals	LgeCup App	LgeCup Goals	Europe App	Europe Goals	Totals App	Totals Goals
Hanson, Alfred (1932/38)	–	–	166	50	11	2	–	–	–	–	177	52
Hardy, Sam (1905/12)	–	–	219	–	20	–	–	–	–	–	239	–
Harkness, Steve (1989/94)	20/1	1	7/4	–	2	–	3/3	–	3/2	–	35/10	1
Harley, Jim (1935/48)	–	–	117	–	16	–	–	–	–	–	133	–
Harrington (1920/21)	–	–	4	–	–	–	–	–	–	–	4	–
Harrop, James (1907/12)	–	–	133	4	6	–	–	–	–	–	139	4
Harrower, Jimmy (1957/61)	–	–	96	21	6	1	3	–	–	–	105	22
Harston, Ted (1937/38)	–	–	5	3	–	–	–	–	–	–	5	3
Hartill, Ted (1935/36)	–	–	5	–	–	–	–	–	–	–	5	–
Hartley, Abraham (1897/98)	–	–	7	1	5	–	–	–	–	–	12	1
Hateley, Tony (1967/69)	–	–	42	17	7	8	2	–	5	3	56	28
Heighway, Steve (1970/81)	–	–	312/17	50	33/3	8	38	7	61/3	11	444/23	76
Henderson (1931/32)	–	–	5	–	–	–	–	–	–	–	5	–
Henderson, Hugh (1893/95)	–	–	24	10	2	2	–	–	–	–	26	12
Hewitt, Charlie (1907/08)	–	–	16	6	–	–	–	–	–	–	16	6
Hewitt, Joe (1903/10)	–	–	153	67	11	2	–	–	–	–	164	69
Heydon, Jack (1950/53)	–	–	63	–	4	–	–	–	–	–	67	–
Hickson, Dave (1959/61)	–	–	60	37	4	–	3	1	–	–	67	38
Hignett, A (1907/08)	–	–	1	–	–	–	–	–	–	–	1	–
Hignett, Alan (1964/65)	–	–	1	–	–	–	–	–	–	–	1	–
Hoare, J (1903/04)	–	–	7	–	–	–	–	–	–	–	7	–
Hobson, Alfred (1936/46)	–	–	26	–	2	–	–	–	–	–	28	–
Hodgson, David (1982/84)	–	–	21/7	4	3	1	6/3	3	3/4	2	33/14	10
Hodgson, Gordon (1925/36)	–	–	359	232	19	8	–	–	–	–	378	240
Holden, A (1912/14)	–	–	2	–	–	–	–	–	–	–	2	–

Player	FAPL		League		FACup		LgeCup		Europe		Totals	
	App	Goals	App	Goals	App	Goals	App	Goals	App	Goals	App	Goals
Holmes, J (1895/98)	-	-	42	-	2	-	-	-	-	-	44	-
Hood (1937/38)	-	-	3	-	-	-	-	-	-	-	3	-
Hooper, Mike (1986/93)	8/1	-	92/1	-	11	-	19	-	4	-	134/2	-
Hopkin, Fred (1921/31)	-	-	335	9	24	2	-	-	-	-	359	11
Houghton, Ray (1987/92)	-	-	147/6	28	26/1	4	14	3	4	2	191/7	37
Howe, Fred (1934/38)	-	-	89	36	5	4	-	-	-	-	94	36
Howell, 'Rabbi' (1897/1901)	-	-	59	-	9	-	-	-	-	-	68	-
Hughes, Abel (1893/94)	-	-	-	-	-	-	-	-	-	-	1	-
Hughes, Emlyn (1966/79)	-	-	474	35	62	1	46	3	75	9	657	48
Hughes, James (1903/09)	-	-	45	2	2	-	-	-	-	-	47	2
Hughes, Laurie (1945/58)	-	-	303	-	23	-	-	-	-	-	326	-
Hunt, Roger (1959/70)	-	-	401/3	245	44	18	10	5	29/2	17	484/5	285
Hunter, 'Sailor' (1899/1902)	-	-	37	10	7	3	-	-	-	-	44	13
Hunter, T (1899/1902)	-	-	5	-	-	-	-	-	-	-	5	-
Hunter, William (1908/09)	-	-	-	-	-	-	-	-	-	-	1	-
Hutchison, Don (1990/94)	33/9	7	0/3	-	1/2	-	7/1	2	3	1	49/7	10
Hysen, Glenn (1989/91)	-	-	70/2	2	13	-	6	1	-	-	89/2	3
Ireland, Bob (1930/31)	-	-	1	-	-	-	-	-	-	-	1	-
Irvine (1986/87)	-	-	0/2	-	0/1	-	0/1	-	-	-	0/4	-
Irwin, Colin (1979/81)	-	-	26	-	4	-	6	-	4/1	-	40/4	3
Jackson, Brian (1951/58)	-	-	124	12	7	-	-	-	-	-	131	12
Jackson, James (1925/33)	-	-	212	7	12	-	-	-	-	-	224	7
James (1930/33)	-	-	8	2	-	-	-	-	-	-	8	2
James, David (1992/94)	42/1	-	-	-	-	-	1	-	1	-	44/1	-
Jenkinson, Will (1919/20)	-	-	13	-	-	-	-	-	-	-	13	-

Player	FAPL App	FAPL Goals	League App	League Goals	FACup App	FACup Goals	LgeCup App	LgeCup Goals	Europe App	Europe Goals	Totals App	Totals Goals
Johnson, David (1976/82)	–	–	128/20	55	17/2	6	15/3	9	14/5	8	174/30	78
Johnson, Dick (1919/25)	–	–	78	28	5	2	–	–	–	–	83	30
Johnson, Tom (1933/36)	–	–	37	8	2	–	–	–	–	–	39	8
Johnston, Craig (1981/88)	–	–	165/25	30	14/4	4	32/3	3	13/4	2	324/36	39
Jones, Alan (1959/63)	–	–	5	–	–	–	–	–	–	–	5	–
Jones, Bill (1946/54)	–	–	257	17	21	–	–	–	–	–	278	17
Jones, Harold (1953/54)	–	–	1	–	–	–	–	–	–	–	1	–
Jones, Joey (1975/78)	–	–	72	3	9	–	4	–	12	–	97	3
Jones, John (1924/25)	–	–	4	–	–	–	–	–	–	–	4	–
Jones, Mervyn (1951/53)	–	–	4	–	1	–	–	–	–	–	5	–
Jones, Rob (1991/94)	69	–	28	1	13	–	7/1	–	4/1	–	121/2	1
Jones, Ron (1937/39)	–	–	5	–	–	–	–	–	–	–	5	–
Jowitt, C (1896/97)	–	–	1	–	–	–	–	–	–	–	1	–
Kane (1934/36)	–	–	6	–	–	–	–	–	–	–	6	–
Kaye, Harold (1945/47)	–	–	1	–	1	–	–	–	–	–	2	–
Keech, W (1895/96)	–	–	6	–	–	–	–	–	–	–	6	–
Keegan, Kevin (1971/77)	–	–	230	68	28	14	23	6	40	12	321	100
Keetley (1923/24)	–	–	9	3	–	–	–	–	–	–	9	3
Kelly (1892/93)	–	–	3	–	–	–	–	–	–	–	3	–
Kelso (1892/93)	–	–	1	–	–	–	–	–	–	–	1	–
Kelvin (1892/93)	–	–	4	–	–	–	–	–	–	–	4	–
Kemp, Dirk (1936/400)	–	–	30	–	3	–	–	–	–	–	33	–
Kennedy, Alan (1978/85)	–	–	247/2	15	21	–	45	2	34	4	347/2	21
Kennedy, Ray (1974/82)	–	–	272/3	51	28	3	35	6	46	12	381/3	72
Kerr, Neil (1894/95)	–	–	12	3	–	–	–	–	–	–	12	3

Player	FAPL		League		FACup		LgeCup		Europe		Totals	
	App	Goals	App	Goals	App	Goals	App	Goals	App	Goals	App	Goals
Kettle, Brian (1975/77)	–	–	3	–	–	–	–	–	–	–	3	–
Kewley, Kevin (1977/78)	–	–	/1	–	–	–	–	–	–	–	/1	–
Kinghorn, William (1938/39)	–	–	19	4	–	–	–	–	–	–	19	4
Kippax, Peter (1948/49)	–	–	1	–	–	–	–	–	–	–	1	–
Kozma, Istvan (1991/93)	0/1	–	3/2	–	0/2	–	0/1	–	–	–	3/6	–
Kyle, P (1899/1900)	–	–	4	–	1	–	–	–	–	–	5	–
Lacey, Billy (1911/24)	–	–	229	18	28	11	–	–	–	–	257	29
Lambert, Ray (1945/56)	–	–	308	2	33	–	–	–	–	–	341	2
Lane, Frank (1972/73)	–	–	1	–	–	–	1	–	–	–	2	–
Lathom, George (1904/08)	–	–	18	–	1	–	–	–	–	–	19	–
Lawler, Chris (1962/76)	–	–	406	41	47	4	27	5	66	11	546	61
Lawrence, Tommy (1962/71)	–	–	306	–	42	–	6	–	33	–	387	–
Lawrenson, Mark (1981/88)	–	–	233/7	11	24	2	49	2	26/2	2	332/9	17
Lawson, Hector (1923/25)	–	–	12	–	4	–	–	–	–	–	16	–
Leavy, H (1910/11)	–	–	5	–	–	–	–	–	–	–	5	–
Lee, Sammy (1977/86)	–	–	190/7	13	17	–	39	2	33	4	279/7	19
Leishman, Tommy (1959/63)	–	–	107	6	9	–	3	1	–	–	119	7
Lester H (1911/13)	–	–	2	–	–	–	–	–	–	–	2	–
Lewis, Harry (1919/220)	–	–	59	10	11	2	–	–	–	–	70	12
Lewis, Kevin (1960/63)	–	–	71	39	8	3	2	2	–	–	81	44
Liddell, Billy (1945/61)	–	–	495	216	42	13	–	–	–	–	537	229
Lindsay, Alec (1969/77)	–	–	168/2	12	22	1	23	1	31	4	244/2	18
Lindsay, J (1928/30)	–	–	14	2	2	1	–	–	–	–	16	3
Lipsham, J (1906/07)	–	–	3	–	–	–	–	–	–	–	3	–
Livermore, Doug (1967/71)	–	–	13/3	–	1	–	1	–	–	–	14/3	–

Player	FAPL		League		FACup		LgeCup		Europe		Totals	
	App	Goals	App	Goals	App	Goals	App	Goals	App	Goals	App	Goals
Livingstone, G. (1902/03)	–	–	31	4	1	–	–	–	–	–	32	4
Longworth, E. (1910/28)	–	–	342	–	28	–	–	–	–	–	370	–
Low, Norman (1934/37)	–	–	13	–	–	–	–	–	–	–	13	–
Lowe, Harry (1911/20)	–	–	122	2	13	–	–	–	–	–	135	2
Lowry, Tom (1964/65)	–	–	1	–	–	–	–	–	–	–	1	–
Lucas, Tommy (1919/330)	–	–	341	3	25	–	–	–	–	–	366	3
Lumsden, J (1897/98)	–	–	6	2	2	–	–	–	–	–	8	2
MacDonald, Kevin (1984/89)	–	–	29/11	2	10	1	9/2	1	3	–	51/13	3
McAvoy, Doug (1947/49)	–	–	2	–	–	–	–	–	–	–	2	–
McBain, Neil (1927/29)	–	–	12	–	–	–	–	–	–	–	12	–
McBride, John (1892/95)	–	–	50	7	2	–	–	–	–	–	52	7
McCallum, D (1902/03)	–	–	2	–	–	–	–	–	–	–	2	–
McCann, W (1894/95)	–	–	15	–	2	–	–	–	–	–	17	–
McCarthy (1893/94)	–	–	1	–	–	–	–	–	–	–	1	–
McCartney, John (1892/98)	–	–	146	5	16	–	–	–	–	–	162	5
McConnell, John (1909/12)	–	–	50	–	3	–	–	–	–	–	53	1
McCowie, Andrew (1896/99)	–	–	33	11	2	–	–	–	–	–	35	11
McDermott, Terry (1974/83)	–	–	221/11	54	23	4	36	5	30/1	12	310/12	75
McDevitt (1923/25)	–	–	4	–	–	–	–	–	–	–	4	–
McDonald, John (1909/12)	–	–	76	4	2	–	–	–	–	–	78	4
McDougall, J (1913/15)	–	–	7	1	1	–	–	–	–	–	8	1
McDougall, Jimmy (1928/38)	–	–	339	12	18	–	–	–	–	–	357	12
McFarlane (1928/30)	–	–	2	–	–	–	–	–	–	–	2	–
McGuigan, Andy (1900/02)	–	–	31	14	4	–	–	–	–	–	35	14
McInnes, Jimmy (1937/40)	–	–	48	2	3	–	–	–	–	–	51	2

Player	FAPL App	FAPL Goals	League App	League Goals	FACup App	FACup Goals	LgeCup App	LgeCup Goals	Europe App	Europe Goals	Totals App	Totals Goals
McKenna, John (1906/07)	–	–	1	33	–	–	–	–	–	–	1	34
McKinlay, Donald (1909/29)	–	–	393	1	40	–	–	–	–	–	433	1
McKinney (1920/21)	–	–	3	1	–	–	–	–	–	–	3	1
McLaughlin, John (1969/75)	–	–	38/2	2	4	1	3	–	8	–	53/2	3
McLean, Duncan (1892/95)	–	–	75	6	5	–	–	–	–	–	80	6
McLean, J (1903/04) -	–	–	4	–	–	–	–	–	–	–	4	–
McLean, Jimmy (1894/96)	–	–	27	–	2	–	–	–	–	–	29	–
McLeod, Tommy (1946/49)	–	–	7	–	–	–	–	–	–	–	7	–
McMahon, Steve (1985/91)	–	–	202/2	29	30	7	27	13	5	–	264/2	49
McManaman, S. (1990/94)	56/5	6	26/6	5	11	3	11/1	5	11	1	115/12	20
McMullan, David (1925/28)	–	–	31	–	4	–	–	–	–	–	35	–
McNab, Jock (1919/28)	–	–	200	6	21	–	–	–	–	–	221	6
McNamara, Tony (1957/58)	–	–	10	3	1	–	–	–	–	–	11	3
McNaughton (1920/21)	–	–	1	–	–	–	–	–	–	–	1	–
McNulty, Tom (1953/58)	–	–	36	–	–	–	–	–	–	–	36	–
McOwen, William (1892/94)	–	–	24	–	3	–	–	–	–	–	27	–
McPherson, Archie (1929/35)	–	–	130	18	3	1	–	–	–	–	133	19
McPherson, W. (1906/08)	–	–	48	16	7	1	–	–	–	–	55	17
McQue, Joe (1892/98)	–	–	126	12	14	2	–	–	–	–	140	14
McQueen, Hugh (1892/95)	–	–	56	16	4	1	–	–	–	–	60	17
McQueen, Matt (1892/99)	–	–	95	6	8	–	–	–	–	–	103	6
McRorie, Daniel (1930/33)	–	–	33	6	2	–	–	–	–	–	35	6
McVean, Malcolm (1892/97)	–	–	115	33	8	4	–	–	–	–	123	37
Maloney, Joe (1952/54)	–	–	12	–	–	–	–	–	–	–	12	–
Marsh, Mike (1987/93)	22/8	2	20/19	–	6/2	–	10/1	3	11/1	–	69/31	5

Player	FAPL App	FAPL Goals	League App	League Goals	FACup App	FACup Goals	LgeCup App	LgeCup Goals	Europe App	Europe Goals	Totals App	Totals Goals
Marshall (1901/02)	–	–	1	–	–	–	–	–	–	–	1	–
Marshall, R (1897/99)	–	–	20	2	1	–	–	–	–	–	21	2
Matthews, R (1919/22)	–	–	9	4	–	–	–	–	–	–	9	4
Matteo, Dominic (1993/94)	9	–	–	–	–	–	2	–	–	–	11	–
Melia, Jimmy (1955/64)	–	–	269	76	18	2	–	–	–	–	287	78
Metcalfe, Arthur (1912/15)	–	–	52	23	11	5	–	–	–	–	63	28
Michael, William (1896/97)	–	–	19	4	4	–	–	–	–	–	23	4
Miller (1892/93)	–	–	21	22	–	–	–	–	–	–	21	22
Miller (1928/29)	–	–	3	2	–	–	–	–	–	–	3	2
Miller, John (1919/20)	–	–	8	–	–	–	–	–	–	–	8	–
Miller, Tom (1911/21)	–	–	127	52	19	6	–	–	–	–	146	58
Milne, Gordon (1960/67)	–	–	234/2	18	27	1	–	–	16	–	277/2	19
Minshull, Ray (1946/50)	–	–	28	–	3	–	–	–	–	–	31	–
Mitchell, Frank (1920/22)	–	–	18	–	–	–	–	–	–	–	18	–
Molby, Jan (1984/94)	19/2	5	164/19	37	25/4	4	22/3	10	7	1	237/28	57
Molyneux, Bill (1964/65)	–	–	1	–	–	–	–	–	–	–	1	–
Molyneux, John (1955/62)	–	–	229	2	17	1	3	–	–	–	249	3
Money, Richard (1980/81)	–	–	12/2	–	1	–	1	–	1	–	15/2	–
Mooney (1986/87)	–	–	–	–	–	–	0/1	–	–	–	0/1	–
Moran, Ronnie (1952/65)	–	–	343	14	32	2	–	–	4	–	379	16
Morgan, Hugh (1897/1900)	–	–	59	15	10	3	–	–	–	–	69	18
Morris, Fred (1958/60)	–	–	47	14	1	–	–	–	–	–	48	14
Morris, Richard (1901/05)	–	–	38	5	1	–	–	–	–	–	39	5
Morrissey, Johnny (1957/61)	–	–	36	6	1	–	–	–	–	–	37	6
Morrison, Tom (1927/35)	–	–	240	4	14	–	–	–	–	–	254	4

Player	FAPL		League		FACup		LgeCup		Europe		Totals	
	App	Goals	App	Goals	App	Goals	App	Goals	App	Goals	App	Goals
Muir, Alex (1947/48)	–	–	4	–	–	–	–	–	–	–	4	–
Murdoch, Bobby (1957/59)	–	–	17	5	2	2	–	–	–	–	19	7
Murray (1937/30)	–	–	4	1	–	–	–	–	–	–	4	1
Murray, David (1904/06)	–	–	15	–	–	–	–	–	–	–	15	–
Neal, Phil (1974/86)	–	–	453/2	41	66	4	45	3	69	12	633/2	60
Nicholl, Robert (1894/97)	–	–	23	2	4	1	–	–	–	–	27	3
Nicholl, Jimmy (1913/15)	–	–	52	12	7	2	–	–	–	–	59	14
Nicholson, John (1959/60)	–	–	1	–	–	–	–	–	–	–	1	–
Nickson, Fred (1945/46)	–	–	3	–	–	–	–	–	–	–	3	–
Nicol, Steve (1982/94)	52/3	1	265/10	36	51	3	41	4	17/2	2	426/15	46
Nieuwenhuys, B. (1933/47)	–	–	239	74	21	5	–	–	–	–	260	79
Ogrizovic, Steve (1977/81)	–	–	4	–	–	–	–	–	–	–	4	–
Ogston, John (1966/67)	–	–	1	–	–	–	–	–	–	–	1	–
Orr, Ronald (1907/12)	–	–	108	35	4	3	–	–	–	–	112	38
Oxley, Cyril (1925/26)	–	–	31	6	3	–	–	–	–	–	34	6
Pagnam, Frederick (1941/20)	–	–	37	28	2	2	–	–	–	–	39	30
Paisley, Bob (1945/54)	–	–	253	10	25	3	–	–	–	–	278	13
Parkinson, Jack (1899/1914)	–	–	203	123	19	5	–	–	–	–	222	128
Parr, Steve (1951/53)	–	–	20	–	–	–	–	–	–	–	20	–
Parry, Edward (1920/25)	–	–	13	–	–	–	–	–	–	–	13	–
Parry, Maurice (1900/09)	–	–	207	3	14	–	–	–	–	–	221	3
Patterson, George (1938/39)	–	–	2	–	1	1	–	–	–	–	3	1
Patne, Jimmy (1948/56)	–	–	224	37	21	5	–	–	–	–	245	42
Peake, Ernest (1908/14)	–	–	51	5	4	1	–	–	–	–	55	6
Pearson (1892/93)	–	–	1	–	–	–	–	–	–	–	1	–

Player	FAPL		League		FACup		LgeCup		Europe		Totals	
	App	Goals	App	Goals	App	Goals	App	Goals	App	Goals	App	Goals
Pearson, Albert (1919/21)	–	–	44	4	8	–	–	–	–	–	52	4
Penman (1920/21)	–	–	1	–	–	–	–	–	–	–	1	–
Peplow, Steve (1969/70)	–	–	2	–	–	–	–	–	–	–	2	–
Perkins, William (1893/1903)	–	–	107	–	9	–	–	–	–	–	116	–
Perry, Fred (1955/56)	–	–	1	–	–	–	–	–	–	–	1	–
Peters (1938/39)	–	–	1	–	–	–	–	–	–	–	1	–
Piechnik, Torben (1992/94)	16/1	–	–	–	2	–	5	–	–	–	23/1	–
Pither (1926/28)	–	–	12	–	–	–	–	–	–	–	12	–
Platt, Peter (1902/04)	–	–	44	1	1	–	–	–	–	–	45	1
Polk, Stan (1946/48)	–	–	13	–	–	–	–	–	–	–	13	–
Pratt, David (1922/27)	–	–	77	1	8	–	–	–	–	–	85	1
Price, John (1955/56)	–	–	1	–	–	–	–	–	–	–	1	–
Priday, Bob (1945/49)	–	–	33	6	6	1	–	–	–	–	39	7
Pursell, Bob (1911/20)	–	–	99	–	13	–	–	–	–	–	112	–
Race, Henry (1927/30)	–	–	43	18	–	–	–	–	–	–	43	18
Raisbeck, Alex (1898/1907)	–	–	312	19	28	2	–	–	–	–	340	21
Ramsden, Bernard (1937/48)	–	–	60	–	6	–	–	–	–	–	66	–
Rawlings, Archie (1923/26)	–	–	63	8	4	2	–	–	–	–	67	10
Raybould, Steve (1899/1907)	–	–	211	119	13	8	–	–	–	–	224	127
Redknapp, Jamie (1991/94)	56/8	6	5/1	1	5	–	10	1	5/1	–	81/10	8
Reid, Tom (1925/29)	–	–	51	31	4	–	–	–	–	–	55	31
Richardson (1892/93)	–	–	1	–	–	–	–	–	–	–	1	–
Riley, Arthur (1925/39)	–	–	322	–	16	–	–	–	–	–	338	–
Roberts, J (1933/34)	–	–	–	–	–	–	–	–	–	–	–	–
Roberts, Syd (1931/37)	–	–	57	10	4	3	–	–	–	–	61	13

Player	FAPL		League		FACup		LgeCup		Europe		Totals	
	App	Goals	App	Goals	App	Goals	App	Goals	App	Goals	App	Goals
Robertson, John (1900/02)	–	–	42	1	4	–	–	–	–	–	46	1
Robertson, T. (1897/1902)	–	–	126	34	15	3	–	–	–	–	141	37
Robinson, Michael (1983/85)	–	–	26/4	6	2	1	11/1	4	6/1	2	45/6	13
Robinson, Robert (1903/12)	–	–	254	64	17	1	–	–	–	–	271	65
Rogers, Frederick (1934/39)	–	–	70	–	5	–	–	–	–	–	75	–
Rogers, T (1906/11)	–	–	38	–	2	–	–	–	–	–	40	–
Rosenthal, R.e (1990/94)	16/14	6	16/28	15	5/2	–	2/7	1	1/4	–	40/55	22
Ross (1892/93)	–	–	17	–	–	–	–	–	–	–	17	–
Ross, Ian (1966/72)	–	–	42/6	2	9/1	–	3	–	5/2	1	59/9	4
Ross, Jimmy (1894/97)	–	–	78	37	7	3	–	–	–	–	85	40
Rowley, Antonio (1954/58)	–	–	58	37	3	1	–	–	–	–	61	38
Rowley, Arthur (1952/54)	–	–	13	–	–	–	–	–	–	–	13	–
Ruddock, Neil (1993/94)	39	3	–	–	2	–	5	1	–	–	46	4
Rudham, Doug (1954/60)	–	–	63	–	3	–	–	–	–	–	66	–
Rush, I. (1980/87, 1988/94)	72/1	28	329/10	183	48/2	36	69	41	33/1	21	549/14	309
Russell, Colin (1980/81)	–	–	0/1	–	–	–	–	–	–	–	0/1	–
Rylands, Dave (1973/74)	–	–	1	–	1	–	–	–	–	–	1	–
Salisbury, William (1928/29)	–	–	16	2	1	–	–	–	–	–	17	3
Sambrooke, J (1922/23)	–	–	2	–	–	–	–	–	–	–	2	–
Satterthwaite, C. (1899/1902)	–	–	46	12	–	–	–	–	–	–	46	12
Saul, Percy (1906/09)	–	–	75	–	8	–	–	–	–	–	83	–
Saunders, Dean (1991/92)	6	1	36	10	8	2	5	2	5	9	60	24
Saunders, Roy (1952/59)	–	–	132	1	12	–	–	–	–	–	144	1
Savage, Robert (1931/28)	–	–	100	2	5	–	–	–	–	–	105	2
Scott, A (1929/31)	–	–	3	–	1	–	–	–	–	–	4	2

Player	FAPL App	FAPL Goals	League App	League Goals	FACup App	FACup Goals	LgeCup App	LgeCup Goals	Europe App	Europe Goals	Totals App	Totals Goals
Scott, Elisha (1912/34)	-	-	430	-	37	-	-	-	-	-	467	-
Scott, T (1911/13)	-	-	10	-	-	-	-	-	-	-	10	-
Scott, Tom (1924/28)	-	-	17	4	1	-	-	-	-	-	18	4
Seagraves, Mark (1985/86)	-	-	-	-	1	-	1	-	0	-	2	-
Sealey, John (1964/65)	-	-	1	1	1	-	-	-	-	-	2	1
Shafto, John (1937/39)	-	-	17	6	3	1	-	-	-	-	20	7
Shannon, Les (1947/49)	-	-	11	1	-	-	-	-	-	-	11	1
Shears (1925/29)	-	-	16	-	-	-	-	-	-	-	16	-
Sheedy, Kevin (1980/82)	-	-	1/2	-	-	-	2	2	-	-	3/2	2
Sheldon, Jackie (1913/21)	-	-	129	17	18	3	-	-	-	-	147	20
Shepherd, Bill (1948/52)	-	-	53	-	4	-	-	-	-	-	57	-
Shield (1935/36)	-	-	1	-	-	-	-	-	-	-	1	-
Shields, Sam (1949/50)	-	-	-	-	-	-	-	-	-	-	-	-
Shone, Danny (1921/26)	-	-	76	23	5	3	-	-	-	-	81	26
Sidlow, Cyril (1946/51)	-	-	149	-	16	-	-	-	-	-	165	-
Slater, Bert (1959/62)	-	-	99	-	9	-	3	-	-	-	111	-
Sloan, Donald (1908/09)	-	-	6	5	-	-	-	-	-	-	6	5
Smith (1892/93)	-	-	10	5	-	-	-	-	-	-	10	5
Smith (1937/38)	-	-	1	-	-	-	-	-	-	-	1	-
Smith, Jack (1951/54)	-	-	57	14	2	-	-	-	-	-	59	14
Smith, Jimmy (1929/32)	-	-	61	38	1	-	-	-	-	-	62	38
Smith, S (1903/04)	-	-	2	1	-	-	-	-	-	-	2	1
Smith, Tommy (1962/78)	-	-	467	36	52	2	30	2	83/1	8	632/1	48
Smyth, Sammy (1952/54)	-	-	45	20	-	-	-	-	-	-	45	20
Souness, Graeme (1977/84)	-	-	246/1	38	24	2	45	9	35/1	7	350/2	56

Player	FAPL		League		FACup		LgeCup		Europe		Totals	
	App	Goals	App	Goals	App	Goals	App	Goals	App	Goals	App	Goals
South, Alex (1954/55)	-	-	6	1	1	-	-	-	-	-	7	1
Spackman, Nigel (1986/89)	-	-	35/12	1	5	-	6/1	-	-	-	46/13	1
Speakman, J (1909/20)	-	-	33	-	1	-	-	-	-	-	34	-
Speedie, Eddie (1945/54)	-	-	8/4	6	1/1	-	-	-	-	-	9/5	6
Spicer (1990/91)	-	-	158	2	10	-	-	-	-	-	168	2
Staniforth, F (1913/14)	-	-	3	-	-	-	-	-	-	-	3	-
Staunton, Steve (1986/91)	-	-	55/10	-	14/2	1	7/2	4	-	-	76/14	5
Steele, William (1931/35)	-	-	120	-	8	-	-	-	-	-	128	-
Stevenson, 'General' (1898/1900)	-	-	21	-	2	-	-	-	-	-	23	-
Stevenson, Willie (1962/68)	-	-	188	15	24	1	-	-	25/1	1	237/1	17
Stewart, James (1909/14)	-	-	64	27	4	-	-	-	-	-	68	27
Stewart, Paul (1992/94)	28/4	1	-	-	1	-	6	-	2	2	37/4	3
St John, Ian (1961/71)	-	-	334/2	95	48/1	12	7	1	30/2	10	419/5	118
Storer, Harry (1895/1900)	-	-	106	-	15	-	-	-	-	-	121	-
Storton, Trevor (1972/74)	-	-	5	-	1	-	4	-	1/1	-	11/1	-
Stott, James (1893/94)	-	-	16	14	2	-	-	-	-	-	18	14
Strong, Geoff (1964/70)	-	-	150/5	29	23	1	4	-	16	2	193/5	32
Stubbins, Albert (1946/53)	-	-	161	75	19	8	-	-	-	-	180	83
Tanner, Nicky (1988/93)	2/2	-	34/3	-	2	-	7/1	-	6/2	-	48/5	-
Taylor, Harold (1932/37)	-	-	69	6	2	-	-	-	-	-	71	6
Taylor, Phil (1935/54)	-	-	314	34	31	-	-	-	-	-	345	34
Tennant, Jack (1933/35)	-	-	39	-	3	-	-	-	-	-	42	-
Thomas, Michael (1991/94)	7/8	1	16/1	3	7	2	-	-	1	-	33/9	6
Thompson (1929/31)	-	-	5	-	1	-	-	-	-	-	6	-
Thompson, Max (1973/76)	-	-	1	-	-	-	-	-	0/1	-	1/1	-

Player	FAPL App	FAPL Goals	League App	League Goals	FACup App	FACup Goals	LgeCup App	LgeCup Goals	Europe App	Europe Goals	Totals App	Totals Goals
Thompson, Peter (1963/72)	–	–	318/4	41	37/1	5	9	2	40/3	6	404/8	54
Thompson, Phil (1971/83)	–	–	337/3	7	36	–	42/1	1	44/3	4	459/7	12
Thomson, Bobby (1962/64)	–	–	6	–	1	–	–	–	–	–	7	–
Tomley, Frederick (1954/55)	–	–	2	–	–	–	–	–	–	–	2	–
Toshack, John (1970/78)	–	–	169/3	74	24	8	13	3	30/6	10	236/9	95
Toswill, J (1912/13)	–	–	11	1	–	–	–	–	–	–	11	1
Twentyman, Geoff (1953/60)	–	–	170	18	14	1	–	–	–	–	184	19
Underwood, Dave (1953/56)	–	–	45	–	5	–	–	–	–	–	50	–
Uren, Harold (1907/12)	–	–	43	2	3	–	–	–	–	–	46	2
Van Den Berg, H. (1937/40)	–	–	22	4	–	–	–	–	–	–	22	4
Venison, Barry (1986/92)	–	–	103/7	1	16/4	–	13/3	–	0/3	1	132/17	2
Waddle, Alan (1973/77)	–	–	11/5	1	2	–	–	–	0/1	–	16/6	1
Wadsworth, Harold (1919/24)	–	–	54	3	–	–	–	–	–	–	54	3
Wadsworth, Walter (1914/26)	–	–	217	7	23	1	–	–	–	–	240	8
Walker, John (1897/1902)	–	–	121	30	12	1	–	–	–	–	133	31
Wall, Peter (1967/1970)	–	–	31	–	6	–	2	–	3	–	42	–
Wallace, Gordon (1962/67)	–	–	19/1	3	–	–	–	–	1	2	20/1	5
Walsh, Jimmy (1923/28)	–	–	68	24	8	3	–	–	–	–	76	27
Walsh, Paul (1984/87)	–	–	63/14	25	6/2	3	10/2	4	6	3	85/18	35
Walters, Mark (1991/94)	33/18	11	18/7	3	4/1	–	9/2	4	7/1	1	71/29	19
Wark, John (1983/87)	–	–	64/6	28	11/2	6	6/4	3	9	5	90/12	42
Watkinson, Will (1946/50)	–	–	24	2	–	–	–	–	–	–	24	2
Watson (1988/90)	–	–	3/1	–	1/1	–	1/1	–	–	–	5/2	–
Welfare, J (1912/13)	–	–	4	–	–	–	–	–	–	–	4	–
West, Alfred (1903/11)	–	–	128	5	12	1	–	–	–	–	140	6

Player	FAPL App	FAPL Goals	League App	League Goals	FACup App	FACup Goals	LgeCup App	LgeCup Goals	Europe App	Europe Goals	Totals App	Totals Goals
Wheeler, Johnny (1956/62)	–	–	164	21	10	2	3	–	–	–	177	23
Whelan, Ronnie (1980/94)	40	2	311/12	43	40/1	7	47/4	14	22/1	6	460/18	72
White, Dick (1955/62)	–	–	203	–	10	1	3	–	–	–	216	1
White, W (1901/02)	–	–	6	1	–	–	–	–	–	–	6	1
Whitham, Jack (1970/72)	–	–	15	7	–	–	1	–	–	–	16	7
Whitehead, J (1894/96)	–	–	3	–	–	–	–	–	–	–	3	–
Whitehurst, Albert (1928/29)	–	–	8	2	–	–	–	–	–	–	8	2
Whitworth, George (1951/52)	–	–	9	–	–	–	–	–	–	–	9	–
Wilkie, Thomas (1895/99)	–	–	59	1	6	1	–	–	–	–	65	2
Wilkinson, Barry (1953/60)	–	–	78	–	1	–	–	–	–	–	79	–
Williams, Bryan (1948/53)	–	–	31	5	3	–	–	–	–	–	34	5
Wilson, Charlie (1897/1905)	–	–	84	3	6	–	–	–	–	–	90	3
Wilson, D (1899/1900)	–	–	2	–	–	–	–	–	–	–	2	–
Wilson, Dave (1966/67)	–	–	0/1	–	–	–	–	–	–	–	0/1	–
Worgan, A (1893/95)	–	–	2	2	–	–	–	–	–	–	2	2
Woan, Don (1950/51)	–	–	2	–	–	–	–	–	–	–	2	–
Wright, Dave (1929/34)	–	–	93	35	7	–	–	–	–	–	100	35
Wright, Mark (1991/94)	63/4	3	21	–	14	–	3/2	1	7	1	108/6	5
Wright, Vic (1933/37)	–	–	81	31	4	2	–	–	–	–	85	33
Wyllie (1892/93)	–	–	22	11	–	–	–	–	–	–	22	11
Yeats, Ron (1961/71)	–	–	357/1	13	50	2	7	–	36	2	450/1	15
Younger, Tommy (1956/59)	–	–	120	–	7	–	–	–	–	–	127	–

Full Record in Cup Competitions – *FA Cup*

1892/93

1st Qual Round	Nantwich	(a)	4-0	Miller 3, Unknown
2nd Qual Round	Newtown	(h)	9-0	Wyllie 3, McVean 2, McCartney, H McQueen, Cameron, Townsend (og)
3rd Qual Round	Northwich Victoria	(a)	1-2	Wyllie

1893/94

1st Round	Grimsby Town	(h)	3-0	Bradshaw 2, McQueen
2nd Round	Preston North End	(h)	3-2	Henderson 2, McVean
3rd Round	Bolton Wanderers	(a)	0-3	

1894/95

1st Round	Barnsley St Peter's	(a)	2-1†	McVean, Ross
(agreed as 1-1 draw following Barnsley protest)				
Replay	Barnsley St Peter's	(h)	4-0	Bradshaw, Drummond, McVean, McQueen
2nd Round	Nottingham Forest	(h)	0-2	

1895/96

1st Round	Millwall	(h)	4-1	Ross, Becton, Allan, Bradshaw
2nd Round	Wolves	(a)	0-2	

1896/97

1st Round	Burton Swifts	(h)	4-3	Hannah, Allan, Cleghorn, Ross
2nd Round	West Brom. Albion	(a)	2-1	McVean, Neill
3rd Round	Nottingham Forest	(h)	1-1	Becton
Replay	Nottingham Forest	(a)	1-0	Allan
Semi-Final	Aston Villa	(n)	0-3	

1897/98

1st Round	Hucknall St John's	(h)	2-0	
2nd Round	Newton Heath	(a)	0-0	
Replay	Newton Heath	(h)	2-1	Wilkie, Cunliff
3rd Round	Derby County	(a)	1-1	
Replay	Derby County	(h)	1-5	Becton (pen)

1898/99

1st Round	Blackburn Rovers	(h)	2-0	Cox, Allan
2nd Round	Newcastle United	(h)	3-1	Morgan, Raisbeck, Higgins (og)
Semi-Final	Sheffield United	(n)	2-2	Allan, Morgan
Replay	Sheffield United	(n)	4-4	Walker, Allan, Boyle (og), Cox
Replay	Sheffield United	(n)	1-0	Allan
(match abandoned)				

Replay	Sheffield United	(n)	0-1	
3rd Round	West Brom. Albion	(a)	2-0	

1899/1900

1st Round	Stoke City	(a)	0-0	
Replay	Stoke City	(h)	1-0	Hunter
2nd Round	West Brom. Albion	(h)	1-1	Cox
Replay	West Brom. Albion	(a)	1-2	Robertson

1900/01

1st Round	Notts County	(a)	0-2	

1901/02

1st Round	Everton	(h)	2-2	T Robertson (pen), Hunter
Replay	Everton	(a)	2-0	Raisbeck, Hunter
2nd Round	Southampton	(a)	1-4	Fleming

1902/03

1st Round	Manchester Utd	(a)	1-2	Raybould

1903/04

1st Round	Blackburn Rovers	(a)	1-3	Raybould

1904/05

1st Round	Everton	(h)	1-1	
Replay	Everton	(a)	1-2	Goddard

1905/06

1st Round	Leicester Fosse	(h)	2-1	Raybould, Goddard
2nd Round	Barnsley	(h)	1-0	West
3rd Round	Brentford	(h)	2-0	Hewitt, Goddard
4th Round	Southampton	(h)	3-0	Raybould 3
Semi-Final	Everton,	(n)	0-2	

1906/07

1st Round	Birmingham	(h)	2-1	Raybould 2
2nd Round	Oldham Athletic	(a)	1-0	McPherson
3rd Round	Bradford City	(h)	1-0	Cox
4th Round	Sheffield Wed.	(a)	0-1	

1907/08

1st Round	Derby County	(h)	4-2	Cox, Gorman, Bradley, Parkinson
2nd Round	Brighton	(h)	1-1	Cox
Replay	Brighton	(a)	3-0	Bradley 2, Cox
3rd Round	Newcastle United	(a)	1-3	Saul

1908/09

1st Round	Lincoln City	(h)	5-1	Orr 3, Hewitt, Parkinson
2nd Round	Norwich City	(h)	2-3	Cox, Robinson

1909/10

| 1st Round | Bristol City | (a) | 0-2 | |

1910/11

| 1st Round | Gainsborough Trin. | (h) | 3-2 | Bowyer 2, Goddard |
| 2nd Round | Everton | (a) | 1-2 | Parkinson |

1911/12

| 1st Round | Leyton | (h) | 1-0 | Parkinson |
| 2nd Round | Fulham | (a) | 0-3 | |

1912/13

1st Round	Bristol City	(h)	3-0	Goddard (pen), Peake, Lacey
2nd Round	Arsenal	(a)	4-1	Metcalfe 3, Lacey
3rd Round	Newcastle United	(h)	1-1	Lacey
Replay	Newcastle United	(a)	0-1	

1913/14

1st Round	Barnsley	(h)	1-1	Lacey
Replay	Barnsley	(a)	1-0	Lacey
2nd Round	Gillingham	(h)	2-0	Lacey, Ferguson
3rd Round	West Ham United	(a)	1-1	Miller
Replay	West Ham United	(h)	5-1	Lacey 2, Miller 2, Metcalfe
4th Round	Q.P.R.	(h)	2-1	Sheldon, Miller
Semi-Final	Aston Villa	(n)	2-0	Nicholl 2
Final	Burnley	(n)	0-1	

1914/15

| 1st Round | Stockport County | (h) | 3-0 | Pagnam 2, Metcalfe |
| 2nd Round | Sheffield United | (a) | 0-1 | |

1919/20

1st Round	South Shields	(a)	1-1	Lewis
Replay	South Shields	(h)	2-0	Lewis, Sheldon
2nd Round	Luton Town	(a)	2-0	Lacey 2
3rd Round	Birmingham	(h)	2-0	Sheldon, Miller
4th Round	Huddersfield Town	(a)	1-2	Miller

1920/21

1st Round	Manchester Utd	(h)	1-1	Chambers
Replay	Manchester Utd	(a)	2-1	Lacey, Chambers
2nd Round	Newcastle Utd	(a)	0-1	

1921/22

1st Round	Sunderland	(a)	1-1	Forshaw
Replay	Sunderland	(h)	5-0	Forshaw 2, Chambers 2, Wadsworth
2nd Round	West Brom. Albion	(a)	0-1	

1922/23

1st Round	Arsenal	(h)	0-0	
Replay	Arsenal	(a)	4-1	Chambers 2, Johnson, McKinlay (pen)
2nd Round	Wolves	(a)	2-0	Johnson, Forshaw
3rd Round	Sheffield Utd	(h)	1-2	Chambers

1923/24

1st Round	Bradford City	(h)	2-1	Chambers 2
2nd Round	Bolton Wanderers	(a)	4-1	Walsh 3, Chambers
3rd Round	Southampton	(a)	0-0	
Replay	Southampton	(h)	2-0	Chambers, Forshaw
4th Round	Newcastle Utd	(a)	0-1	

1924/25

1st Round	Leeds Utd	(h)	3-0	Shone 2, Hopkin
2nd Round	Bristol City	(a)	1-0	Rawlings
3rd Round	Birmingham	(h)	2-1	Rawlings, Shone
4th Round	Southampton	(a)	0-1	

1925/26

3rd Round	Southampton	(a)	0-0	
Replay	Southampton	(h)	1-0	Forshaw
4th Round	Fulham	(a)	1-3	Forshaw

1926/27

3rd Round	Bournemouth	(a)	1-1	Hodgson
Replay	Bournemouth	(h)	4-1	Hopkin, Chambers 3
4th Round	Southport	(h)	3-1	Hodgson, Chambers, Edmed
5th Round	Arsenal	(a)	0-2	

1927/28

3rd Round	Darlington	(h)	1-0	Chambers
4th Round	Cardiff City	(a)	1-2	Edmed (pen)

1928/29

3rd Round	Bristol City	(a)	2-0	Salisbury, Hodgson
4th Round	Bolton Wanderers	(h)	0-0	
Replay	Bolton Wanderers	(a)	2-5†	Lindsay, Hodgson

1929/30

3rd Round	Cardiff City	(h)	1-2	McPherson

1930/31

3rd Round	Birmingham City	(h)	0-2	

1931/32

3rd Round	Everton	(a)	2-1	Gunson, Hodgson
4th Round	Chesterfield	(a)	4-2	Barton 4
5th Round	Grimsby Town	(h)	1-0	Gunson

6th Round	Chelsea	(h)	0-2

1932/33

3rd Round	West Brom Albion	(a)	0-2

1933/34

3rd Round	Fulham	(h)	1-1	
Replay	Fulham	(a)	3-2†	Hanson, Bradshaw, Roberts
4th Round	Tranmere Rovers	(h)	3-1	English 2, Nieuwenhuys
5th Round	Bolton Wanderers	(h)	0-3	

1934/35

3rd Round	Yeovil & Petters	(a)	6-2	Nieuwenhuys, Wright, Hodgson 2, Roberts 2
4th Round	Blackburn Rovers	(a)	0-1	

1935/36

3rd Round	Swansea Town	(h)	1-0	Wright
4th Round	Arsenal	(h)	0-2	

1936/37

3rd Round	Norwich City	(a)	0-3

1937/38

3rd Round	Crystal Palace	(a)	0-0	
Replay	Crystal Palace	(h)	3-1†	Shafto, Collins (og), Fagan(pen)
4th Round	Sheffield Utd	(a)	1-1	Hanson
Replay	Sheffield Utd	(h)	1-0	Johnson (og)
5th Round	Huddersfield Town	(h)	0-1	

1938/39

3rd Round	Luton Town	(h)	3-0	
4th Round	Stockport County	(h)	5-1	
5th Round	Wolves	(a)	1-4	Fagan (pen)

1945/46

3rd Round (leg 1)	Chester	(a)	2-0	Liddell, Fagan
3rd Round (leg 2)	Chester	(h)	2-1	Fagan 2
(Liverpool won 4-1 on aggregate)				
4th Round (leg 1)	Bolton Wanderers	(a)	0-5	
4th Round (leg 2)	Bolton Wanderers	(h)	2-0	Balmer, Nieuwenhuys
(Bolton Wanderers won 5-2 on aggregate)				

1946/47

3rd Round	Walsall	(a)	5-2	Foulkes (og), Done, Liddell, Balmer 2
4th Round	Grimsby Town	(h)	2-0	Stubbins, Done
5th Round	Derby County	(h)	1-0	Balmer
6th Round	Brimingham City	(h)	4-1	Stubbins 3, Balmer

Semi-Final	Burnley		0-0†	Played at Ewood Park
Replay	Burnley		0-1	Played at Maine Road

1947/48

3rd Round	Nottingham Forest	(h)	4-1	Priday, Stubbins 2, Liddell
4th Round	Manchester Utd	(a)	0-3	

1948/49

3rd Round	Nottingham Forest	(a)	2-2†	Fagan, Paisley
Replay	Nottingham Forest	(h)	4-0	Payne, Balmer 2, Stubbins
4th Round	Notts County	(h)	1-0	Liddell
5th Round	Wolves	(a)	1-3	Done

1949/50

3rd Round	Blackburn Rovers	(a)	0-0	
Replay	Blackburn Rovers	(h)	2-1	Payne, Fagan
4th Round	Exeter City	(h)	3-1	Baron, Fagan, Payne
5th Round	Stockport County	(a)	2-1	Fagan, Stubbins
6th Round	Blackpool	(h)	2-1	Fagan, Liddell
Semi-Final	Everton	(n)	2-0	Paisley, Liddell
Final	Arsenal	(n)	0-2	

1950/51

3rd Round	Norwich City	(a)	1-3	Balmer

1951/52

3rd Round	Workington	(h)	1-0	Payne
4th Round	Wolves	(h)	2-1	Paisley, Done
5th Round	Burnley	(a)	0-2	

1952/53

3rd Round	Gateshead	(a)	0-1	

1953/54

3rd Round	Bolton Wanderers	(a)	0-1	

1954/55

3rd Round	Lincoln City	(a)	1-1	Evans
Replay	Lincoln City	(h)	1-0†	Evans
4th Round	Everton	(h)	4-0	Liddell, A'Court, Evans 2
5th Round	Huddersfield Town	(h)	0-2	

1955/56

3rd Round	Accrington Stanley	(h)	2-0	Liddell 2
4th Round	Scunthorpe United	(h)	3-3	Liddell 2, Payne
Replay	Scunthorpe United	(a)	2-1†	Liddell, Arnell
5th Round	Manchester City	(a)	0-0	
Replay	Manchester City	(h)	1-2	Arnell

1956/57

3rd Round	Southend United	(a)	1-2	Wheeler

1957/58

3rd Round	Southend United	(h)	1-1	Smith (og)
Replay	Southend United	(a)	3-2	Molyneux, White, Rowley
4th Round	Northampton Town	(h)	3-1	Liddell, Collins (og), Bimpson
5th Round	Scunthorpe United	(a)	1-0	Murdoch
6th Round	Blackburn Rovers	(a)	1-2	Murdoch

1958/59

3rd Round	Worcester City	(a)	1-2	Twentyman (pen)

1959/60

3rd Round	Leyton Orient	(h)	2-1	Hunt 2
4th Round	Manchester United	(h)	1-3	Wheeler

1960/61

3rd Round	Coventry City	(h)	3-2	Hunt, Lewis, Harrower
4th Round	Sunderland	(h)	0-2	

1961/62

3rd Round	Chelsea	(h)	4-3	St John 2, Hunt, A'Court
4th Round	Oldham Athletic	(a)	2-1	St John 2
5th Round	Preston North End	(h)	0-0	
Replay	Preston North End	(a)	0-0†	
Second replay	Preston North End	(n)	0-1	

1962/63

3rd Round	Wrexham	(a)	3-0	Hunt, Lewis, Melia
4th Round	Burnley	(a)	1-1	Lewis
Replay	Burnley	(h)	2-1†	St John, Moran (pen)
5th Round	Arsenal	(a)	2-1	Melia, Moran (pen)
6th Round	West Ham Utd	(h)	1-0	Hunt
Semi-Final	Leicester City	(n)	0-1	

1963/64

3rd Round	Derby County	(h)	5-0	Arrowsmith 4, Hunt
4th Round	Port Vale	(h)	0-0	
Replay	Port Vale	(a)	2-1†	Hunt, Thompson
5th Round	Arsenal	(a)	1-0	
6th Round	Swansea Town	(h)	1-2	Thompson

1964/65

3rd Round	West Brom. Albion	(a)	2-1	Hunt, St John
4th Round	Stockport County	(h)	1-1	Milne
Replay	Stockport County	(a)	2-0	Hunt 2
5th Round	Bolton Wanderers	(a)	1-0	Callaghan
6th Round	Leicester City	(a)	0-0	
Replay	Leicester City	(h)	1-0	Hunt
Semi-Final	Chelsea	(n)	2-0	Thompson, Stevenson (pen)
Final	Leeds United	(n)	2-1†	Hunt, St John

1965/66

3rd Round	Chelsea	(h)	1-2	Hunt

1966/67

3rd Round	Watford	(a)	0-0	
Replay	Watford	(h)	3-1	St John, Hunt, Lawler
4th Round	Aston Villa	(h)	1-0	St John
5th Round	Everton	(a)	0-1	

1967/68

3rd Round	Bournemouth	(a)	0-0	
Replay	Bournemouth	(h)	4-1	Hateley, Thompson, Hunt, Lawler
4th Round	Walsall	(a)	0-0	
Replay	Walsall	(h)	5-2	Hateley 4, Strong
5th Round	Tottenham Hotspur	(a)	1-1	Hateley
Replay	Tottenham Hotspur	(h)	2-1	Hunt, Smith (pen)
6th Round	West Brom. Albion	(a)	0-0	
Replay	West Brom. Albion	(h)	1-1†	Hateley
Second replay	West Brom. Albion	(n)	1-2	Hateley

1968/69

3rd Round	Doncaster Rovers	(h)	2-0	Hunt, Callaghan
4th Round	Burnley	(h)	2-1	Smith (pen), Hughes
5th Round	Leicester City	(a)	0-0	
Replay	Leicester City	(h)	0-1	

1969/70

3rd Round	Coventry City	(a)	1-1	
Replay	Coventry City	(h)	3-0	Ross, Thompson, Graham
4th Round	Wrexham	(h)	3-1	Graham 2, St John
5th Round	Leicester City	(h)	0-0	
Replay	Leicester City	(a)	2-0	Evans 2
6th Round	Watford	(a)	0-1	

1970/71

3rd Round	Aldershot	(h)	1-0	McLaughlin
4th Round	Swansea Town	(h)	3-0	Toshack, St John, Lawler
5th Round	Southampton	(h)	1-0	Lawler
6th Round	Tottenham Hotspur	(h)	0-0	
Replay	Tottenham Hotspur	(a)	1-0	Heighway
Semi-Final	Everton	(n)	2-1	Evans, Hall
Final	Arsenal	(n)	1-2†	Heighway

1971/72

3rd Round	Oxford United	(a)	3-0	Keegan 2, Lindsay
4th Round	Leeds United	(h)	0-0	
Replay	Leeds United	(a)	0-2	

1972/73

3rd Round	Burnley	(a)	0-0	
Replay	Burnley	(h)	3-0	Toshack 2, Cormack
4th Round	Manchester City	(h)	0-0	
Replay	Manchester City	(a)	0-2	

1973/74

3rd Round	Doncaster Rovers	(h)	2-2	Keegan 2
Replay	Doncaster Rovers	(a)	2-0	Heighway, Cormack
4th Round	Carlisle United	(h)	0-0	
Replay	Carlisle United	(a)	2-0	Boersma, Toshack
5th Round	Ipswich Town	(h)	2-0	Hall, Keegan
6th Round	Bristol City	(a)	1-0	Toshack
Semi-Final	Leicester City	(n)	0-0	
Replay	Leicester City	(n)	3-1	Hall, Keegan, Toshack
Final	Newcastle United	(n)	3-0	Keegan 2, Heighway

1974/75

3rd Round	Stoke City	(h)	2-0	Heighway, Keegan
4th Round	Ipswich Town	(a)	0-1	

1975/76

3rd Round	West Ham Utd	(a)	2-0	Keegan, Toshack
4th Round	Derby County	(a)	0-1	

1976/77

3rd Round	Crystal Palace	(h)	0-0	
Replay	Crystal Palace	(a)	3-2	Keegan, Heighway 2
4th Round	Carlisle United	(h)	3-0	Keegan, Toshack, Heighway
5th Round	Oldham Athletic	(h)	3-1	Keegan, Case, Neal (pen)
6th Round	Middlesbrough	(h)	2-0	Fairclough, Keegan
Semi-Final	Everton	(n)	2-2	McDermott, Case
Replay	Everton	(n)	3-0	Neal (pen), Case, Kennedy
Final	Manchester Utd	(n)	1-2	Case

1977/78

3rd Round	Chelsea	(a)	2-4	Johnson, Dalglish

1978/79

3rd Round	Southend United	(a)	0-0	
Replay	Southend United	(h)	3-0	
4th Round	Blackburn Rovers	(h)	1-0	
5th Round	Burnley	(h)	3-0	Johnson 2, Souness
6th Round	Ipswich Town	(a)	1-0	Dalglish
Semi-Final	Manchester Utd	(n)	2-2	Dalglish, Hansen
Replay	Manchester Utd	(n)	0-1	

1979/80

3rd Round	Grimsby Town	(h)	5-0	Souness, Johnson 3, Case
4th Round	Nottingham Forest	(a)	2-0	Dalglish, McDermott
5th Round	Bury	(h)	2-0	Fairclough 2
6th Round	Tottenham Hotspur	(a)	1-0	McDermott
Semi-Final	Arsenal	(n)	0-0	
Replay	Arsenal	(n)	1-1†	Fairclough
Second replay	Arsenal	(n)	1-1†	Dalglish
Third replay	Arsenal	(n)	0-1	

1980/81

3rd Round	Altrincham	(h)	4-1	McDermott, Dalglish 2, Kennedy
4th Round	Everton	(a)	1-2	Case

1981/82

3rd Round	Swansea City	(a)	4-0	Hansen, Rush 2, Lawrenson
4th Round	Sunderland	(a)	3-0	Dalglish 2, Rush
5th Round	Chelsea	(a)	0-2	

1982/83

3rd Round	Blackburn Rovers	(a)	2-1	Hodgson, Rush
5th Round	Brighton & Hove Alb	(h)	1-2	Johnston

1983/84

3rd Round	Newcastle United	(h)	4-0	Robinson, Rush 2, Johnston
4th Round	Brighton & Hove Alb	(a)	0-2	

1984/85

3rd Round	Aston Villa	(h)	3-0	Rush 2, Wark
4th Round	Tottenham Hotspur	(h)	1-0	Rush
5th Round	York City	(a)	1-1	Rush
Replay	York City	(h)	7-0	Whelan 2, Wark 3, Neal, Walsh
6th Round	Barnsley	(a)	4-0	Rush 3, Whelan
Semi-Final	Manchester Utd	(n)	2-2†	Whelan, Walsh
Replay	Manchester Utd	(n)	1-2	McGrath (og)

1985/86

3rd Round	Norwich City	(h)	5-0	MacDonald, Walsh, McMahon, Whelan, Wark
4th Round	Chelsea	(a)	2-1	Rush, Lawrenson
5th Round	York City	(a)	1-1	Molby (pen)
Replay	York City	(h)	3-1†	Wark, Molby, Dalglish
6th Round	Watford	(h)	0-0	
Replay	Watford	(a)	2-1†	Molby (pen), Rush
Semi-Final	Southampton	(n)	2-0†	Rush 2
Final	Everton	(n)	3-1	Rush 2, Johnston

1986/87

3rd Round	Luton Town	(a)	0-0	
Replay	Luton Town	(h)	0-0	
Second replay	Luton Town	(a)	0-3	

1987/88

3rd Round	Stoke City	(a)	0-0	
Replay	Stoke City	(h)	1-0	Beardsley
4th Round	Aston Villa	(a)	2-0	Barnes, Beardsley
5th Round	Everton	(a)	1-0	Houghton
6th Round	Manchester City	(a)	4-0	Houghton, Beardsley, Johnston, Barnes
Semi-Final	Nottingham Forest	(n)	2-1	Aldridge 2
Final	Wimbledon	(n)	0-1	

1988/89

3rd Round	Carlisle United	(a)	3-0	Barnes, McMahon 2
4th Round	Millwall	(a)	2-0	Rush, Aldridge
5th Round	Hull City	(a)	3-2	Barnes, Aldridge 2
6th Round	Brentford	(h)	4-0	McMahon, Barnes, Beardsley 2
Semi-Final	Nottingham Forest	(n)	0-0*	
	*(*match abandoned after 6 minutes)*			
rematch	Nottingham Forest	(n)	3-1	Aldridge 2, Laws (og)
Final	Everton	(n)	3-2	Aldridge, Rush 2

1989/90

3rd Round	Swansea City	(a)	0-0	
Replay	Swansea City	(h)	8-0	Barnes 2, Whelan, Rush 3, Beardsley, Nicol
4th Round	Norwich City	(a)	0-0	
Replay	Norwich City	(h)	3-1	Nicol, Barnes, Beardsley
5th Round	Southampton	(h)	3-0	Rush, Beardsley, Nicol
6th Round	Queens Park Rangers	(a)	2-2	Barnes, Rush
Replay	Queens Park Rangers	(h)	1-0	Beardsley
Semi-Final	Crystal Palace	(n)	3-4	Rush, McMahon, Barnes

1990/91

3rd Round	Blackburn Rovers	(a)	1-1	(og)
Replay	Blackburn Rovers	(h)	3-0	Houghton, Rush, Staunton
4th Round	Brighton & Hove Alb	(h)	2-2	Rush 2
Replay	Brighton & Hove Alb	(a)	3-2	Rush, McMahon 2
5th Round	Everton	(h)	0-0	
Replay	Everton	(a)	4-4	Beardsley 2, Rush, Barnes
Second replay	Everton	(a)	0-1	

227

1991/92

3rd Round	Crewe Alexandra	(a)	4-0	Barnes 3, McManaman
4th Round	Bristol Rovers	(a)	1-1	Saunders
Replay	Bristol Rovers	(h)	2-1	Saunders, McManaman
5th Round	Ipswich Town	(a)	0-0	
Replay	Ipswich Town	(h)	3-2	McManaman, Houghton, Molby
6th Round	Aston Villa	(h)	1-0	Thomas
Semi-Final	Portsmouth	(n)	1-1	Whelan
Replay	Portsmouth	(n)	0-0	
	(Liverpool won 3-1 on penalties)			
Final	Sunderland	(n)	2-0	Rush, Thomas

1992/93

3rd Round	Bolton Wanderers	(a)	2-2	Winstanley (og), Rush
Replay	Bolton Wanderers	(h)	0-2	

1993/94

3rd Round	Bristol City	(a)	(1-1)*	(Rush)
	*(*match abandoned after 65 minutes)*			
rematch	Bristol City	(a)	1-1	Rush
Replay	Bristol City	(h)	0-1	

Full Record in Cup Competitions – *League Cup*

1960/61

2nd Rnd (leg1)	Luton Town	(h)	1-1	Leishman
2nd Rnd (leg2)	Luton Town	(a)	5-2	Lewis 2, Hickson, Hunt 2
3rd Round	Southampton	(h)	1-2	Hunt

1967/68

2nd Rnd (leg1)	Bolton Wanderers	(h)	1-1	Thompson
2nd Rnd (leg2)	Bolton Wanderers	(a)	2-3	Smith (pen), Callaghan

1968/69

2nd Round	Sheffield United	(h)	4-0	Hunt, Lawler, Callaghan, Thompson
3rd Round	Swansea Town	(h)	2-0	Lawler, Hunt
4th Round	Arsenal	(a)	1-2	Lawler

1969/70

2nd Round	Watford	(a)	2-1	Slater (og), St John
3rd Round	Manchester City	(a)	2-3	Evans, Graham

1970/71

2nd Round	Mansfield Town	(a)	0-0	
Replay	Mansfield Town	(h)	3-2†	Hughes, Smith (pen), Evans
3rd Round	Swindon Town	(a)	0-2	

1971/72

2nd Round	Hull City	(h)	3-0	Lawler, Heighway, Hall (pen)
3rd Round	Southampton	(h)	1-0	Heighway
4th Round	West Ham Utd	(a)	1-2	Graham

1972/73

2nd Rnd (leg1)	Carlisle United	(a)	1-1	Keegan
2nd Rnd (leg2)	Carlisle United	(h)	5-1	Keegan, Boersma 2, Lawler, Hieghway
3rd Round	West Brom. Albion	(a)	1-1	Heighway
Replay	West Brom. Albion	(h)	2-1†	Hughes, Keegan
4th Round	Leeds United	(h)	2-2	Keegan, Toshack
Replay	Leeds United	(a)	1-0	Keegan
5th Round	Tottenham Hotspur	(h)	1-1	Hughes
Replay	Tottenham Hotspur	(a)	1-3	Callaghan

1973/74

2nd Rnd (leg1)	West Ham United	(a)	2-2	
2nd Rnd (leg2)	West Ham United	(h)	1-0	Toshack
3rd Round	Sunderland	(a)	2-0	Keegan, Toshack
4th Round	Hull City	(a)	0-0	
Replay	Hull City	(h)	3-1	Callaghan 3
5th Round	Wolves	(a)	0-1	

1974/75

2nd Round	Brentford	(h)	2-1	Kennedy, Boersma
3rd Round	Bristol City	(a)	0-0	
Replay	Bristol City	(h)	4-0	Heighway 2, Kennedy 2
4th Round	Middlesbrough	(h)	0-1	

1975/76

2nd Round	York City	(a)	1-0	Lindsay (pen)
3rd Round	Burnley	(h)	1-1	Case
Replay	Burnley	(a)	0-1	

1976/77

2nd Rnd (leg1)	West Brom. Albion	(h)	1-1	Callaghan
2nd Rnd (leg1)	West Brom.h Albion	(a)	0-1	

1977/78

2nd Round	Chelsea	(h)	2-0	Dalglish, Case
3rd Round	Derby County	(a)	2-0	Fairclough 2
4th Round	Coventry City	(h)	2-2	Fairclough, Neal (pen)
Replay	Coventry City	(a)	2-0	Case, Dalglish
5th Round	Wrexham	(a)	3-1	Dalglish 3
Semi-Final (leg1)	Arsenal	(h)	2-1	Dalglish, Kennedy
Semi-Final (leg2)	Arsenal	(a)	0-0	

(Liverpool won 2-1 on aggregate)

Final	Nottingham Forest	(n)	0-0†	
Replay	Nottingham Forest	(n)	0-1	

1978/79

2nd Round	Sheffield United	(a)	0-1	

1979/80

2nd Round (leg1)	Tranmere Rovers	(a)	0-0	
Replay	Tranmere Rovers	(h)	4-0	Thompson, Dalglish 2, Fairclough
3rd Round	Chesterfield	(h)	3-1	Fairclough, Dalglish, McDermott
4th Round	Exeter City	(h)	2-0	Fairclough 2
5th Round	Norwich City	(a)	3-1	Johnson 2, Dalglish
Semi-Final (leg1)	Nottingham Forest	(a)	0-1	
Semi-Final (leg2)	Nottingham Forest	(h)	1-1	Fairclough

1980/81

2nd Rnd (leg1)	Bradford City	(a)	0-1	
2nd Rnd (leg2)	Bradford City	(h)	4-0	Dalglish 2, R Kennedy, Johnson
3rd Round	Swindon Town	(h)	5-0	Lee 2, Dalglish, Cockerill (og), Fairclough
4th Round	Portsmouth	(h)	4-1	Dalglish, Johnson 2, Souness
5th Round	Brimingham City	(h)	3-1	Dalglish, McDermott, Johnson
Semi-Final	Manchester City	(a)	1-0	R Kennedy
Replay	Manchester City	(h)	1-1	Dalglish
Final	West Ham United	(n)	1-1†	A Kennedy
Replay	West Ham United	(n)	2-1	Dalglish, Hansen

1981/82

2nd Rnd (leg1)	Exeter City	(h)	5-0	Rush 2, McDermott, Dalglish, Whelan
2nd Rnd (leg2)	Exeter City	(a)	6-0	Rush 2, Dalglish, Neal, Sheedy, Marker (og)
3rd Round	Middlesbrough	(h)	4-1	Sheedy, Rush, Johnson 2
4th Round	Arsenal	(a)	0-0	
Replay	Arsenal	(h)	3-0†	Johnston, McDermott (pen), Dalglish
5th Round	Barnsley	(h)	0-0	
Replay	Barnsley	(a)	3-1	Souness, Johnson, Dalglish
Semi-Final (leg1)	Ipswich Town	(a)	2-0	McDermott, Rush
Semi-Final (leg2)	Ipswich Town	(h)	2-2	Rush, Dalglish
Final	Tottenham Hotspur	(n)	3-1†	Whelan 2, Rush

1982/83

2nd Rnd (leg1)	Ipswich Town	(a)	2-1	Rush 2

2nd Rnd (leg2)	Ipswich Town	(h)	2-0	Whelan, Lawrenson
3rd Round	Rotherham United	(h)	1-0	Johnston
4th Round	Norwich City	(h)	2-0	Lawrenson, Fairclough
5th Round	West Ham United	(h)	2-1	Hodgson, Souness
Semi-Final (leg1)	Burnley	(h)	3-0	Souness, Neal (pen), Hodgson
Semi-Final (leg2)	Burnley	(a)	0-1	
Final	Manchester United	(n)	2-1†	Kennedy, Whelan

1983/84

2nd Rnd (leg1)	Brentford	(a)	4-1	Rush 2, Robinson, Souness
2nd Rnd (leg2)	Brentford	(h)	4-0	Souness (pen), Hodgson, Dalglish, Robinson
3rd Round	Fulham	(a)	1-1	Rush
Replay	Fulham	(h)	1-1	Dalglish
Second replay	Fulham	(a)	1-0†	Souness
4th Round	Birmingham City	(a)	1-1	Souness
Replay	Birmingham City	(h)	3-0	Nicol, Rush 2 (1 pen)
5th Round	Sheffield Wednesday	(a)	2-2	Nicol, Neal (pen)
Replay	Sheffield Wednesday	(h)	3-0	Rush 2, Robinson
Semi-Final	Walsall	(h)	2-2	Whelan 2
Replay	Walsall	(a)	2-0	Rush, Whelan
Final	Everton	(n)	0-0†	
Replay	Everton	(n)	1-0	Souness

1984/85

2nd Rnd (leg1)	Stockport County	(a)	0-0	
2nd Rnd (leg1)	Stockport County	(h)	2-0†	Robinson, Whelan
3rd Round	Tottenham Hotspur	(a)	0-1	

1985/86

2nd Rnd (leg1)	Oldham Athletic	(h)	3-0	McMahon 2, Rush
2nd Rnd (leg2)	Oldham Athletic	(a)	5-2	Whelan 2, Wark, Rush, MacDonald
3rd Round	Brighton & Hove Alb	(h)	4-0	Walsh 3, Dalglish
4th Round	Manchester United	(h)	2-1	Molby 2 (1 pen)
5th Round	Ipswich Town	(h)	3-0	Walsh, Whelan, Rush
Semi-Final (leg1)	Queens Park Rangers	(a)	0-1	
Semi-Final (leg2)	Queens Park Rangers	(h)	2-2	MacMahon, Johnston

1986/87

2nd Rnd (leg1)	Fulham	(h)	10-0	MacMahon 4, Rush 2, Wark2, Whelan, Nicol
2nd Rnd (leg2)	Fulham	(a)	3-2	MacMahon, Parker (og), Molby
3rd Round	Leicester City	(h)	4-1	McMahon 3, Dalglish
4th Round	Coventry City	(a)	0-0	
Replay	Coventry City	(h)	3-1	Molby 3

5th Round	Everton	(a)	1-0	Rush
Semi-Final (leg1)	Southampton	(a)	0-0	
Semi-Final (leg2)	Southampton	(h)	3-0	Whelan, Dalglish, Molby
Final	Arsenal	(n)	1-2	Rush

(The first game when Ian Rush scored but Liverpool lost)

1987/88
2nd Rnd (leg1)	Blackburn Rovers	(a)	1-1	Nicol
2nd Rnd (leg2)	Blackburn Rovers	(h)	1-0	Aldridge
3rd Round	Everton	(h)	0-1	

1988/89
2nd Rnd (leg1)	Walsall	(h)	1-0	Gillespie
2nd Rnd (leg2)	Walsall	(a)	3-1	Barnes, Rush, Molby
3rd Round	Arsenal	(h)	1-1	Barnes
Replay	Arsenal	(a)	0-0	
Second replay	Arsenal	(n)	2-1	McMahon, Aldridge
4th Round	West Ham United	(a)	1-4	Aldridge

1989/90
2nd Rnd (leg1)	Wigan Athletic	(h)	5-2	Hysen, Rush 2, Barnes, Beardsley
2nd Rnd (leg2)	Wigan Athletic	(h)	3-0	Staunton 3
3rd Round	Arsenal	(a)	0-1	

1990/91
2nd Rnd (leg1)	Crewe Alexandra	(h)	5-1	Gillespie, Houghton, Rush 2, McMahon
2nd Rnd (leg2)	Crewe Alexandra	(a)	4-1	Rush 3, Staunton
3rd Round	Manchester United	(a)	1-3	Houghton

1991/92
2nd Rnd (leg1)	Stoke City	(h)	2-2	Rush 2
2nd Rnd (leg2)	Stoke City	(a)	3-2	Saunders, McManaman, Walters
3rd Round	Port Vale	(h)	2-2	McManaman, Rush
Replay	Port Vale	(a)	4-1	Saunders, McManaman, Walters, Houghton
4th Round	Peterborough United	(a)	0-1	

1992/93
2nd Rnd (leg1)	Chesterfield	(h)	4-4	Rosenthal, Hutchison, Walters, Wright
2nd Rnd (leg2)	Chesterfield	(a)	4-1	Hutchison, Redknapp, Walters, Rush
3rd Round	Sheffield United	(a)	0-0	
Replay	Sheffield United	(h)	3-0	McManaman 2, Marsh (pen)
4th Round	Crystal Palace	(h)	1-1	Marsh (pen)

| Replay | Crystal Palace | (a) | 1-2† | Marsh (pen) |

1993/94

2nd Rnd (leg1)	Fulham	(a)	3-1	Rush, Clough, Fowler
2nd Rnd (leg2)	Fulham	(h)	5-0	Fowler 5
3rd Round	Ipswich Town	(h)	3-2	Rush 3
4th Round	Wimbledon	(h)	1-1	Molby
Replay	Wimbledon	(a)	2-2	Ruddock, Segers (og)

(Wimbledon won 4-3 on penalties)

Cup Final Squads – *FA Cup*

Date	Opponents	Venue	Score	Att.

25/4/14   v Burnley   The Crystal Palace   0-1   72,778
Team: Campbell, Longworth, Pursell, Fairfoul, Ferguson, McKinaly, Sheldon,
Metcalfe, Miller, Lacey, Nicholl

29/4/50   v Arsenal   Wembley   0-2   100,000
Team: Sidlow, Lambert, Spicer, Taylor, Jones, Hughes, Payne, Baron, Stubbins,
Fagan, Liddell

1/5/64   v Leeds United   Wembley   2-1†   100,000
Team: Lawrence, Lawler, Byrne, Milne, Yeats, Stevenson, Callaghan, Hunt, St
John, Smith, Thompson. *Scorers:* Hunt 93, St John 111

8/5/71   v Arsenal   Wembley   1-2†
Team: Clemence, Lawler, Lindsay, Smith, Lloyd, Hughes, Callaghan, Evans
(Thompson), Heighway, Toshack. *Scorer:* Heighway 92

4/5/74   v Newcastle United   Wembley   3-0
Team: Clemence, Smith, Lindsay, Thompson, Cormack, Hughes, Keegan, Hall,
Heighway, Toshack, Callaghan. *Scorers:* Keegan 57, 88, Heighway 75

21/5/76   v Manchester United   Wembley   1-2   100,000
Team: Clemence, Neal, Jones, Smith, Kennedy, Hughes, Keegan, Case, Heighway,
Johnson (Callaghan). *Scorer:* Case 52

10/5/86   v Everton   Wembley   3-1
Team: Grobbelaar, Lawrenson, Beglin, Nicol, Whelan, Hansen, Dalglish, Johnston,
Rush, Molby, MacDonald. *Scorers:* Rush 2, Johnston

14/5/88   v Wimbledon   Wembley   0-1
Team: Grobbelaar, Gillespie, Ablett (Molby), Nicol, Johnston, Hansen, Beardsley,
Aldridge, Houghton, Barnes, McMahon

20/5/89   v Everton   Wembley   3-2
Team: Grobbelaar, Ablett, Staunton, Nicol, Whelan, Hansen, Beardsley, Aldridge,
Houghton (Rush), Barnes, McMahon. *Scorers:* Aldridge, Rush (2)

9/5/92   v Sunderland   Wembley   2-0
Team: Grobbelaar, R Jones, Burrows, Nicol, Molby, Wright, Saunders, Houghton, Rush, McManaman, Thomas*Scorers:*Rush, Thomas

Cup Final Squads – *League Cup*

Date	Opponents	Venue	Score

18/3/78   v Nottingham Forest   Wembley   0-0†
Team: Clemence, Neal, Smith, Thompson, Kennedy (Fairclough), Hughes, Dalglish, Case, Heighway, McDermott, Callaghan

22/3/78   v Nottingham Forest   Old Trafford   0-1
Team: Clemence, Neal, Smith, Thompson, Kennedy , Hughes, Dalglish, Case (Fairclough), Heighway, McDermott, Callaghan

14/3/81   v West Ham Utd   Wembley   1-1†
Team: Clemence, Neal, A Kennedy , Thompson, R Kennedy, Hansen, Dalglish, Lee, Rush, McDermott, Souness. *Scorer:* A Kennedy

1/4/81   v West Ham Utd   Villa Park   2-1
Team: Clemence, Neal, A Kennedy , Thompson, R Kennedy, Hansen, Dalglish, Lee, Rush, McDermott, Case. *Scorers:* Dalglish, Hansen

13/3/82   v Tottenham Hotspur   Wembley   3-1†
Team: Grobbelaar, Neal, A Kennedy , Thompson, Whelan, Lawrenson, Dalglish, Lee, Rush, McDermott (Johnson). Souness. *Scorers:* Whelan 2, Rush

26/3/83   v Manchester Utd   Wembley   2-1†
Team: Grobbelaar, Neal, Kennedy , Lawrenson, Whelan, Hansen, Dalglish, Lee, Rush, Johnston (Fairclough), Souness. *Scorers:* Kennedy, Whelan

25/3/84   v Everton   Wembley   0-0†
Team: Grobbelaar, Neal, Kennedy , Lawrenson, Whelan, Hansen, Dalglish, Lee, Rush, Johnston (Robinson). Souness

28/3/84   v Everton   Maine Road   1-0
Team: Grobbelaar, Neal, Kennedy , Lawrenson, Whelan, Hansen, Dalglish, Lee, Rush, Johnston, Souness. *Scorer:* Souness

5/4/87   v Arsenal   Wembley   1-2
Team: Grobbelaar, Gillespie, Venison, Lawrenson, Whelan, Hansen, Walsh, Johnston, Rush, Molby, Wark. *Scorer:* Rush

Cup Final Squads – *European Cup*

Date	Opponents	Venue	Score

25/5/77 v Bor. Moenchengladbach Rome 3-1
Team: Clemence, Neal, Jones, Smith, Kennedy, Hughes, Keegan, Case, Heighway, Callaghan, McDermott. *Scorers:* McDermott, Smith, Neal (pen)

10/5/78 v FC Bruges Wembley 1-0
Team: Clemence, Neal, Thompson, Hansen, Kennedy, Hughes, Dalglish, Case (Heighway), Fairclough, McDermott, Souness. *Scorer:* Dalglish

27/5/81 v Real Madrid Paris 1-0
Team: Clemence, Neal, A Kennedy, Thompson, R Kennedy, Hansen, Dalglish (Case), Lee, Johnson, McDermott, Souness. *Scorer:* R Kennedy

30/5/84 v AS Roma Rome 1-1
Team: Grobbelaar, Neal, Kennedy, Lawrenson, Whelan, Hansen, Dalglish (Robinson), Lee, Rush, Johnston (Nicol), Souness. *Scorer:* Neal
(*Liverpool won 4-2 on penalties: Neal, Souness, Rush, Kennedy*)

29/5/85 v Juventus Brussels 0-1
Team: Grobbelaar, Neal, Beglin, Lawrenson (Gillespie), Nicol, Hansen, Dalglish, Whelan, Rush, Walsh (Johnston), Wark

Cup Final Squads – *European Cup Winners' Cup*

Date	Opponents	Venue	Score

5/5/66 v Borussia Dortmund Glasgow 1-2†
Team: Lawrence, Lawler, Byrne, Milne, Yeats, Stevenson, Callaghan, Hunt, St John, Smith, Thompson. *Scorer:* Hunt

Cup Final Squads – *UEFA Cup*

Date	Opponents	Venue	Score

10/5/73 v Borussia Moenchengladbach h 3-0
Team: Clemence. Lawler, Lindsay, Smith, Lloyd, Hughes, Keegan, Cormack, Toshack, Heighway (Hall), Callaghan. *Scorers:* Keegan 2, Lloyd

23/5/73 v Bor Moenchengladbach (a) 0-2
Team: Clemence, Lawler, Lindsay, Smith, Lloyd, Hughes, Keegan, Cormack, Heighway (Boersma), Toshack, Callaghan

28/4/76 v FC Bruges (h) 3-2
Team: Clemence, Neal, Smith, Thompson, Kennedy, Hughes, Keegan, Fairclough, Heighway, Toshack (Case), Callaghan. *Scorers:* Kennedy, Case, Keegan (pen)

19/5/76   v FC Bruges   (a)   1-1
Team: Clemence, Neal, Smith, Thompson, Kennedy, Hughes, Keegan, Case,
Heighway, Toshack (Fairclough), Callaghan. *Scorer:* Keegan

Cup Final Squads – *World Club Championship*

Date	Opponents	Venue	Score
13/12/81	v Flamengo	Tokyo	0-3

Team: Grobbelaar, Neal, Lawrenson, Thompson, R Kennedy, Hansen, Dalglish,
Lee, Johnston, McDermott (Johnson), Souness

9/12/84	v Independiente	Tokyo	0-1

Team: Grobbelaar, Neal, A Kennedy, Gillespie, Nicol, Hansen, Dalglish, Molby,
Rush, Johnston, Wark (Whelan)

Cup Final Squads – *European Super Cup*

Date	Opponents	Venue	Score
22/11/77	v SV Hamburg	(a)	1-1

Team: Clemence, Neal, Jones (Smith), Thompson, R Kennedy, Hughes, Dalglish,
Case (Johnson), Heighway, Fairclough, Callaghan. *Scorer:* Fairclough

6/12/77	v SV Hamburg	(h)	6-0

Team: Clemence, Neal, Smith, Thompson, R Kennedy, Hughes, Dalglish,
McDermott, Heighway (Johnson), Fairclough, Case. *Scorers:* Thompson,
McDermott 3, Fairclough, Dalglish

4/12/78	v Anderlecht	(a)	1-3

Team: Clemence, Neal, A Kennedy, Hughes, R Kennedy, Hansen, Dalglish, Case,
Johnson (Heighway), McDermott, Souness. *Scorer:* Case

16/1/79	v Anderlecht	(h)	2-1

Team: Ogrizovic, Neal, Hughes, Thompson, R Kennedy, Hansen, Dalglish, Case,
Fairclough, McDermott, Souness. *Scorers:* Hughes, Fairclough

Liverpool in Europe – *European Cup*

1964/65

1st (1st)	Reykjavik	(a)	5-0	Wallace 2, Hunt 2, Chisnall
1st (2nd)	Reykjavik	(h)	6-1	Byrne, St John 2, Hunt, Graham, Stevenson
2nd (1st)	Anderlecht	(h)	3-0	St John, Hunt, Yeats
2nd (2nd)	Anderlecht	(a)	1-0	Hunt
3rd (1st)	FC Cologne	(a)	0-0	
3rd (2nd)	FC Cologne	(h)	0-0	
3rd (replay)	FC Cologne	(n)	2-2	St John, Hunt

(Liverpool won on the toss of a coin)

Semi-Final (1st)	Internazionale	(h)	3-1	Hunt, Callaghan, St John
Semi-Final (2nd)	Internazionale	(a)	0-3	

1966/67

Prelim (1st)	Petrolul Ploesti	(h)	2-0	St John, Callaghan
Prelim (2nd)	Petrolul Ploesti	(a)	1-3	Hunt
Prelim (replay)	Petrolul Ploesti	(n)	2-0	St John, Thompson
1st (1st)	Ajax	(a)	1-5	Lawler
1st (2nd)	Ajax	(h)	2-2	Hunt 2

1973/74

1st (1st)	Jeunesse D'Esch	(a)	1-1	Hall
1st (2nd)	Jeunesse D'Esch	(h)	2-0	Mond (og), Toshack
2nd (1st)	Red Star Belgrade	(a)	1-2	Lawler
2nd (2nd)	Red Star Belgrade	(h)	1-2	Lawler

1976/77

1st (1st)	Crusaders	(h)	2-0	Neal (pen), Toshack
1st (2nd)	Crusaders	(a)	5-0	Keegan, Johnson 2, McDermott, Heighway
2nd (1st)	Trabzonspor	(a)	0-1	
2nd (2nd)	Trabzonspor	(h)	3-0	Heighway, Johnson, Keegan
3rd (1st)	St Etienne	(a)	0-1	
3rd (2nd)	St Etienne	(h)	3-1	Keegan, Kennedy, Fairclough
Semi-Final (1st)	FC Zurich	(a)	3-1	Neal 2 (1 pen), Heighway
Semi-Final (2nd)	FC Zurich	(h)	3-0	Case 2, Keegan
Final	B. Monchengladbach	(n)	3-1	McDermott, Smith, Neal (pen)

1977/78

2nd (1st)	Dynamo Dresden	(h)	5-1	Hansen, Case 2, Neal (pen), Kennedy
2nd (2nd)	Dynamo Dresden	(a)	1-2	Heighway
3rd (1st)	Benfica	(a)	2-1	Case, Hughes
3rd (2nd)	Benfica	(h)	4-1	Callaghan, Dalglish, McDermott, Neal

Semi-Final (1st)	B. Monchengladbach	(a)	1-2	Johnson
Semi-Final (2nd)	B. Monchengladbach	(h)	3-0	Kennedy, Dalglish, Case
Final	FC Bruges	(n)	1-0	Dalglish

1978/79

1st (1st)	Nottingham Forest	(a)	0-2	
1st (2nd)	Nottingham Forest	(h)	0-0	

1979/80

1st (1st)	Dynamo Tbilisi	(h)	2-1	Johnson, Case
1st (2nd)	Dynamo Tbilisi	(a)	0-3	

1980/81

1st (1st)	Oulu Palloseura	(a)	1-1	McDermott
1st (2nd)	Oulu Palloseura	(h)	10-1	Souness 3 (1 pen), McDermott 3, Lee, R Kennedy, Fairclough 2
2nd (1st)	Aberdeen	(a)	1-0	McDermott
2nd (2nd)	Aberdeen	(h)	4-0	Miller (og), Neal, Dalglish, Hansen
3rd (1st)	CSKA Sofia	(h)	5-1	Souness 3, Lee, McDermott
3rd (2nd)	CSKA Sofia	(a)	1-0	Johnson
Semi-Final (1st)	Bayern Munich	(h)	0-0	
Semi-Final (2nd)	Bayern Munich	(a)	1-1	R Kennedy
	(Liverpool go through on the away goals rule)			
Final	Real Madrid	(n)	1-0	A Kennedy

1981/82

1st (1st)	Oulu Palloseura	(a)	1-0	Dalglish
1st (2nd)	Oulu Palloseura	(h)	7-0	Dalglish, McDermott 2, R Kennedy, Johnson, Rush, Lawrenson
2nd (1st)	AZ 67 Alkmaar	(a)	2-2	Johnson, Lee
2nd (2nd)	AZ 67 Alkmaar	(h)	3-2	McDermott (pen), Rush, Hansen
3rd (1st)	CSKA Sofia	(h)	1-0	Whelan
3rd (2nd)	CSKA Sofia	(a)	0-2	

1982/83

1st (1st)	Dundalk	(a)	4-1	Whelan 2, Rush, Hodgson
1st (2nd)	Dundalk	(h)	1-0	Whelan
2nd (1st)	JK Helsinki	(a)	0-1	
2nd (2nd)	JK Helsinki	(h)	5-0	Dalglish, Johnston, Neal, Kennedy 2
3rd (1st)	Widzew Lodz	(a)	0-2	
3rd (2nd)	Widzew Lodz	(h)	3-2	Neal (pen), Rush, Hodgson

1983/84

1st (1st)	BK Odense	(a)	1-0	Dalglish
1st (2nd)	BK Odense	(h)	5-0	Robinson 2, Dalglish 2, Clausen (og)
2nd (1st)	Atletico Bilbao	(h)	0-0	
2nd (2nd)	Atletico Bilbao	(a)	1-0	Rush
3rd (1st)	Benfica	(h)	1-0	Rush
3rd (2nd)	Benfica	(a)	4-1	Whelan 2, Johnston, Rush
Semi-Final (1st)	Dinamo Bucharest	(h)	1-0	Lee
Semi-Final (2nd)	Dinamo Bucharest	(a)	2-1	Rush 2
Final	AS Roma	(n)	1-1†	Neal

(Liverpool won 4-2 on penalties: Neal, Souness, Rush, Kennedy)

1984/85

1st (1st)	Lech Poznan	(a)	1-0	Wark
1st (2nd)	Lech Poznan	(h)	4-0	Wark 3, Walsh
2nd (1st)	Benfica	(h)	3-1	Rush 3
2nd (2nd)	Benfica	(a)	0-1	
3rd (1st)	Austria Vienna	(a)	1-1	Nicol
3rd (2nd)	Austria Vienna	(h)	4-1	Walsh 2, Nicol, Obermayer (og)
Semi-Final (1st)	Panathinaikos	(h)	4-0	Wark, Rush 2, Beglin
Semi-Final (2nd)	Panathinaikos	(a)	1-0	Lawrenson
Final	Juventus	(n)	0-1	

Liverpool in Europe – *European Cup Winners' Cup*

1965/66

Prelim (1st)	Juventus	(a)	0-1	
Prelim (2nd)	Juventus	(h)	2-0	Lawler, Strong
1st (1st)	Standard Liege	(h)	3-1	Lawler 2, Thompson
1st (2nd)	Standard Liege	(a)	2-1	Hunt, St John
2nd (1st)	Honved	(a)	0-0	
2nd (2nd)	Honved	(h)	2-0	Lawler, St John
Semi-Final (1st)	Celtic	(a)	0-1	
Semi-Final (2nd)	Celtic	(h)	2-0	Smith, Strong
Final	Borussia Dortmund	(n)	1-2†	Hunt.

1971/72

1st (1st)	Servette Geneva	(a)	1-2	Lawler
1st (2nd)	Servette Geneva	(h)	2-0	Hughes, Heighway
2nd (1st)	Bayern Munich	(h)	0-0	
2nd (2nd)	Bayern Munich	(a)	1-3	Evans

1974/75

1st (1st)	Stromgodset Drammen	(h)	11-0	Lindsay (pen), Boersma 2, Thompson 2, Heighway, Cormack, Hughes, Smith, Callaghan, Kennedy*
1st (2nd)	Stromgodset Drammen	(a)	1-0	Kennedy
2nd (1st)	Ferencvaros	(h)	1-1	Keegan
2nd (2nd)	Ferencvaros	(a)	0-0	

(Ferncvaros go through on the away goals rule)

* *Only two players, Clemence and Hall, did not score*

1992/93

1st (1st)	Apollon Limassol	(h)	6-1	Stewart 2, Rush 4
1st (2nd)	Apollon Limassol	(a)	2-1	Rush, Hutchison
2nd (1st)	Spartak Moscow	(a)	2-4	Wright, McManaman
2nd (2nd)	Spartak Moscow	(h)	0-2	

Liverpool in Europe – UEFA Cup (includes European Fairs Cup)

1967/68

1st (1st)	Malmo	(a)	2-0	Hateley 2
1st (2nd)	Malmo	(h)	2-1	Yeats, Hunt
2nd (1st)	TSV Munchen	(h)	8-0	St John, Hateley, Smith (pen), Hunt 2, Thompson, Callaghan 2
2nd (2nd)	TSV Munchen	(a)	1-2	Callaghan
3rd (1st)	Ferencvaros	(a)	0-1	
3rd (2nd)	Ferencvaros	(h)	0-1	

1968/69

1st (1st)	Atletico Bilbao	(a)	1-2	Hunt
1st (2nd)	Atletico Bilbao	(h)	2-1	Lawler, Hughes

(Atletico Bilbao go through on the toss of a coin)

1969/70

1st (1st)	Dundalk	(h)	10-0	Evans 2, Lawler, Smith 2, Graham 2, Lindsay, Thompson, Callaghan
1st (2nd)	Dundalk	(a)	4-0	Thompson 2, Graham, Callaghan
2nd (1st)	Vitoria Setubal	(a)	0-1	
2nd (2nd)	Vitoria Setubal	(h)	3-2	Smith (pen), Evans, Hunt

(Vitoria Setubal go through on away goals rule)

1970/71

1st (1st)	Ferencvaros	(h)	1-0	Graham
1st (2nd)	Ferencvaros	(a)	1-1	Hughes

2nd (1st)	Dinamo Bucharest	(h)	3-0	Lindsay, Lawler, Hughes
2nd (2nd)	Dinamo Bucharest	(a)	1-1	Boersma
3rd (1st)	Hibernian	(a)	1-0	Toshack
3rd (2nd)	Hibernian	(h)	2-0	Heighway, Boersma
4th (1st)	Bayern Munich	(h)	3-0	Evans 3
4th (2nd)	Bayern Munich	(a)	1-1	Ross
Semi-Final (1st)	Leeds United	(h)	0-1	
Semi-Final (2nd)	Leeds United	(a)	0-0	

1972/73

1st (1st)	Eintracht Frankfurt	(h)	2-0	Keegan, Hughes
1st (2nd)	Eintracht Frankfurt	(a)	0-0	
2nd (1st)	AEK Athens	(h)	3-0	Boersma, Cormack, Smith (pen)
2nd (2nd)	AEK Athens	(a)	3-1	Hughes 2, Boersma
3rd (1st)	Dynamo Berlin	(a)	0-0	
3rd (2nd)	Dynamo Berlin	(h)	3-1	Boersma, Heighway, Toshack
4th (1st)	Dynamo Dresden	(h)	2-0	Hall, Boersma
4th (2nd)	Dynamo Dresden	(a)	1-0	Keegan
Semi-Final (1st)	Tottenham Hotspur	(h)	1-0	Lindsay
Semi-Final (2nd)	Tottenham Hotspur	(a)	1-2	Heighway
(Liverpool go through on the away goals rule)				
Final (1st)	B. Moenchengladbach	(h)	3-0	Keegan 2, Lloyd
Final (2nd)	B. Moenchengladbach	(a)	0-2	

1975/76

1st (1st)	Hibernian	(a)	0-1	
1st (2nd)	Hibernian	(h)	3-1	Toshack 3
2nd (1st)	Real Sociedad	(a)	3-1	Heighway, Callaghn, P Thompson
2nd (2nd)	Real Sociedad	(h)	6-0	Toshack, Kennedy 2, Fairclough, Heighway, Neal
3rd (1st)	Slask Wroclaw	(a)	2-1	Kennedy, Toshack
3rd (2nd)	Slask Wroclaw	(h)	3-0	Case 3
4th (1st)	Dynamo Dresden	(a)	0-0	
4th (2nd)	Dynamo Dresden	(h)	2-1	Case, Kegan
Semi-Final (1st)	Barcelona	(a)	1-0	Toshack
Semi-Final (2nd)	Barcelona	(h)	1-1	P Thompson
Final (1st)	FC Bruges	(h)	3-2	Kennedy, Case, Keegan (pen)
Final (2nd)	FC Bruges	(a)	1-1	Keegan

1990/91

1st (1st)	Kuusysil	(h)	6-1	Saunders 4, Houghton 2
1st (2nd)	Kuusysil	(a)	0-1	
2nd (1st)	Auxerre	(a)	0-2	
2nd (2nd)	Auxerre	(h)	3-0	Molby (pen), Marsh, Walters

3rd (1st)	Tirol	(a)	2-0	Saunders 2	
3rd (2nd)	Tirol	(h)	4-0	Saunders 3, Venison	
4th (1st)	Genoa	(a)	0-2		
4th (2nd)	Genoa	(h)	1-2	Rush	

Liverpool in the FA Charity Shield

10/5/22   v Huddersfield Town   Old Trafford   0-1   20,000
Team: Scott, Longworth, McKinlay, McNab, Wadsworth, Bromilow, Lacey, Chambers, Beadles, Hopkin

15/8/64   v West Ham Utd   Anfield   2-2   38,858
Team: Lawrence, Byrne, Moran, Milne, Yeats, Stevenson, Callaghan, Hunt, Arrowsmith (Chisnall), Wallace, Thompson. *Scorers*: Wallace, Byrne

14/8/65   v Manchester Utd   Old Trafford   2-2   48,502
Team: Lawrence, Lawler, Byrne, Milne, Yeats, Stevenson, Callaghan, Hunt, St John, Smith, Strong. *Scorers:* Stevenson, Yeats

13/8/66   v Everton   Goodison Park   1-0   63,329
Team: Lawrence, Lawler, Byrne, Smith, Yeats, Stevenson, Callaghan, Hunt, St John, Strong, Thompson. *Scorer:* Hunt

7/8/71   v Leicester City   0-1   25,014
Team: Clemence, Lawler, Lindsay, Smith, Lloyd, Hughes, Callaghan, Evans, Heighway, Graham, Hall

10/8/74   v Leeds Utd   Wembley   1-1   67,000
Team: Clemence, Smith, Lindsay, Thompson, Cormack, Hughes, Keegan, Hall, Heighway, Boersma, Callaghan. *Scorer:* Boersma

14/8/76   v Southampton   Wembley   1-0   76,500
Team: Clemence, Neal, Jones, Thompson, Kennedy, Hughes, Keegan, Case, Heighway, Toshack, Callaghan. *Scorer:* Toshack

13/8/77   v Manchester Utd   Wembley   0-0   82,000
Team: Clemence, Neal, Jones, Thompson, Kennedy, Hughes, Dalglish, Case, Fairclough, McDermott, Callaghan

11/8/79   v Arsenal   Wembley   3-1   92,000
Team: Clemence, Neal, A Kennedy, Thompson, R Kennedy, Hansen, Dalglish, Case, Johnson, McDermott, Souness. *Scorers:* McDermott 2, Dalglish

9/8/80   v West Ham Utd   Wembley   1-0   90,000
Team: Clemence, Neal, A Kennedy, Thompson, R Kennedy, Hansen, Dalglish, Case, Johnson, McDermott, Souness. *Scorer:* McDermott

21/8/82   v Tottenham Hotspur   Wembley   1-0   82,500
Team: Grobbelaar, Neal, A Kennedy, Lawrenson, Thompson, Hansen, Dalglish (Hodgson), Lee, Rush, Whelan, Souness. *Scorer:* Rush

20/8/83   v Manchester Utd   Wembley   0-2   92,000
Team: Grobbelaar, Neal, A Kennedy, Lawrenson, Thompson (Johnston), Hansen, Dalglish, Lee, Rush, Robinson (Hodgson), Souness

18/8/84   v Everton   Wembley   0-1   100,000
Team: Grobbelaar, Neal, A Kennedy, Lawrenson, Whelan, Hansen, Dalglish, Lee (Walsh), Rush, Nicol, Wark

16/8/86   v Everton   Wembley   1-1   88,231
Team: Grobbelaar (Hooper), Venison, Beglin, Lawrenson, Whelan, Hansen, McMahon, John ston, Rush, Molby, MacDonald (Dalglish) *Scorer:* Rush

20/8/88   v Wimbledon   Wembley   2-0   54,000
Team: Grobbelaar, Gillespie, Venison, Ablett, Whelan, Watson, Beardsley, Aldridge, Houghton, Barnes, McMahon*Scorers:* Aldridge 2

12/8/89   v Arsenal   Wembley   1-0   63,000
Team: Grobbelaar, Hysen, Burrows, Nicol, Whelan, Hansen, Beardsley, Venison, Rush, Barnes. McMahon*Scorer:* Beardsley

18/8/90   v Manchester Utd   Wembley   1-1   66,558
Team: Grobbelaar, Hysen, Burrows, Venison, Whelan, Ablett, Beardsley (Rosenthal), Houghton, Rush, Barnes, McMahon*Scorer:* Barnes (pen)

8/8/92   v Leeds Utd   Wembley   3-4   61,291
Team: Grobbelaar, Tanner, Burrows, Marsh (Hutchison), Whelan, Wright, Saunders, Stewart, Rush, Rosenthal (Kozma), Walters*Scorers:* Rush, Saunders, Strachan (og)

Liverpool Home Internationals

The records below are the international appearances made by Liverpool players when they have been registered as palyers at the club. They do not include appearances at World Cup '94. An asterisk (*) denotes an appearance as substitute. The year's referred to are seasons rather than calendar years so, for example, 1994 stands for the 1993-94 season. The record for some overseas players may be incomplete.

Player	Country	Apps	Opponents
A'Court	England	5	1957: N Ireland 1958: Brazil, Austria, USSR, Wales
Aldridge	Ireland	18	1987: Scotland, Bulgaria, Belgium, Brazil, Luxembourg 1988: Bulgaria, Poland, Norway, England, USSR, Netherlands 1989: N Ireland, Tunisia, Spain, France*, Hungary, Malta* 1990: W Germany
Allan	Scotland	1	1897: England
Bamber	England	1	1921: Wales
Barnes	England	41	1988: W Germany, Turkey, Yugoslavia, Israel, Netherlands, Scotland, Colombia, Switzerland, Ireland, Netherlands, USSR 1989: Sweden, Greece, Albania, Poland, Denmark 1990: Sweden, Italy, Brazil, Denmark, Uruguay, Tunisia, Ireland, Netherlands, Egypt, Belgium, Cameroon 1991: Hungary, Poland, Cameroon,Ireland, Turkey, USSR, Argentina 1992: Czechoslovakia, Finland 1993: San Marino, Turkey, Netherlands, Poland, United States, Germany
Beardsley	England	34	W Germany, Turkey, Yugoslavia, Israel, Netherlands, Hungary, Scotland, Colombia, Switzerland, Ireland, Netherlands 1989: Denmark, Sweden, Saudi Arabia, Greece*, Albania*, Albania, Poland, Denmark 1990: Sweden, Poland, Italy, Brazil, Uruguay*, Tunisia*, Ireland, Egypt*, Cameroon*, W Germany, Italy 1991: Poland*, Ireland, Ireland, USSR*
Becton	England	1	1897: Wales
Beglin	Ireland	11	1984: China 1985: Mexico, Denmark, Italy, Israel, England, Norway, Switzerland, USSR, Denmark 1986: Wales 1987: Belgium*, Scotland, Poland
Bjornebye	Sweden	14	1993: Sweden, Holland, Holland, San Marino, England, England, China, Qatar, Turkey, USA, Poland, Poland, Turkey, Wales
Bradshaw	England	1	1897: Ireland
Bromilow	England	5	1921: Wales 1922: Wales, Scotland 1923: Belgium 1925: N Ireland

Player	Country	Apps	Opponents
Callaghan	England	4	1966: Finland, France 1977: Switzerland, Luxembourg
Campbell	Scotland	3	1920: Wales, Ireland, England
Chambers	England	8	1921: Scotland, Wales, Belgium 1922: Ireland 1923: Wales, Belgium, Scotland, Ireland
Clemence	England	56	1972: Wales 1973: Wales 1974: E Germany, Bulgaria, Yugoslavia, Czechoslovakia, Portugal 1975: W Germany, Cyprus, N Ireland, Wales, Scotland, Switzerland, Czechoslovakia, Portugal 1976: Wales, Wales, N Ireland, Scotland, Brazil, Finland, Ireland, Finland, Italy 1977: Netherlands, Luxembourg, Scotland, Brazil, Argentina, Uruguay, Switzerland, Luxembourg, Italy 1978: W Germany, N Ireland, Scotland, Denmark, Ireland 1979: N Ireland, N Ireland, Scotland, Bulgaria, Austria*, Denmark, Bulgaria 1980: Ireland, Argentina, Wales, Scotland, Belgium, Spain, Romania 1981: Spain, Brazil, Switzerland, Hungary
Clough	England	14	1989: Chile 1991: Argentina*, Australia, Malta 1992: France, Czechoslovakia, CIS, 1993: Spain, Turkey*, Poland*, Norway*, USA, Brazil, Germany
Cox	England	3	1901: Ireland 1902: Scotland 1903: Scotland
Dalglish	Scotland	55	1977: E Germany, Czechoslovakia, Wales 1978: Bulgaria, N Ireland*, Wales, England, Peru, Iran, Netherlands, Austria, Norway, Portugal 1979: Wales, England, Argentina, Norway, Peru, Austria, Belgium, Belgium 1980: Portugal, N Ireland, Wales, England, Poland, Hungary, Sweden, Portugal 1981: Israel, Sweden, N Ireland, Portugal* 1982: Spain, Netherlands, N Ireland, Wales, England, New Zealand, Brazil*, Belgium 1983: Switzerland, Uruguay, Belgium, E Germany 1984: Yugoslavia, Iceland, Spain 1985: Wales, E Germany, Australia 1986: Romania 1987: Bulgaria*, Luxembourg

Player	Country	Apps	Opponents
Dunlop	Scotland	1	1906: England
Gillespie	Scotland	12	1988: Belgium, Bulgaria, Sp 1989: Norway, France, Chile 1990: Yugoslavia, East Germany, Poland, Malta, Brazil* 1991: Bulgaria
Grobbelaar	Zimbabwe	15	1993: S Africa, S Africa, Togo, Togo, Mauritius, Mauritius, Egypt, Egypt, Egypt, Zambia, Zambia, Angola, Angola, Guinea, Cameroon
Hansen	Scotland	26	1979: Wales, Argentina, Belgium 1980: Portugal, Sweden, Portugal 1981: Israel, Sweden, N Ireland, Portugal 1982: Spain, N Ireland*, Wales, England, New Zealand, Brazil, USSR, E Germany, Switzerland, Belgium 1983: Switzerland 1985: Wales* 1986: Romania* 1987: Ireland, Ireland, Luxembourg
Hardy	England	14	1907: Ireland, Wales, Scotland 1908: Scotland 1909: Ireland, Wales, Scotland, Hungary, Hungary, Austria 1910: Ireland, Wales, Scotland 1912: Ireland
Heighway	Ireland	32	1971: Poland, Sweden, Sweden, Italy, Austria 1973: USSR 1975: USSR, Turkey, USSR 1976: Turkey, Norway 1977: England, France, France, Spain, Bulgaria 1978: Bulgaria, Norway, Denmark 1979: N Ireland, Bulgaria 1980: Bulgaria, USA, N Ireland, England, Cyprus, Argentina 1981: Belgium, France, Cyprus, Wales, Belgium
Hodgson	England	3	1930: N Ireland, Wales 1931: Scotland
Howell	England	1	1899: Scotland
Hughes, E	England	59	1969: Netherlands, Portugal 1970: Belgium, Wales, N Ireland, Scotland, E Germany 1971: Malta, Greece, Malta, Wales, Switzerland, Greece 1972: W Germany, W Germany, Wales, N Ireland, Scotland, Wales 1973: Wales, Scotland, Wales, Scotland, Poland, USSR, Italy, Austria, Poland Italy 1974: Wales, N Ireland, Scotland, Argentina,

Player	Country	Apps	Opponents
			E. Germany, Bulgaria, Yugoslavia, Czechoslovakia, Portugal 1975: Cyprus*, N. Ireland 1976: Italy 1977: Luxembourg, Wales, Scotland, Brazil, Argentina, Uruguay, Switzerland, Luxembourg, Italy 1978: W Germany, N Ireland, Scotland, Hungary, Denmark, Ireland 1979: N Ireland, Wales, Sweden
Hughes, J	Wales	3	1905: Scotland, England, Ireland
Hughes, L	England	3	1950: Chile, USA, Spain
Hunt	England	34	1962: Austria 1963: E Germany 1964: Scotland, USA, Portugal, Wales 1965: Spain 1966: Poland, W Germany, Scotland, Finland, Norway, Poland, Uruguay, Mexico, France, Argentina, Portugal, W Germany, N Ireland, Czechoslovakia, Wales 1967: Spain, Austria, Wales, N Ireland, USSR 1968: Spain, Spain, Sweden, Yugoslavia, USSR, Romania 1969: Romania
Hysen	Sweden	2	1991: Denmark, Germany
Johnson	England	5	1980: Ireland, Argentina, N Ireland, Scotland, Belgium
Jones, J	Wales	18	1975: Austria 1976: England, Scotland, W Germany, Scotland 1977: Czechoslovakia, Scotland, England, N Ireland Kuwait, Kuwait, Scotland, Czechoslovakia, W Germany 1978: Iran, England, Scotland, N Ireland
Jones, R	England	4	1992: France 1994: Poland, Greece, Norway
Jones, W	England	2	1950: Portugal, Belgium
Keegan	England	29	1972: Wales 1973: Wales 1974: Wales, N Ireland, Argentina, E Germany, Bulgaria, Yugoslavia, Czechoslovakia 1975: W Germany, Cyprus, Cyprus, N Ireland, Scotland, Switzerland. Czechoslovakia, Portugal 1976: Wales, Wales, N Ireland, Scotland, Brazil, Finland, Ireland, Finland, Italy 1977: Netherlands, Luxembourg, Wales
Kennedy, A	England	2	1984: N Ireland, Wales

Player	Country	Apps	Opponents
Kennedy, R	England	17	1976: Wales, Wales, N Ireland, Scotland 1977: Luxembourg, Wales, Scotland, Brazil*, Argentina*, Switzerland, Luxembourg 1979: Bulgaria 1980: Spain, Argentina, Wales, Belgium*, Italy
Kozma	Hungary	3	1992: Ireland, USSR, Bulgaria
Lacey	Ireland	12	1913: Wales, 1914: Wales, England, Scotland 1919: England, 1920: Wales, Scotland, England 1921: Scotland, Wales, England 1922: Scotland
Lambert	Wales	5	1946: Scotland 1947: England 1949: Portugal, Belgium, Switzerland
Lathom	Wales	8	1905: Scotland, England 1906: Scotland 1907: Ireland, Scotland, England 1908: England 1909: Ireland
Lawler	England	4	1971: Malta, Wales, Scotland, Switzerland
Lawrence	Scotland	3	1963: Ireland 1969: W Germany, Wales
Lawrenson	Ireland	27	1982: Netherlands, France 1983: Netherlands, Spain, Iceland, Malta, Spain 1984: Iceland, Netherlands, Malta, Israel, USSR, Norway, Denmark 1985: Italy, England, Norway, Switzerland, USSR, Denmark 1986: Switzerland, USSR, Denmark 1987: Belgium, Scotland 1988: Bulgaria, Israel
Lee	England	14	1982: Greece, Luxembourg 1983: Wales, Greece, Hungary, Scotland, Australia, Denmark, Hungary, Luxembourg 1984: France, N Ireland, Wales, Chile*
Liddell	Scotland	28	1946: Wales, N Ireland 1947: N Ireland, Wales 1948: England 1949: Wales 1950: England, Portugal, France, Wales N Ireland, Austria 1951: England, N Ireland, Wales 1952: England, USA, Denmark, Sweden, Wales, N Ireland 1953: England, Wales 1955: Portugal, Yugoslavia, Austria, Hungary, N Ireland
Lindsay	England	4	1974: Argentina, E Germany, Bulgaria, Yugoslavia
Lloyd	England	3	1971: Wales, Switzerland 1972: N Ireland

Player	Country	Apps	Opponents
Longworth	England	5	1920: Scotland 1921: Belgium 1923 Wales, Belgium, Scotland
Lucas	England	3	1921: Ireland 1924: France 1926: Belgium
Matthews	Wales	1	1921: Ireland
McDermott	England	25	1977: Switzerland, Luxembourg 1979: N Ireland, Wales, Sweden, Denmark, Romania, Switzerland 1980: Ireland, N Ireland, Scotland, Belgium*, Spain, Norway, Romania, Switzerland 1981: Romania*, Brazil, Switzerland*, Hungary, Norway, Hungary 1982: Wales*, Netherlands, Scotland*, Iceland
McDougall	Scotland	2	1931: Austria, Italy
McGarvey	Scotland	2	1979: N Ireland*, Argentina
McKinlay	Scotland	2	1922: Wales, Ireland
McMahon	England	17	1988: Israel, Hungary, Colombia, USSR 1989: Denmark* 1990: Sweden, Poland, Italy, Yugoslavia*, Brazil, Czechoslovakia*, Denmark, Ireland*, Egypt, Belgium, Italy 1991: Ireland
McMullan	N Ireland	3	1925: England 1926: Wales 1927: Scotland
McNab	Scotland	1	1923: Wales
Melia	England	2	1963: Scotland, Switzerland
Miller	Scotland	1	1920: England
Milne	England	14	1963: Brazil, Czechoslovakia, E Germany, Wales, Rest of the World, N Ireland 1964: Scotland, Uruguay, Portugal, Ireland, Brazil, Argentina, N Ireland, Belgium
Molby	Denmark	25	1984: Austria, Norway, Switzerland, Ireland 1985: Sweden, USSR, Switzerland, Norway, Ireland 1986: Norway, N Ireland, Poland, Scotland, Uruguay, W Germany, Spain, Finland, USSR 1987: Finland, USSR 1988: Hungary, England, Italy 1991: Wales, Yugoslavia
Morgan	Scotland	1	1899: England
Morris	Wales	5	1903: Scotland, Ireland 1904: England, Scotland, Ireland

Player	Country	Apps	Opponents
Neal	England	50	1976: Wales, Italy 1977: Wales, Scotland, Brazil, Argentina, Uruguay, Switzerland, Italy 1978: W Germany, N Ireland, Scotland, Hungary, Denmark, Ireland 1979: N Ireland, N Ireland, Scotland, Bulgaria, Austria, Denmark, N Ireland 1980: Spain, Argentina, Wales, Belgium, Italy, Romania, Switzerland 1981: Spain, Brazil, Hungary, Norway, Hungary 1982: Wales, Netherlands, Iceland, France*, Kuwait, Denmark, Greece, Luxembourg 1983: Wales, Greece, Hungary, N Ireland, Scotland, Australia, Australia, Denmark
Nicol	Scotland	27	1984: Yugoslavia, Iceland, Spain 1985: Wales, Wales, E Germany, Australia 1986: England, Denmark, W Germany, Uruguay 1988: Hungary, Bulgaria, Saudi Arabia, Spain, Colombia, England 1989, Norway, Yugoslavia, Cyprus 1990: Yugoslavia, France 1991: Switzerland, USSR, San Marino 1992: Switzerland
Parkinson	England	2	1910: Wales, Scotland
Parry, E	Wales	5	1922: Scotland 1923: England, Ireland 1925: N Ireland 1926: N Ireland
Parry, M	Wales	16	1901: Scotland, England, Ireland 1902: Ireland, England, Scotland 1903: England , Scotland 1904: England, Ireland 1906: England, 1908: Scotland, England, Ireland 1909: Scotland, England
Peake	Wales	10	1909: Scotland, England, Ireland 1910: Scotland, Ireland 1911: Ireland 1912: England 1913: Ireland, England 1914: Ireland
Raisbeck	Scotland	8	1900: England 1901: England 1902: England 1903: Wales, England 1904: England 1906: England 1907: England
Rosenthal	Israel		1993: Cyprus, France, Austria, Finland 1994: Poland, Austria, Sweden, Sweden, Bulgaria, Bulgaria, France

Player	Country	Apps	Opponents
Rush	Wales	63	1980: Scotland*, N Ireland 1981: England*, Iceland*, USSR 1982: England, Scotland, N Ireland, France, Norway, Yugoslavia 1983: England, Bulgaria, Norway, Romania, Bulgaria, Yugoslavia 1984: Scotland, England, N Ireland, Iceland 1985: Norway, Scotland, Spain, Scotland, Hungary 1986: Saudi Arabia, Ireland, Uruguay 1987: Finland, Finland, USSR, Czechoslovakia 1989: Netherlands, Finland, Sweden, W Germany 1990: Finland, Ireland 1991: Denmark, Belgium, Belgium, Luxembourg, Ireland, Poland, W Germany 1992: Germany , Luxembourg, Romania 1993: Faeroes, Cyprus Belgium, Belgium, Czechoslovakia, Faeroes, RCS, Romania, Norway 1994: Czechoslovakia, Cyprus, Romania, Norway, Sweden
Saunders	Wales	8	1992: Brazil, Germany , Ireland, Romania, Netherlands, Argentina, Japan 1993: Faeroes
Scott	N Ireland†	27	1920: Scotland, England 1921: Scotland, Wales, England 1925: Wales, England 1926: Wales, Scotland, England 1927: Scotland, Wales, England 1928: Wales, Scotland, England 1929: Wales, Scotland, England 1930: England 1931: Wales 1932: Scotland, England, Wales 1933: Scotland, England, Wales
Sidlow	Wales	7	1946: Scotland, England 1947: England, Scotland 1948: N Ireland, Scotland 1949: England
Smith	England	1	1971: Wales
Souness	Scotland	37	1978: Bulgaria, Wales, England*, Netherlands, Austria, Norway 1979: Wales, N Ireland, England, Peru, Austria, Belgium 1980: Portugal, N Ireland, Portugal 1981: Israel, Israel, N Ireland, Portugal 1982: Spain, Wales, England, New Zealand, Brazil, USSR, E Germany, Switzerland, Belgium 1983: Switzerland, Wales, England, Canada*, Canada, Uruguay, N Ireland 1984: Wales

Player	Country	Apps	Opponents
St John	Scotland	14	1961: Czechoslovakia, N Ireland, Wales, Czechoslovakia 1962: England, Uruguay, Wales, N Ireland 1963: England, Norway, Ireland*, Spain, N Ireland 1965: England
Staunton	Ireland	25	1989: Tunisia, Spain, Spain, Malta, Hungary 1990: W Germany, N Ireland, Malta, Wales, USSR, Finland, Turkey, Malta, England, Egypt, Hungary, Romania, Italy, 1991: Morocco, Turkey, England, England, Wales, Poland, Chile, United States
Taylor	England	3	1947: Wales, N Ireland, Sweden
Thompson, P	England	16	1964: Portugal, Ireland, United States, Brazil, Portugal, Argentina, N Ireland, Belgium, Wales, Netherlands 1965: Scotland, N Ireland 1967: N Ireland 1968: W Germany 1969: Netherlands* 1970: Scotland
Thompson, PB	England	41	1976: Wales, Wales, N Ireland, Scotland, Brazil, Italy, Finland, Finland 1978: Ireland*, Czechoslovakia 1979: N Ireland, Scotland, Bulgaria, Austria, Denmark, N Ireland, Bulgaria 1980: Ireland, Spain, Argentina, Wales, Scotland, Belgium, Italy, Spain, Norway, Romania 1981: Hungary, Norway, Hungary 1982: Wales, Netherlands, Scotland, Finland, France, Czechoslovakia, Kuwait, W Germany, Spain, W Germany, Greece
Toshack	Wales	26	1971: Scotland, England, N Ireland, Finland, Finland 1972: England, England 1973: England, Poland, Scotland, England 1974: Austria, Hungary, Luxembourg 1975: Hungary, Luxembourg, Scotland, England 1976: Yugoslavia, England, Yugoslavia, Scotland 1977: Kuwait, Kuwait, Scotland, Czechoslovakia
Wark	Scotland	3	1984: England, France, Yugoslavia
Whelan	Ireland	48	1981: Czechoslovakia* 1982: Netherlands*, France 1983: Iceland, Malta, Spain 1984: Israel, USSR, Norway 1985: Italy*, Israel, England, Norway*, Switzerland* 1986: Wales,

Player	Country	Apps	Opponents
			USSR* 1987: Belgium*, Scotland, Bulgaria, Belgium, Brazil, Luxembourg 1988: Luxembourg, Bulgaria, Poland, Norway, England, USSR, Netherlands 1989: N Ireland, France, Hungary, Spain, Malta 1990: W Germany, N Ireland, Malta, Wales, Netherlands* 1991: Morocco, England 1992: Switzerland 1993: Latvia, Wales*, Lithuania* 1994: Lithuania*, Spain, Russia, Holland
Wright	England	3	1992: France, Finland 1993: Spain
Yeats	Scotland	2	1964: Wales 1965: Italy
Younger	Scotland	16	1956: Wales, N Ireland, Yugoslavia 1957: England, Spain, Switzerland, W Germany, Spain, N Ireland, Switzerland, Wales 1958: England, Hungary, Poland, Yugoslavia, Paraguay

† Before 1924 for Ireland

Miscellaneous

Managers

J. McKenna/WE Barclay (1892-1896)
1893: Lancashire League
champions
1894: Division Two champions
1896: Division Two champions

Tom Watson (1896-1915)
1901: League champions
1905: Division Two champions
1906: League champions

Dave Ashworth (1920-1923)
1922: League champions
1923: League champions

Matt McQueen (1923-1928)
none

George Patterson (1928-1936)
none

George Kay (1936-1951)
1947: League champions

Don Welsh (1951-1956)
none

Phil Taylor (1956-1959)
none

Bill Shankly (1959-1974)
1962: Division Two champions
1964: League champions
1965: FA Cup winners
1966: League champions
1973: League champions
UEFA Cup winners
1974: FA Cup winners

Bob Paisley (1974-1983)
1976: League champions
UEFA Cup winners
1977: League champions
European Cup winners
1978: European Cup winners
1979: League champions
1980: League champions
1981: League Cup winners
European Cup winners
1982: League champions
League Cup winners
1983: League champions
League Cup winners

Joe Fagan (1983-1985)
1984: League champions
League Cup winners
European Cup winners

Kenny Dalglish (1985-1991)
1986: League champions
FA Cup winners
1988: League champions
1989: FA Cup winners
1990: League champions

Graeme Souness (1991-1994)
1992: FA Cup winners

Roy Evans (1994-date)

Graeme Souness

At the end of the FA Cup third round replay on the 25th January 1994 against Bristol City, which Liverpool lost 1-0 at home, there were calls from the fans for Graeme Souness to resign or be sacked. Asked after the game if he would accede to these wishes the normally bullish Souness said *"I will have to wait until the cold light of day to answer that."*

It was a slightly surprising response from the Liverpool manager who had always vowed that he wouldn't be shouted out of his job. He had said from the very start of his tenure that quick success couldn't be guaranteed and that it would take the club anything up to five years to rebuild the infrastructure to provide for future success. We'll never know whether he wold have been successful in the long term because on the Friday, two days after the game, he handed in his notice. It was the news that the fans wanted to hear: a poll conducted on Radio City said that 81% of the fans wished him to leave.

Souness's resignation letter was written with a quiet dignity that bore no malice to those involved with the club:

"After a great deal of soul-searching I have concluded that the best thing for the club and me is that we should part company.

"I took this job believing that I could return the club to its former glory but that has proved more difficult than I expected.

"Liverpool Football Club has, and always will have, a very special place in my heart, and I can only wish the club well and every success in the future."

Souness's Millions

Transfers In...

Player	From	Fee
Mark Wright	Derby County	£2,200,000
Dean Saunders	Derby County	£2,900,000
Mark Walters	Rangers	£1,250,000
Rob Jones	Crewe	£600,000
Michael Thomas	Arsenal	£1,500,000
Istvan Kozma	Dunfermline	£300,000
Lee Jones	Wrexham	£300,000
David James	Watford	£1,000,000
Paul Stewart	Tottenham	£2,300,000
Torben Piechnik	Copenhagen	£500,000
Stig Bjornebye	Rosenborg	£600,000
Nigel Clough	Nottingham Forest	£2,275,000
Neil Ruddock	Tottenham	£2,500,000
Julian Dicks	West Ham	swap
	Total	**£18,225,000**

Transfers Out...

Player	From	Fee
Peter Beardsley	Everton	£1,000,000
Steve Staunton	Aston Villa	£1,100,000
Jimmy Carter	Arsenal	£500,000
Steve McMahon	Manchester City	£900,000
Gary Ablett	Everton	£750,000
Barry Venison	Newcastle	£250,000
Ray Houghton	Aston Villa	£900,000
Dean Saunders	Aston Villa	£2,300,000
Istvan Kozma	Ujpest	free
Mike Marsh	West Ham	swap
David Burrows	West Ham	swap
Mike Hooper	Newcastle	£550,000
Ronny Rosenthal	Tottenham	£250,000
	Total:	**£8,500,000**
	Deficit:	**£9,725,000**

The Records

As a Manager

Graeme Souness arrived at Anfield as manager in April, 1991. His sole trophy was the FA Cup in 1992.

Season	League	FA Cup	League Cup	Euro
90/91	2nd	–	–	–
91/92	6th	Winners	4th Round	UEFA Cup quarter finals
92/93	6th	3rd Round	4th Round	CWC 2nd round
93/94	5th*	3rd Round	4th Round	–

* Position when Souness resigned

As a Player

Graeme Souness's record as a Liverpool player was rather better. In six seasons he picked up twelve medals in three major competitions including three in his final season, 1983-84, when Liverpool won an unprecedented treble of League Championship, League Cup and European Cup.

League Championship	1978-79, 1979-80, 1981-82, 1982-83, 1983-84
League Cup	1980-81, 1981-82, 1982-83, 1983-84
European Cup	1977-78, 1980-81, 1983-84

Pontins League – Reserve Team

Date	Opponents	Venue	Score
Aug 19	York City	(h)	3-1
Aug 26	Bolton Wanderers	(a)	2-2
Sept 8	Leeds United	(h)	1-4
Sept 14	Coventry City	(h)	5-1
Sept 23	Newcastle United	(h)	1-1
Sept 29	Wolverhampton Wanderers	(a)	0-0
Oct 7	Notts County	(h)	3-0
Oct 19	Leicester City	(h)	1-0
Oct 28	Aston Villa	(a)	0-4
Nov 10	Manchester United	(a)	0-0
Nov 13	Everton	(h)	1-0
Nov 17	Nottingham Forest	(a)	2-2
Dec 2	Sheffield Wednesday	(h)	3-3
Dec 9	Sunderland	(a)	0-1
Jan 13	Derby County	(a)	1-3
Jan 18	Notts County	(a)	0-2
Jan 28	Bolton Wanderers	(h)	1-1
Jan 31	Leicester City	(a)	3-1
Feb 5	Sheffield United	(a)	1-2
Feb 8	Coventry City	(a)	0-3
Feb 22	Everton	(a)	1-0
Mar 1	Sunderland	(h)	2-2
Mar 16	Newcastle United	(a)	0-1
Mar 22	Wolverhampton Wanderers	(h)	2-1
Mar 28	Sheffield United	(h)	0-0
Apr 19	Manchester United	(h)	0-1
Apr 21	Leeds United	(a)	0-2
Apr 23	Aston Villa	(h)	1-1
Apr 25	Nottingham Forest	(h)	2-3
Apr 27	Blackburn Rovers	(a)	0-3
May 9	Derby County	(a)	1-0
May 11	York City	(a)	0-2

Pontin's League First Division

	P	W	D	L	F	A	Pts
Manchester United	34	22	7	5	77	38	73
Aston Villa	34	18	9	7	61	29	63
Bolton Wanderers	34	15	10	9	88	65	55
Wolverhampton Wanderers	34	15	9	10	45	38	54
Derby County	34	14	8	12	55	51	50
Nottingham Forest	34	14	8	12	55	51	50
Sunderland	34	12	13	9	47	53	49
Blackburn Rovers	34	14	7	13	40	47	49
Leeds United	34	13	8	13	42	48	47
Coventry City	34	13	7	14	42	41	46
Sheffield United	34	12	9	13	57	60	45
Notts County	34	12	8	14	43	50	44
Everton	34	12	7	15	54	50	43
Liverpool	34	10	11	13	42	51	41
Newcastle United	34	10	8	16	46	53	38
Sheffield Wednesday	34	7	12	15	46	63	33
Leicester City	34	8	7	19	37	58	31
York City	34	6	10	18	36	67	28

The History of Liverpool

In 1892 Anfield was home to a successful Football League side – Everton. The owner of the ground and patron of the club, John Houlding, had wanted to raise the rent but was met with stiff resistance. After much squabbling the rest of the club went off to find a new ground, taking the team with them; Houlding was left with the ground. Undeterred he decided to form his own team – Liverpool.

Rebuffed by the Football League, then in its fifth year, Liverpool played for a year in the Lancashire League which of course they won. Their strip was blue and white quarters with the familiar all red not being adopted until the 1898-99 season.

After the success of their one season in the Lancashire League Liverpool were invited to play in an enlarged second division of the Football League, an invitation which they accepted. Liverpool went through the 1893-94 league season unbeaten and sailed into the first division. There they completed their record run of 31 games undefeated before they finally ran out of steam and were relegated back down again. Another season in the second division but only the one as Liverpool finally established themselves as a major side. They won the league for the first time in 1900-01 and, after yet another one season trip to the second division, in 1905-06.

Liverpool reached the FA Cup final in 1914, losing 1-0 to Burnley, and won two consecutive league titles in 1921-22 and 1922-23. The thirties, however, were a relatively barren period. Although Liverpool never left the top division they were never in the running for any trophies. The first season back after the Second World War saw Liverpool take the title in a season which spilled over into June because of bad weather but thereafter followed a steady decline. They reached the FA Cup final at Wembley in 1950, losing 2-0 to Arsenal, and were relegated from the first division at the end of the 1953-54 season. This time there was no quick return to the top division, Liverpool slumping to their lowest ever league position – 11th in the second division. 1955-56 saw Liverpool just miss out on promotion but third place was deemed insufficient and Welsh became the first, and so far only, Liverpool manager to be dismissed. His replacement, Phil Taylor, steadied the ship but Liverpool spent the next three years as the nearly boys of the second division finishing third once more and fourth twice but failing to gain promotion. Taylor resigned and his successor was bought in from Huddersfield Town – Bill Shankly.

Again Liverpool finished third for two more seasons before Shankly led Liverpool to the second division title. In those three years some 24 players left the club but it was not just the team that Shanks built, it was an entire system. For all its stars, any Liverpool team that followed was always greater than the sum of its parts. No-one was bigger than the club and the most important people were always acknowledged to be the fans.

Out of the second division Liverpool won the league title in the 1963-64 and 1965-66 seasons, triumphs which sandwiched their first ever FA Cup victory. Liverpool won 2-1 against Leeds after extra time. 1964-65 was also Liverpool's first of 21 consecutive seasons in European football. They reached the semi-finals of the European Cup in 1965 and the final of the Cup Winners Cup in 1966 losing 2-1 after extra time to Borussia Dortmund.

The next six years saw Liverpool consistent league finishers never failing to finish in the top five but without managing to take the title itself and failing, once again in the FA Cup losing (2-1 after extra time, again) to double winners Arsenal in 1971.

By the early seventies Shankly had completely rebuilt the side and in 1972-73 Liverpool won the league title and their first European trophy, the UEFA Cup, beating Borussia Moenchengladbach 3-2 over two legs. The next season was Shankly's last in charge, Liverpool winning the FA Cup against a much fancied Newcastle United side 3-0.

In Shankly's reign Liverpool had risen from being a second division club with potential to a respected European force and had equalled Arsenal's record eight league titles. More than that he had set the foundation for future success unparalleled in the English game.

With Shankly's resignation the Liverpool system he had created took over and Bob Paisley was promoted from within. Paisley's first season in charge was unique - it was the only one when his team didn't win a trophy. Liverpool continued to gather strength both at home and abroad. In 1975-76 Liverpool won a record ninth league title and the UEFA Cup for the second time this time beating FC Bruges 4-3 across two games. Liverpool did even better the following year. They won the league title again, and reached the final of the FA Cup where they lost 2-1 to Manchester United somewhat against the run of play. Four days later the Reds picked themselves up from the disappointment of that defeat and won the European Cup. 26,000 Liverpool fans travelled to Rome to see the game against Borussia Moenchengladbach virtually turning the game into a home tie. The Liverpool players responded appropriately, winning 3-1 and in considerable style. Liverpool were Champions of Europe.

The following season Liverpool finished second in the league to Nottingham Forest and also lost to them in the League Cup final - 1-0 in a replay after a goalless game at Wembley - but there was no stopping Liverpool in Europe. They took their second European crown winning 1-0 at

Wembley against FC Bruges.

Nottingham Forest again proved a thorn in the Liverpool side in 1978-79, winning their first round European Cup tie but they couldn't stop Liverpool in the league. The Reds went on to amass a record equalling 68 points under the old system of two points for a win. Liverpool scored 85 goals to a miserly count of only 16 conceded – the fewest ever in a league season with Liverpool's goal difference of 69 also being a record.

Liverpool won the league title yet again in the 1979-80 season and reached the semi-final stages of both domestic cup competitions but failed in the European Cup's first round.

In all the seventies brought Liverpool two UEFA Cups, two European Cups, an FA Cup and no fewer than five league championships. Those five gave Liverpool a total of twelve league titles and established them as being by far and away the most successful English league club ever.

In the 1980s Liverpool set about improving that record. The 1980-81 league season was Liverpool's worst since the mid-sixties – they finished fifth – but they made up for that poor showing by winning their first ever League Cup title. 1-1 after extra time at Wembley, Liverpool needed a replay to overcome West Ham United 2-1. In the European Cup Liverpool won their third title beating Real Madrid 1-0 in Paris.

The next two seasons were remarkably similar. Liverpool won the league title as expected and the League Cup as well beating Tottenham Hotspur in 1981-82 3-1 after extra time and Manchester United in 1982-83 2-1 after extra time. In both seasons Liverpool exited the European Cup at the quarter final stage and the FA Cup in the fifth round. The 1982-83 season was the last with Bob Paisley in charge. Under his guidance Liverpool had won a phenomenal 13 major trophies – a record for any English manager. But for all his successes one trophy had eluded him, the FA Cup.

Paisley's successor also came from within the Liverpool system – Joe Fagan. He was only in charge for two seasons but in his very first the record books had to be rewritten once more. Liverpool won the league title – yet again – becoming one of only three clubs to have made it three years in succession, joining Arsenal and Huddersfield Town who both achieved it before the war.

In addition Fagan led Liverpool to a record fourth League Cup title beating cross-city rivals Everton 1-0 after a two goalless hours at Wembley. It was the first and only time that an English trophy has been won four times on the trot by one club. The final jewel in the crown was the European Cup which Liverpool won for a fourth time beating AS Roma in Rome 4-2 on penalties after a 1-1 draw after extra time. The European Cup title gave Liverpool a total of three titles in the one season, another first for an English league club.

The following year Liverpool had to watch in anguish as Everton won the league title and came within an ace of being only the third team since the war to "do the double" of FA Cup and league title. Liverpool's only hope of a trophy came in the European Cup where they reached the final against Juventus, the best team in Italy. Liverpool had never lost a European Cup final and went to Brussels for Joe Fagan's last game in charge confident of giving him the send off of a life time. Instead the events in the Heysel Stadium turned to catastrophe. Rioting Liverpool supporters tore down a fence segregating the fans and caused a stampede of innocent Italian fans trying to get out of the way of a rain of kicks, punches, stones and bars. The stampede led to a dead-end and, crushed up against each other, the crowd caused a wall to collapse. 39 people died and more than 400 were injured. In the mayhem that followed no-one seemed to know what had happened. Some people had died but no-one knew how many and while bodies were carried from the stadium it was the turn of some Italian fans to over-react. The game went ahead in an effort to prevent further bloodhsed but Juventus's 1-0 victory went almost unnoticed.

In the aftermath of the game the blame was passed around: Liverpool football club for the behaviour of their fans, the Belgian police for losing control, UEFA for choosing the venue in the first place but the real culprits were those whose violent behaviour had caused the stampede. The result was a blanket ban from European competition for all English clubs with an extra three year ban for Liverpool.

Throughout a period in English football when hooligans had plagued the game Liverpool had remained relatively free of this scourge. The good behaviour of Liverpool fans had become a proud boast of the club until Heysel when a minority brought shame on the club. Eventually 14 Liverpool fans were convicted of manslaughter by the Belgian courts.

A new season and a new manager. Liverpool surprised everyone by their appointment of Kenny Dalglish as their first ever player-manager. In his first season in charge Dalglish led his team to an achievement that had eluded all his illustrious predecessors – the double of league championship and FA Cup. The latter was achieved against Everton at Wembley with the Reds coming from behind to record a notable 3-1 victory. Liverpool could not maintain the momentum however and finished the following season empty-handed, second in the league to Everton and second in the League Cup final to Arsenal (1-2).

The 1987-88 season saw Liverpool set off at a canter. They didn't lose their first league game until they faced Everton at Goodison Park in March by which time they had equalled the first division record of 29 games from the start of a season without defeat. Liverpool had the league wrapped up early on and only little-fancied Wimbledon stood between them and a second double in three years. The Dons proved an insurmountable hurdle winning 1-0 with their keeper Dave Beasant becoming the first to save an FA Cup final penalty. Liverpool had to settle for "only" one trophy.

1988-89 saw Liverpool well-placed for yet another try at the double. A typical good run of results in the New Year brought them into contention in the league chase and they were still in the FA Cup. In the semi-finals they were pitted against Nottingham Forest at Sheffield Wednesday's Hillsborough ground but the game itself was stopped after 6 minutes when Liverpool fans started tumbling over the fence from the Leppings Lane End. In the confusion police at first feared crowd trouble but the cause wasn't hooliganism – people were being crushed to death. 95 fans lost their lives that day and the catastrophe shook the city of Liverpool to its foundations. Nearly everyone, it seemed, knew of someone who had perished. It put the relative importance of football into harsh perspective. The following morning, a Sunday, thousands of fans started arriving spontaneously at Anfield. The gates were opened and the ground was converted into a mass shrine. The Kop terracing was carpetted with wreathes of flowers and was hung with thousands of scarves and banners as the people of Liverpool struggled to come to terms with their loss. The club responded magnificently and the players led memorial services and attended fans' funerals.

Liverpool didn't play a game for three weeks as they mourned their dead. The supporters who had enjoyed the highest level of success now had to cope with the lowest depths of despair. The aftermath of the Hillsborough disaster was a report compiled by Justice Taylor. The state of the nation's ageing football grounds – too many relics from before the war – was roundly condemned. Proposals were made – all-seater grounds in particular – in an effort to make sure that no similar disaster should ever occur again.

When football restarted Liverpool won their FA Cup semi-final replay to set up another final confrontation with Everton. Once more Liverpool triumphed, winning the tie 3-2.

Becasue of the postponement of games the FA Cup final was not the final game of the season – instead it was a home tie against Arsenal at the end of May. As chance would have it Arsenal were second in the league to Liverpool and needing to win 2-0 to take the title. Instead of setting out to win the game Liverpool appeared to be trying to contain Arsenal and, despite going a goal down, looked like they would try and defend their slender advantage. Arsenal punished Liverpool's negative approach and scored a second goal at the very end of play to steal the title from Anfield.

Liverpool responded by winning their 18th league title the following season, 1989-90, but the 1990s saw a period of unrest at Liverpool start with the shock mid-season resignation of Kenny Dalglish. He cited the pressure of the job as his reason for leaving. Graeme Souness was brought in from Rangers as replacement and he promised a revolution in the way the club was run. 1991-92 was his first full season in charge and Liverpool returned to Europe after their Heysel ban. It was an unsuccessful foray in the UEFA Cup which saw Liverpool defeated home and away by Genoa of Italy in the quarter finals.

Much changed under Souness's leadership but, apart from a 2-0 FA Cup final win against second division Sunderland in 1991-92, the trophies were not forthcoming. Souness himself was the cause of much anxiety needing a triple heart bypass operation before Liverpool's Wembley appearance. Liverpool sank to their lowest league position in 27 years – 6th place – and didn't improve the year after. Liverpool suffered humiliating early exits from the FA and Cup Winners Cups and spent much of the first Premier League season barely above the relegation zone and only managed another 6th place in the league thanks to a late revival. The board of Liverpool took the decision to stand by Souness as manager for another season, despite calls for his head from many supporters, and the 1993-94 season kicked off with much promise. But in the FA Cup Liverpool were again knocked out in the third round by a team from a lower division. This time it was the turn of first division Bristol City to win at Anfield and it was more than the Reds' fans could stomach. A few days later Souness handed in his resignation and Roy Evans was announced as his successor shortly afterwards.

Evans had been Souness's assistant and his appointment – Bob Paisley's choice, no less – meant a return to the glory days of promotion from within. Whether it means a return to the glory days remains to be seen. At the end of the 1993/94 season Liverpool finished in 8th place in the league, their lowest position in over thirty years of top-flight football. Whatever the 1994-95 season brings, it is likely to bring change.

Liverpool
The Season in Statistics

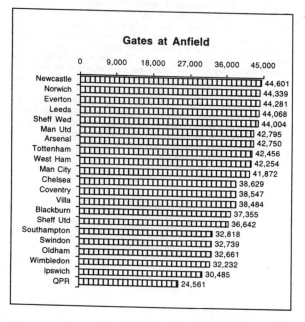

Gates at Anfield

Newcastle	44,601
Norwich	44,339
Everton	44,281
Leeds	44,068
Sheff Wed	44,004
Man Utd	42,795
Arsenal	42,750
Tottenham	42,456
West Ham	42,254
Man City	41,872
Chelsea	38,629
Coventry	38,547
Villa	38,484
Blackburn	37,355
Sheff Utd	36,642
Southampton	32,818
Swindon	32,739
Oldham	32,661
Wimbledon	32,232
Ipswich	30,485
QPR	24,561

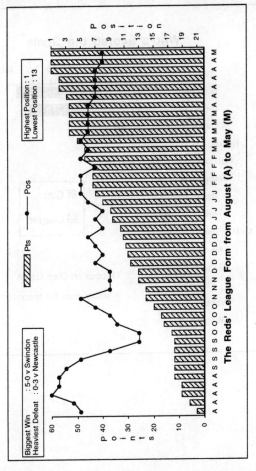

The Reds' League Form from August (A) to May (M)

Biggest Win : 5-0 v Swindon
Heaviest Defeat : 0-3 v Newcastle

Highest Position : 1
Lowest Position : 13

Pts

Pos

267

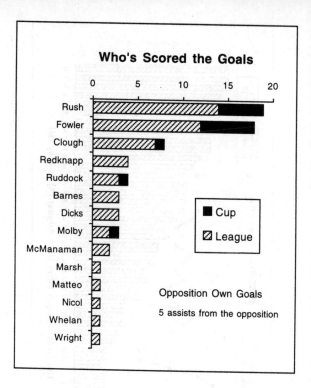

Who's Scored the Goals

Opposition Own Goals

5 assists from the opposition

How the Goals were Scored

Chart showing goals scored "Against" and "For" across categories: Inside Area, Outside Area, Header, Close Range, Penalty, Volley, Own Goal, Free Kick. Horizontal axis marked 0 to 22.

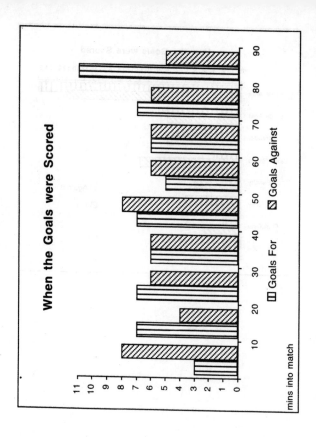

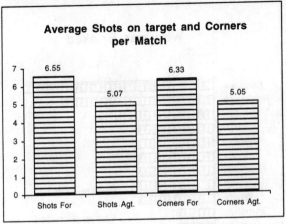

Average Shots on target and Corners per Match

	Shots For	Shots Agt.	Corners For	Corners Agt.
Value	6.55	5.07	6.33	5.05

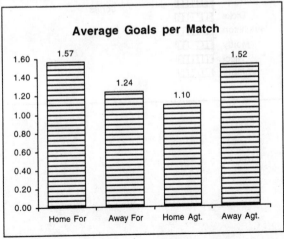

Average Goals per Match

	Home For	Away For	Home Agt.	Away Agt.
Value	1.57	1.24	1.10	1.52

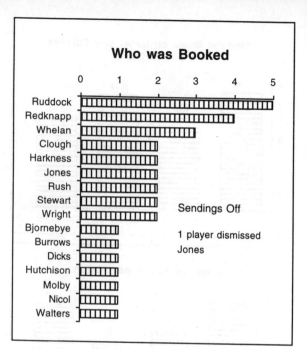

272

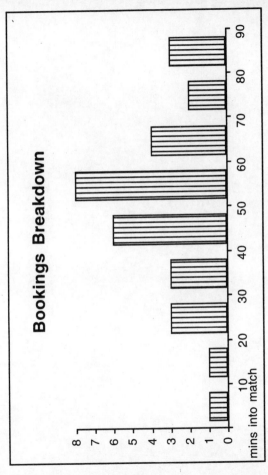

Bookings Breakdown

mins into match

Farewell to the Kop

Liverpool's last home game of the 1993-94 league season against Norwich City was also the last in front of a standing Kop. It was a poignant moment as it brought back memories of so many days of glory at Anfield, days when the singing of the Kop choir lifted the Liverpool team to a higher level and cowed the opposition. It also brought back memories of the Hillsborough tragedy as it was in the aftermath of that catastrophe that the Taylor Report recommended that the major football grounds in this country should become all-seater stadia.

For such a famous terracing the Kop had humble beginnings. It was constructed as a tinder bank back in 1906 on the strength of Liverpool's second championship success. The then Sports Editor of the Liverpool Echo, Ernest Edwards, took one look at the huge mound and decided that it reminded him of the Spion Kop – a hill in South Africa and site of a famous battle in the Boer War where so many local soldiers from the Lancashire Regiment had lost their lives. The name stuck and it has been the Spion Kop – or more often and more simply just 'The Kop' – ever since.

In 1928 the old terracing was in need of improvement and a new structure was built, a structure which lasted substantially unchanged until the end of the 1993-94 season. It was designed by architect Mr J Watson Cabre from Crosby and became the first roofed Kop in the country.

It was huge, being some 425 feet long, 131 feet wide and 80 feet high – big enough, it was claimed, to fit in 91 standard houses in one layer alone. Someone worked out that, if the steps of the Kop were laid out end to end, it would be longer than the entire length of the Liverpool docks. The new stand was designed to accommodate 28,000 people – all standing of course. Two thirds of that number had a completely unrestricted view of the pitch, without any intervening stanchions getting in the way. Of course, there was always the head of the fellow in front to block the view but experienced terrace-goers have long developed the ability to find the best spot from which to view the action. For the start of the 1928-29 season the admission price was raised to one shilling. It was a steep price in those days but the club claimed that it was worth it as the fans would enjoy the *"pleasure and efficiency"* of the new structure. They weren't wrong as over 40,000 turned out to see the first visitors – Bury – beaten 3-0.

In the following years the Kop became the most famous football terrace in the world. It wasn't just the size of the crowd or the volume of their support that impressed but their appreciation of the game. Visiting goalkeepers would sometimes quake as they stood defending their goal in front of the Kop but for others it was an experience to be enjoyed. If you got on well with the Kop the Kop would get on well with you. Good football was always applauded – it was just that, if you were playing at Anfield, Liverpool would be playing even better.

Everyone has their own favourite story about the Kop. Tales of humour and friendliness that are not to be found elsewhere in the game. It was always said that playing in front of the Kop was like a one goal start for Liverpool but rarely can this have been more true than for a match back in 1965 against Inter Milan of Italy. The occasion was the first leg semi-final of the European Cup and Bill Shankly's Liverpool were facing the cup holders whose side included such household names of that day as Burgnich, Fachetti, Suarez and Corso. Liverpool in those days were new to the European game and weren't given much chance against the all-conquering Italian giants. That assessment, however, over-looked the potent influence of the Kop. Liverpool had just completed a successful season, winning the FA Cup for the very first time in their history. Anfield was packed to the rafters for the arrival of the European champions with another 20,000 locked out. The crowd waited in great anticipation. It was at this point that Bill Shankly demonstrated another of his gifts – an understanding not just of the game of football but of its importance to people and an understanding of the response of the crowd. He told Gerry Byrne – the FA Cup final hero – and injured England midfielder Gordon Milne to parade the FA Cup around the ground just before kick-off. They did so, but it was the timing of the event that was so crucial. The FA Cup came on display just as the Italian players were running out of the tunnel. The roar of the crowd hit its peak just as Inter Milan came onto the pitch. The Italians were used to playing in front of crowds of 85,000 in the San Siro stadium but they had heard nothing like it. When the Kop started singing Go Back to Italy to the tune of Santa Lucia they were dumbfounded and just stopped in their tracks and looked around bewildered. It was a start from which they didn't recover as Roger Hunt put Liverpool ahead after only five minutes. Mazzola – the Italian World Cup striker – made the scores level but shortly afterwards Ian Callaghan put the Reds in front once more, coming in late after a free-kick. Urged on by the capacity crowd Liverpool pushed forward and scored a third in the second half. Roger Hunt fired in a fierce shot which the Italian keeper Sarti could only parry out to Ian St John who made it 3-1. The champions of Europe had been humbled. There is a down-side to this story and that's the score in the second leg: 3-0 to Inter. It's a pity Liverpool couldn't take the Kop with them on their European travels.

Liverpool's success in Europe has had many high points and a few lows too but for most fans the greatest day was the day Liverpool won their first European Cup. It was the season of 1976/77 and Liverpool had overcome Trabzonspor, St Etienne and FC Zurich to set up a final confrontation with Bundesliga giants Borussia Moenchengladbach (*"Give us a B..."*). The final was in Roma but the Liverpool team did not make the journey alone, far from it. 26,000 fans came from Liverpool for the occasion making the game into virtually a home fixture. That season had been a hectic one for the club. They won the league for the second season running and had reached the final of the FA Cup. That was only a few days before their final in Rome and Liverpool had every reason to feel hard done by as they missed the chance of recording a double of league and FA Cup in losing 2-1 to Manchester

United. That disappointment didn't show when in the European final however. Goals from Terry McDermott, a header from Tommy Smith and a penalty from Phil Neal after Kevin Keegan had been brought down by his frustrated marker, sent the Germans packing. The 1970s were the days when crowds went in for banners. Bearing in mind the Liverpool success on the way to the final over French and Swiss opposition, some fans of Joey Jones came up with this one:

> JOEY ATE THE FROGS' LEGS
> MADE THE SWISS ROLL
> NOW HE'S MUNCHING GLADBACH

Over the years the Kop choir has gained something of a reputation. It has even managed to find its way onto a Pink Floyd record – check out 'Fearless' from their 1971 album 'Meddle'. However, things aren't always as they should be. It's all very well *"You'll never walk alone"* being plastered across the top of the Liverpool crest but what if you don't know the words? Try this:

> *When you walk through a storm*
> *Hold your head up high*
> *And don't be afraid of the dark*
> *At the end of the storm*
> *Is a golden sky*
> *And the sweet silver song of a lark*
> *Walk on through the wind*
> *Walk on through the rain*
> *Tho' your dreams be tossed and blown*
> *Walk on, walk on*
> *With hope in your heart*
> *And you'll never walk alone*
> *You'll never walk alone!*

Words: Oscar Hammerstein II – *Music:* Richard Rogers

Many other crowds in the footballing world are capable of showing fanatical support. Many others have passable singing as part of their heritage too. But few crowds can be so generous in defeat. Not many teams come to Anfield and win but, when their footballing has been of high quality, the Liverpool fans have always been the first to show their approval – it's a true test of sportsmanship. In 1969 Leeds United came to Anfield at the end of the season. Liverpool were still nursing faint hopes of taking the league championship but for Leeds a draw from that game would clinch it. It was nil-nil after ninety minutes and Leeds were crowned as champions and awarded the trophy. Manager Don Revie instructed his incredulous captain, Billy Bremner, to parade the trophy in front of the Kop. Expecting the worst Bremner trotted off only to be greeted on the half-way line by chants of

"Champions, champions". Now, where else would you get that? More recently Arsenal visited Anfield at the end of the 1988-89 season. It was the season of the Hillsborough tragedy and Liverpool were playing an extended season due to the backlog of games. For the third time in four seasons Liverpool were in the hunt for the double of League title and FA Cup. An emotional game at Wembley had seen Liverpool complete the first half of the task by beating Everton 3-2 with a goal from John Aldridge and a couple from Ian Rush. Now all Liverpool needed to do was to avoid defeat at home to Arsenal by more than one goal. For the Arsenal team it was an unenviable task – visit Anfield and win by two goals but they did it. While Liverpool looked uncertain as to whether they should be attacking or defending, the Gunners stuck to their guns. 1-0 up with only a few minutes to play Michael Thomas snatched a second in the dying minutes of the game. It would have been easy for the Kop to go home quietly at the end of a wretched season which had seen nearly a hundred of their compatriots killed in the Sheffield disaster but they stayed on and cheered their approval of a spirited Arsenal performance.

Although the Kop has always been the fans who stood there rather than the concrete and steel, it was the structure itself which became of symbolic importance in the aftermath of the Hillsborough tragedy. On the Sunday after that game thousands of fans turned up at Anfield and the gates were opened. The Kop itself was transformed by a carpet of wreaths, banners and scarves. It covered the terracing from front to back and spread across the pitch until nearly half was covered. It wasn't just all red, there were Everton scarves there too showing that it wasn't just the club but the whole city which was in mourning.

And that, lest we ever forget, is why the Kop has had to come down. That sort of tragedy can simply not be allowed to happen ever again. Construction work is under way and the terracing which has housed so many for so long, which holds more memories than any part of any other stadium you care to mention, is to be replaced. How can the Kop ever be replaced? What will be put in its place?

The New Kop

After the last home game of the 1993-94 season the demolition men moved in. The new stand is scheduled for completion in December 1994 if all goes according to plan.

The new stand was just one of several designs that were considered. It wasn't the cheapest option but the one which could boast the largest capacity. It will seat some 12,000 fans, all of whom will be able to see all of the pitch without any obstructions.

The new Kop will be 92 meters wide and have 72 rows of seats and will be covered by a cantilevered roof. There will be twenty entrances, ten on the Kemlyn road side and ten on the Main Stand side.

Incorporated into the design is a new shop on two storeys – downstairs will be the main retail area with the upstairs devoted to mail order supplies. More importantly there will also be a large bar area for that all-important pre-match refreshment. There are plans to construct a European soccer heritage museum. If built it will run alongside the current visitors' centre in the main stand and give the ground a genuinely international appeal.

On completion the new-look Anfield should have a capacity of something in the region of 40,000 seats and be a ground to compare with the very best. It is just one of the reasons why Anfield has been selected as one of the grounds to play host to international games as part of the European Championships in 1994.

If the gates from the 1993-94 season are anything to go by the club should have no trouble filling the 40,000 seats for virtually every home fixture in seasons to come. Last season nearly half of Liverpool's home games in the Premiership were in front of crowds in excess of 40,000 with the capacity being reached on several occasions.

Can the Kop ever be the same again? When all is said and done that's up to the fans. The Kop itself is only concrete and steel, what makes it special is the fans that fill it. If they're in good voice then there's no reason why they can't carry on lifting their team like they always have done. But, when the stand is completed and the workmen have gone home, Anfield will be left with a lower capacity than before. With gates rising in recent seasons after an extended period of decline – even at Liverpool – and more season ticket sales it can only mean one thing: signs saying 'Ground Full'. So remember... get your tickets in advance or get there early!

FA PREMIER LEAGUE

	Arsenal	Aston Villa	Blackburn Rovers	Chelsea	Coventry City	Crystal Palace	Everton	Ipswich Town	Leeds United	Leicester City	Liverpool	Manchester City	Manchester United	Newcastle United	Norwich City	Nottingham Forest	QPR	Sheffield Wed.	Southampton	Tottenham H.	West Ham United	Wimbledon
Liverpool											•											
Leicester City										•												
Leeds United									•													
Ipswich Town								•														
Everton							•															
Crystal Palace						•																
Coventry City					•																	
Chelsea				•																		
Blackburn R			•																			
Aston Villa		•																				
Arsenal	•																					

RESULTS 1994-95

Results grid chart. Rows (top to bottom): Wimbledon, West Ham Utd, Tottenham Hot, Southampton, Sheffield Wed, QPR, Nottingham F, Norwich City, Newcastle Utd, Man Utd, Man City. Columns (left to right): Arsenal, Aston Villa, Blackburn Rovers, Chelsea, Coventry City, Crystal Palace, Everton, Ipswich Town, Leeds United, Leicester City, Liverpool, Manchester City, Manchester United, Newcastle United, Norwich City, Nottingham Forest, QPR, Sheffield Wed, Southampton, Tottenham H, West Ham United, Wimbledon.

Other Titles from

Sales:
**Derek Searle Associates,
14 High Street, Slough, Berks, SL1 1EE
Telephone: (0753) 539295 – Fax: (0753) 551863**

Distribution:
**Bookpoint Ltd, 39 Milton Park,
Abingdon, Oxon, OX14 4TD
Telephone: (0235) 400400 – Fax: (0235) 861038/832068**

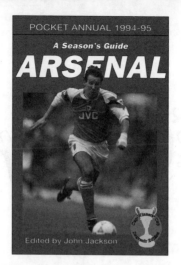

POCKET ANNUAL 1994-95

A Season's Guide

ARSENAL

Edited by John Jackson

Arsenal Pocket Annual 1994-95

Edited by John Jackson, 288 pages, £3.99
ISBN: 1-898351-09-0

Also available as a 10 Copy Counter Pack, £39.90, ISBN: 1-898351-16-3

Re-live the season – match-by-match, fact-by-fact and goal-by-goal as John Jackson provides a report on every Gunners' game as it happened! Look up all the line-ups, appearance details and goal-scoring records of all the current Highbury stars and debate for yourself their current transfer value. The Arsenal Pocket Annual provides complete records for Arsenal in all competitions and against every club – since 1886! Follow the Gunners in the Premiership and on the trail of the three major Cups. Don't leave home without it – it'll even give you directions to all the Premiership grounds. All the facts at your fingertips in a handy pocket size with photos.

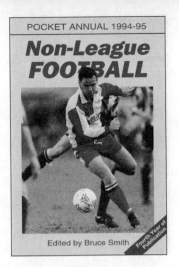

POCKET ANNUAL 1994-95

Non-League FOOTBALL

Fourth Year of Publication

Edited by Bruce Smith

Non-League Football Pocket Annual 1994-95

Edited by Bruce Smith, 288 pages, £3.99
ISBN: 1-898351-07-4

Also available as a 10 Copy Counter Pack, £39.90, ISBN: 1-898351-14-7

Now in its fourth year, Bruce Smith's famous *Non-League Football Annual* is the perfect pocket travelling companion for all followers of the Non-League game. Cram-packed with information and histories on all the major Pyramid clubs, it includes full details and reviews of all the major cup competitions including the FA Cup, FA Trophy and FA Vase. Unique five-year records allow you to see for yourself how the top club sides have fared. There are even appearance records for all the Vauxhall Conference sides. Great for groundhoppers and arm-chair enthusiasts.

POCKET ANNUAL 1994-95

FA Carling PREMIERSHIP

Bruce Smith

FA Carling Premiership Pocket Annual 1994-95

Edited by Bruce Smith, 288 pages, £3.99
ISBN: 1-898351-06-6

Also available as a 10 Copy Counter Pack, £39.90, ISBN: 1-898351-13-9

Having sold out in its first year, the second edition of the *FA Carling Premiership Pocket Annual* has been revamped to make it even clearer, more informative and better value than ever before. It contains a complete Premiership club directory with season reviews, club and player records in the Premiership and former Football League, and is packed with unique statistics and records every fan will want to know. Make sure you have the complete record of this and every Premiership season. Illustrated with detailed guides to all the Premiership League grounds and photographs of all the season's action – and all for just £3.99!

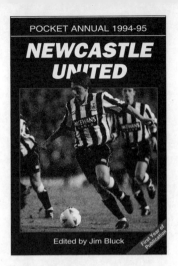

POCKET ANNUAL 1994-95

NEWCASTLE UNITED

Edited by Jim Bluck

First Year of Publication

Newcastle United Pocket Annual 1994-95

Edited by Jim Bluck, 256 pages, £3.99
ISBN: 1-898351-11-2

Also available as a 10 Copy Counter Pack, £39.90, ISBN: 1-898351-18-X

H'away the lads! The Magpies made an incredible impact on the Premiership so don't fail to re-savour every moment with this match-by-match, fact-by-fact, blow-by-blow account of the season as Andy Cole scores the quickest ever 30-goals in Newcastle United's history! With records of all the current Newcastle stars debate their transfer values as estimated by our panel of editors, walk down memory lane as you scan through United's complete record in all competitions and against every other club. Take it with you to matches – it'll slip into your pocket and even give you directions to all the Premiership grounds.

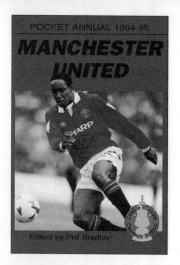

POCKET ANNUAL 1994-95

MANCHESTER UNITED

Edited by Phil Bradley

Manchester United Pocket Annual 1994-95

Edited by Phil Bradley, 288 pages, £3.99
ISBN: 1-898351-08-2

Also available as a 10 Copy Counter Pack, £39.90, ISBN: 1-898351-15-9

The debate was all about *The Treble*. What went right and what went wrong as United set the Premiership alight with their brilliant brand of football? Every match, every goal and all the facts on every player as it's happened since United's formation in 1878 as Newton Heath. Is Ryan Giggs really worth £12 million? Debate for yourself our valuation of him and the other United players. Also included is United's record in all competitions and against every club. Don't leave home without it – it'll even give you directions to all the Premiership grounds.